SORDID
SEX LIVES

SORDiD SEX LiVES

Shocking stories of perversion and
promiscuity from Nero to Nilsen

NIGEL CAWTHORNE

Quercus

CONTENTS

INTRODUCTION

Some of the most revered figures in history and culture have had a little secret – and sometimes it has not been a well-kept one. These famous figures had a strange sexual quirk, what we would nowadays refer to as a perversion. Their kink might not have been illegal, or even unusual, at the time they lived. However, their perversion added, at the very least, an interesting dimension to their character.

Sex is at once the passion that is the most Promethean and the most subject to fashion. In classical Greece, it was common for older men to have sex with young boys in their care. An organization called the Order of Chaeronea tried to promote this practice again in the 19th century. Today it would – rightly – be condemned as paedophilia.

In the early 19th century, there was a 'defloration mania'. Older gentlemen sought out young virgin girls to have sex with. Once deflowered, they would be discarded. The Criminal Law Amendment Act of 1885, passed in the UK, sought to outlaw this by raising the age of consent for females from 13 to 16. Ironically, Oscar Wilde fell foul of an amendment to this act that outlawed acts of 'gross indecency' between males.

In the 18th century, there had been a fashion for flagellation. Brothels were set up where gentlemen could beat or be beaten by prostitutes. And this voguish vice was not confined to the male sex. Women set up flagellation clubs where they could beat each other, in lieu of sex.

Homosexual practices, now widely accepted in the West, have variously been condemned, outlawed, frowned upon, or else considered the height of fashion. Similarly lesbianism – though rarely recognized, let alone outlawed – has sometimes been *à la mode*. Fellatio, cunnilingus, anal sex and even miscegenation – sex between the races – have all been outlawed in various US states. Although these days they are considered normal practice, they were once considered perverted.

This need not bother us here. People who were once persecuted for their sexual orientation or for performing practices now considered the everyday fare of a healthy sex life are not the subject of this book. In these pages, we are concentrating on those who have sailed to the furthest shores of sexual experience and journeyed to erogenous areas that are, if not illegal, at least distasteful.

The reader should be warned that there is material in this book that is disturbing and, if one has that mindset, downright evil. But it is not my position to sanction or condemn. There are the authorities of the Church and state to do that. I am a writer. I merely report so that others can make their own minds up.

What strikes me is how deeply sexual perverts are embedded in society. In this book, we present perverts who were political leaders, murderers, movie stars and, most abundantly of all, artists, composers and writers. This raises the question: Is perversion the wellspring of creativity? It is a question I cannot answer.

Only you and your sexual partners know what you get up to behind the bedroom door. And what they get up to with people other than you may not be the same thing at all. Getting to the 'truth' about human sexuality is impossible. No one is immune to the blandishments of sex. It is no good asking sociologists or psychologists. They are human beings too and must, by that very fact, have a slanted view. Everyone – even those who only have sex with themselves or their God – has an opinion that is biased.

Taking a survey is useless too. When it comes to sex, everyone lies. Some exaggerate; others understate. Ask two people what they did together behind closed doors and you will get completely different stories.

What I have done here is piece together individual stories from written autobiographies and significant interviews, along with the accounts of those who knew these personalities or had sex with them. That way we may reach, if not the truth, then something approaching it.

Many of the people in this book have become mythologized over time. For instance, I find it particularly puzzling that Oscar Wilde – the great writer that he was – is now seen as a saint, a martyr to the cause of gay liberation, when he was not interested in having sex with other men. What he preferred was sex with underage boys. These days he would have fallen foul of the laws against sex offenders. But then so would Paul Gauguin and several of the other characters in this book.

Then there is the strange case of Adolf Hitler. There are white supremacists in Britain and America, and xenophobes in Eastern Europe, who still admire this man. But if they knew what he got up to in the bedroom, they might find it harder to look up to him, unless they were involved in the same degrading practices. Five of Hitler's lovers committed suicide. How bad do you have to be?

Nigel Cawthorne

CLEOPATRA
THE NYMPHOMANIAC WHO TORE APART THE ANCIENT WORLD

69-30 BC

Cleopatra is famous for her affairs with Julius Caesar and Mark Antony, which threatened to undermine the Roman republic. But her sex life was much more extensive – and devious – than that. She married two of her brothers, put on erotic entertainments, enjoyed orgies and was said to have fellated one hundred Roman centurions in a single night. The Greeks called her *Meriochane*, which means 'she who gapes wide for a thousand men'. And, like many upper-class women in ancient Egypt, she liked to show off her body and wore clothing made of the flimsiest see-through fabric.

Cleopatra's full name was Cleopatra VII *Thea Philopator* – Greek for 'Goddess Loving Her Father' – and she believed in keeping it in the family. She married her brother, King Ptolemy XIII, and after he died she married another brother, who became King Ptolemy XIV. Cleopatra served as co-ruler with both of them.

Modern forensic reconstructions have shown that the inbred Cleopatra was not the great beauty she is often assumed to have been. But what she lacked in good looks she more than made up for in sex appeal. The Greek historian Plutarch said: 'We have been told that her beauty was by no means flawless, or even remarkable at first glance, but anyone listening to her for even a moment was captivated by her irresistible charm.'

LEWD JOKES

Cleopatra was thought to have taken her first lover when she was 12, and she first met Mark Antony at the age of 14 when he was a young staff officer. By then she already had a reputation as a nymphomaniac. Known for her lewd jokes and sexually provocative conversation, at 21 Cleopatra quickly captivated the 52-year-old Julius Caesar after, famously, having herself delivered to him in a rolled-up carpet.

Although Caesar was already married, he and Cleopatra went through an Egyptian wedding ceremony, after which he took her and their son Caesarion to Rome, erecting them in one of his homes. He publicly declared his love for her by installing her statue in the temple of Venus, from whom Caesar claimed descent. The idea of deifying a foreigner angered the people of Rome and may have led to Caesar's murder in 44 BC.

After Caesar's death the Roman empire was divided between Octavian (who as Augustus would become Rome's first emperor) in the west and Mark Antony, who married Octavian's sister Octavia, in the east. Determined to seduce Mark Antony, Cleopatra sailed to Tarsus, in modern Turkey, in a barge with a deck of gold, silver oars and purple sails. The Roman biographer Suetonius said her arrival was announced by the music of flutes and lutes. She was dressed as Venus, attended by Cupids and the three Graces.

> 'CLEOPATRA HERSELF LAY BENEATH A CANOPY SPLASHED WITH GOLD, POSED LIKE VENUS IN A PAINTING, WHILE BOYS AS HANDSOME AS EROS GENTLY FANNED HER. APHRODITE HAD ARRIVED TO SPORT WITH DIONYSUS.'
> Plutarch

Knowing Mark Antony's tastes, Cleopatra laid on entertainments featuring the *cineadii* – effeminate men – who performed lewd dances for him. She surrounded him with concubines and eunuchs, along with the 'Inimitables', gilded youth who were said to possess sole knowledge of the supreme refinements of oriental sensuality. They put on erotic theatricals, in one of which another guest played the Greek sea god Glaucus, painted blue and writhing naked on the floor.

According to Plutarch, 'Cleopatra flattered Antony, always dreaming up some fresh delight, careful never to let him stray from her either day or night. She rolled dice with him, drank with him, hunted with him, and faithfully watched him exercise and play war games. And even when he scrambled about the city hiding in doorways and windows, taunting and teasing complete strangers, she went along with it. For Antony liked to disguise himself as a servant and, on occasion, wound up being cursed and sometimes beaten, although most people recognized him. Nonetheless, the Alexandrians enjoyed his crude jokes, and joined in his pranks in their own elegant and cultured way.'

Antony's relationship with Cleopatra caused political problems, and he returned to Rome to patch things up with Octavian – leaving Cleopatra pregnant with twins. Eventually, though, Antony divorced Octavia and returned to marry Cleopatra, making the split with Octavian absolute. Nevertheless Antony wrote to Octavian, trying to heal the rift.

Incest in Ancient Egypt

Since the Macedonian general Ptolemy I had taken control of Egypt after the death of Alexander the Great in 323 BC, the Ptolemaic dynasty had intermarried incestuously to maintain their pure Macedonian blood. But even before that, Egyptian Pharaohs were no strangers to incest, since property passed down the maternal line. When a Pharaoh's wife died, he would marry his daughter and, when she died, his grand-daughter, so as to keep his hands on the family's wealth.

'What has come over you?' he wrote. 'Do you object to my sleeping with Cleopatra? But we are married; and it is not as if this were anything new – the affair started nine years ago. And what about you? Are you faithful to Livia Drusilla? My congratulations if, when you receive this letter, you are not in bed with Tertullia, Terentilla, Rufilla, or Salvia Titisena – or all of them. What does it matter where, or with whom, you have sex?'

DUNG BEETLE WORSHIPPER

Octavian grew angry when Mark Antony taunted him for divorcing his first wife 'because she complained too much about the influence of his concubine', and for openly seducing the wives and daughters of consuls and other officials. Octavian reacted by telling the Senate that Mark Antony had enslaved himself to a queen who worshipped dung beetles. He also claimed that Mark Antony intended to divide the empire up between the children that he had had with Cleopatra and Caesarion, the son that she had borne to Julius Caesar.

War was inevitable, and Octavian defeated Mark Antony and Cleopatra at the Battle of Actium, after which Mark Antony killed himself by falling on his sword. Cleopatra now found herself at the mercy of Octavian. When she threatened to kill herself and destroy her treasure, he sent a silver-tongued freedman to tell her that Octavian was already half in love with her, even at a distance – and soon that distance would shrink. Cleopatra therefore thought she could seduce

Julius Caesar

100–44 BC

Cleopatra's first conquest, Julius Caesar, had a far-from-straightforward love life himself. On military service in the east as a youth, Caesar had a much-publicized homosexual affair with King Nicomedes of Bithynia in northwest Anatolia. The governor of nearby Cilicia, Gnaeus Cornelius Dolabella, called Caesar 'the queen's rival and the inner partner of the royal bed', while the tribune Gaius Scribonius Curio the Elder called Caesar 'the brothel of Nicomedes, and the Bithynian stew'. Later when Caesar pleaded the cause of Nysa, the daughter of Nicomedes, before the Senate, he recounted the king's many kindnesses to him. In reply, the orator Cicero said: 'Pray tell us no more of that. We all know what he gave you and what you gave him in return.' Even Caesar's friend Catullus wrote a poem comparing him to a famous pathic – the 'girl' in a gay relationship. Throughout his life Caesar spent large sums of money on handsome young slaves.

Despite his gay reputation, Caesar had numerous affairs with women. According to Suetonius, he 'spent much energy and money on his lusts, and seduced many women of high rank'. Among them were the wives of his two co-rulers in the First Triumvirate.

Despite Curio's earlier slur, he spoke with some admiration of Caesar's reputation for swinging both ways, calling him 'Every woman's husband and every man's wife'. This was echoed by Suetonius, who said that Caesar was 'a man to every woman and a woman to every man'.

Caesar's assassin Marcus Brutus told the story that a man named Octavius, a well-known practical joker, saluted the triumvir Pompey as king and Caesar as queen and, while entertaining him at dinner, arranged for Caesar to sit among the catamites. Even Caesar's victorious legions in Gaul teased him, singing as they marched: 'The Gauls to Caesar yield, Caesar to Nicomede.' And as they marched across the Rubicon to take Rome, they sang another ribald song:

Lock your wives away, you Romans,
A bald whoremonger home we bring,
In Gaul his tarts cost you all your gold,
So now he'll be just borrowing.

Caesar also loved dark-skinned beauties and fell for Eunoë, a Moor and the wife of a man named Bogudes. He lavished expensive gifts on both the willing wife and the compliant husband.

By the time Caesar died, it was said that his health had been undermined by his incessant debauches. He asked for a bill to be drawn up legitimizing any marriage he made to whatever women he pleased, 'for the procreation of children'. However, before he could have his marriage to Cleopatra recognized, he was stabbed to death in the Senate. His last words were not '*Et tu Brute?*' as is often assumed. It was Shakespeare who put those Latin words, meaning 'You too Brutus', in his mouth. Roman historians said that his last words were in Greek, not Latin, and he said to Brutus '*Kai su, technon?*' – which means 'You too, my child?'

It is likely that Brutus was indeed his son. Brutus's mother, Servilia, was one of Caesar's many mistresses.

Octavian as well. When he arrived in Alexandria and entered her luxurious apartments, he found her draped carelessly across an ornate chaise-longue, her skin softened by freshly drawn asses' milk. Surrounded by busts of Julius Caesar, she pulled out some of his love letters that she had stuffed in her bosom and read them out in a plaintive voice. But for once her seductive powers failed. She was now 39 and no longer the young temptress who had beguiled Julius Caesar. When Octavian was unmoved, she threw herself to her knees before him and begged to be allowed to die. But Octavian wanted her alive so that he could parade her down the Via Sacra in Rome as his captive. He had her food closely examined so that she could not poison herself. Unwilling to be exhibited in chains and publicly humiliated, Cleopatra killed herself using two asps – small poisonous snakes – which were smuggled to her in a basket of figs. When Octavian heard what had happened, he was distraught and tried to revive her. But it was too late.

TIBERIUS
THE ROMAN EMPEROR WHO SET THE BENCHMARK FOR DEPRAVITY

42 BC–AD 37

Tiberius, the second emperor of Rome, is remembered as a depraved pervert who ruled by murder and mayhem. He enjoyed watching people being flogged and forced the noble youths of Rome to be his catamites. According to Suetonius, he had a room in his villa on Capri 'adapted to the purpose of secret wantonness, where he entertained companies of girls and catamites, and assembled from all quarters inventors of unnatural copulations'.

Tiberius's excesses in later life can be put down to the fact that the emperor Augustus – his stepfather – forced him to give up his good and virtuous wife Vipsania, whom he loved, to marry Augustus's daughter Julia, an inveterate adulteress. Earlier Tiberius's mother, Livia, had also been forced to divorce his father and marry Augustus, after his father had supported Mark Antony against Augustus in Rome.

Vipsania remarried, and Tiberius was seen following her through the streets with 'tears in his eyes and intense unhappiness written on his face'. When Augustus heard of this, he gave orders that Tiberius was never to see Vipsania again. Tiberius went into voluntary exile in Rhodes, returning to become emperor in AD 14. He was then allowed to divorce Julia, who had gone off the rails and been sent into exile.

During his time as emperor, Tiberius became increasingly afraid that people were plotting against him. In AD 27, now in his late sixties, he left Rome and moved to the island of Capri, where he spent the remaining 11 years of his life. He built a palace which had a special chamber with numerous couches called a *cellaria* where troupes of naked boys and girls from all over the empire performed for him. They would have sex in front of him in groups of three to 'excite his waning passion'. Then he would indulge in orgies of sodomy, fellatio and coprophilia.

PORNOGRAPHIC FRIEZES

A number of small rooms were furnished with the most obscene pictures and statues he could lay his hands on, and the walls were decorated with pornographic friezes. They also had sex manuals from Elephantis in Egypt 'so that none might want for a pattern for the filthy things they were expected to do', according to Suetonius. In his own bedroom he had a painting of the goddess Atalanta performing fellatio on the warrior Meleager. In the woods and

Suetonius
(AD c.71–c.135)

The sex lives of the first 12 Caesars were recorded in detail by the Roman writer Suetonius in his *Lives of the Caesars*. They were:
- Julius Caesar, lived 100 BC–44 BC
- Augustus, ruled 31 BC–AD 14
- Tiberius, ruled AD 14–37
- Gaius (Caligula), ruled AD 37–41
- Claudius, ruled AD 41–54
- Nero, ruled AD 54–68
- Galba, ruled AD 68–69
- Otho, ruled AD 69
- Vitellius, ruled AD 69
- Vespasian, ruled AD 69–79
- Titus, ruled AD 79–81
- Domitian, ruled AD 81–96

The year 69 was known as the 'Year of Four Emperors'. *Lives of the Caesars* was written during the reign of Hadrian (AD 117–38). Suetonius was Hadrian's secretary and it seems that he was dismissed for sleeping with Hadrian's wife. Hadrian himself was more interested in boys. Suetonius wrote a number of other salacious books, including *Lives of Famous Whores*, which, sadly, has been lost.

glades that surrounded the palace, Tiberius kept young people of both sexes to 'indulge their passions in the guise of Pans and nymphs'. It was also said that he trained young boys from noble families – whom he called his 'minnows' – to dive between his legs when he was swimming to nibble and suck on his private parts. In an even more outlandish version of this story, he was said to cover his genitals with crumbs to entice mullet to nibble on them as he reclined in a warm rock pool. Suetonius, author of *Lives of the Caesars*, claimed that Tiberius had unweaned babies suck on his penis as if it were their mothers' breast. To encourage them, he coated his member with milk and honey.

Suetonius also said that, during a sacrifice, Tiberius took such a fancy to the beautiful boy holding the censer that, before the religious rites were over, he took him aside and sexually abused him, along with his brother who was playing the flute. When they protested about his disgusting behaviour, he had their legs broken.

THE OLD GOAT

Tiberius was just as bad with women, even those of high birth and stainless reputation. A Roman matron named Mallonia was forced into his bed. He was known to be an extremely ugly man in old age and, after she showed a certain repugnance at what was required of her, he had paid informers make false accusations about her. During her trial he kept shouting out 'Are you sorry now?' When Mallonia left court, she went home and, after a tirade against 'that filthy-mouthed, hairy, stinking man', she stabbed herself to death.

It is plain that what she objected to was the wrinkly old Tiberius performing cunnilingus on her, as a joke at his expense was inserted into a play about an 'old goat' savouring does with his tongue. Goat is caper in Latin and is a pun on the name Capri. Indeed, Tiberius's sexual theme park on Capri was known as *Caprineum*, which means 'Goatland'.

Recently discovered inscriptions in his ruined palace have revealed that Tiberius enjoyed triple anal penetration and that every member of his household had to bow down before his wizened, diseased penis every morning. He was also devoted to sexual research, measuring the maximum capacity of the anal cavity and setting up a mile-long daisy-chain with male slaves, each of whom was to be strangled at the moment of orgasm. His ultimate aim, apparently, was for everyone in the empire to participate so that the known world would explode in one giant eruption of semen.

> 'MENTION TIBERIUS AND THE NAME EVOKES A SCEPTRED BUTCHER ILL WITH SATYRIASIS – A TACITURN TYRANT, HIDEOUS AND DEBAUCHED; AN UNCLEAN OLD MAN, DEVISING IN THE CRYPTS OF A PALACE INFAMIES SO MONSTROUS.'
>
> J. Stuart Hay

Though some of the accusations against him are fanciful, there is little doubt that Tiberius was a brutal sadist who had people mercilessly flogged merely for crossing his path. A fisherman offered him a large mullet he had caught and hauled up the cliff at the rear of the palace, but Tiberius had become so afraid of assassination that he ordered the man's face to be scrubbed raw with the fish scales. The poor man cried out in agony, 'Thank heavens, I did not offer Caesar the lobster I caught.'

Julia

39 BC – AD 14

Tiberius's second wife, Julia, was notoriously promiscuous. She was once accused of sleeping with her own father, Augustus. Julia was married off to the ageing admiral Marcus Agrippa, the father of Tiberius's great love Vipsania, but she entertained herself with a series of lovers from Rome's most distinguished families. Asked why her five children looked like her husband, Agrippa, she said: '*Numquam enim nisi navi plena tollo vectorem,*' – 'I do not drop the pilot until the boat is full.' In other words, she was careful not to give herself to another man until she was already pregnant.

After Agrippa died, Julia was engaged to Mark Antony's son Julius Antonius, and then to Cotiso, king of the Getae who lived along the banks of the lower Danube. She made several attempts to seduce Tiberius, who refused her. Then Augustus forced Tiberius to divorce Vipsania and marry Julia. They seemed happy enough to start with, but after their young son died, she gave herself up to serial adultery.

The historian Velleius Paterculus, who lived during Augustus's reign, said: 'His daughter Julia, entirely forgetting what she owed to her father and her husband, exceeded in lust and debauchery the utmost limits of shamelessness.'

Seneca, another contemporary, said: 'She counted her lovers in scores. At night, she revelled through the city streets. She chose for the scene of her embraces the very forum and platform from which her father had promulgated his law against adultery. She made daily rendezvous at the statue of Marysas, for she had now turned from adulteress into whore. She had even sold her favours and sought every indulgence with unknown lovers as a prostitute.'

When one night she staged an orgy in the forum, her father put his foot down. She was sent into a comfortable exile. But once Tiberius came to power, he stopped her allowance and she starved to death. Her daughter, Julia the Younger, had followed her mother's example and was also exiled for adultery. If either of the two Julias were mentioned in his hearing, Augustus would say: 'Would that I was wifeless, and had died childless.'

Hearing this, Tiberius ordered that his face be scrubbed with the lobster too. When his litter was held up by bushes obstructing the road, he ordered the centurion who was supposed to make sure the road was clear to lie on the ground and had him flogged to within an inch of his life.

TORTURED TO DEATH

Not a day went by without someone being sentenced to death. Tiberius took such a delight in cruelty that anyone who actually seemed willing to die was forced to live. He would send friendly letters to people, inviting them to Capri. When they arrived he would have them tortured to death. People were flung off the cliffs into the sea, where sailors waited with poles and oars to beat to death anyone who had survived the fall. One particularly nasty torture he devised was to tie a cord tightly around a man's penis, then force him to drink huge draughts of wine. Many killed themselves rather than visit him on Capri. Despite Tiberius's fear of people plotting against him in Rome, the danger was rather closer to home. He was killed in his bed by Gaius Germanicus Caligula, the very man whom he had chosen to be his successor. Tiberius's last wish was for his corpse to be buggered by a well-endowed slave. No one could be found to perform the task despite the large amount of cash on offer.

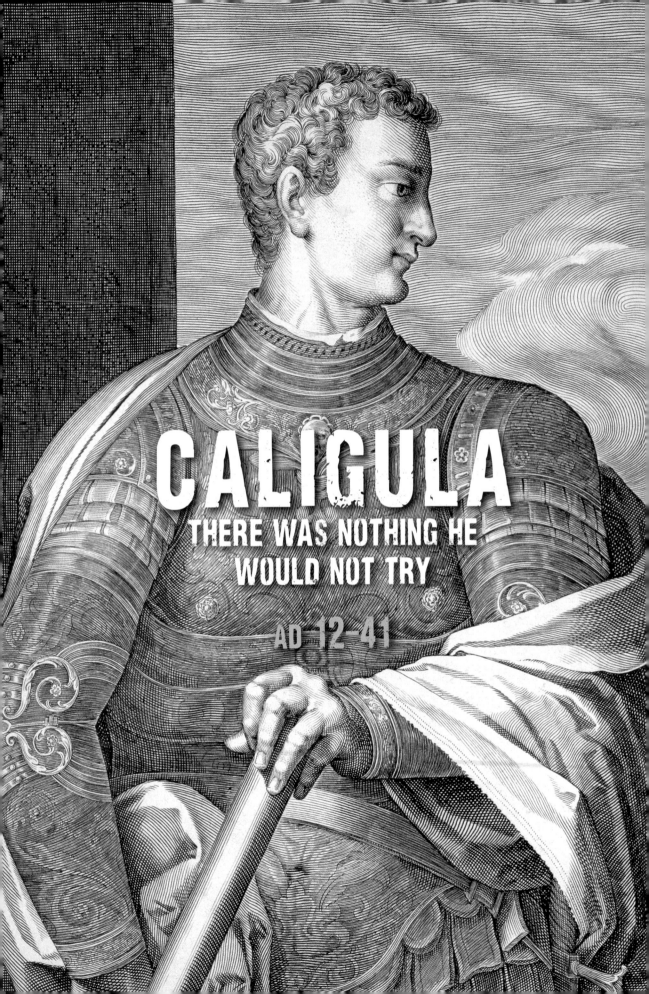

uetonius said that Tiberius's successor, Caligula, 'could not control his natural cruelty and viciousness'. He lived incestuously with his three sisters, prostituting them to his favourites. He had any man or woman he wanted. None dared refuse. He married the wife of one of his generals and took pleasure in displaying her naked to his friends. He often wore women's clothing and ordered torture and brutal executions as mealtime entertainment. Eventually the Praetorian Guard turned against him and stabbed him to death.

Born the son of a Roman general, Gaius Germanicus was nicknamed Caligula – 'Little Boot' – after the army footwear he wore as a child. When he was seven, his father, his mother, Agrippina the Elder, and his two older brothers were executed by the emperor Tiberius in his paranoid purges. But Caligula and his three sisters survived. He was summoned to Capri where he managed to ingratiate himself with Tiberius. There he witnessed the old man's sexual depravity and his fondness for torture and executions. And as Tiberius's favourite, he got to indulge perverted whims of his own.

'Even at that time he could not control his natural cruelty and viciousness,' wrote Suetonius. 'He was a most eager witness of the tortures and executions of those who suffered punishment, revelling at night in gluttony and adultery, disguised in a wig and a long robe, passionately devoted besides to the theatrical arts of dancing and singing, in which Tiberius very willingly indulged him, in the hope that through these his savage nature might be softened. This last was so clearly evident to the shrewd old man, that he used to say now and then that to allow Gaius to live would prove the ruin of himself and of all men.'

Tiberius was right. After Caligula had gone through a number of marriages and affairs, he killed Tiberius, possibly out of revenge for the murder of his father, mother and brothers. The Romans were delighted that Tiberius was dead and crowds cheered Caligula as he made his way to Rome. He celebrated by brutally sacrificing 160 victims and expelling the *spintriae* – homosexual prostitutes – from Rome.

AT THE GAMES

Unlike Julius Caesar or Tiberius, Caligula was a great fan of the games. He was inordinately proud of the size of his penis and liked to flash it at the crowds. He could even be seen masturbating or being attended to by Rome's most skilled and beautiful prostitutes while below, in the ring, victorious gladiators would spell out the emperor's name in their victims' blood, dotting the i with the severed head. Caligula often ordered the death of the loser by removing his thumb, or perhaps his whole fist, from the anus of a catamite from Mesopotamia, where rectal elasticity was said to be greatly prized.

The defeated would be despatched in the most brutal way – chopped up while still alive, prodded with a red-hot poker or finished off by a butcher with a cleaver. Not only did Caligula

> ### 'HE LIVED IN HABITUAL INCEST WITH ALL HIS SISTERS, AND AT A LARGE BANQUET HE PLACED EACH OF THEM IN TURN BELOW HIM, WHILE HIS WIFE RECLINED ABOVE.'
> Suetonius

enjoy the bloodshed, he also enjoyed the gladiators. His favourites were as accomplished in the bedroom as they were in the ring and, after the games, he would appear in the changing room to view the blood-splattered gladiators naked.

INCEST

Since childhood, Caligula had maintained an incestuous relationship with his sister Drusilla. It was said that he was deflowering her when they were caught in bed by his grandmother Antonia. Once he was emperor, he flaunted their affair. They lived openly as man and wife, although she was married to a man of consular rank. Incest, he claimed, was no shame, boasting that his own mother had been born as a result of the emperor Augustus's incest with his daughter, Julia. Caligula could be seen riding round the seedier quarters of Rome with Drusilla, masturbating with one hand and hurling gold coins to the crowds with the other. He also had an amphitheatre built so that, for a small fee, the plebeian rabble could watch him bugger his sister on a solid gold stage, sometimes with some favourite gladiator entering him anally at the same time.

At some point, Caligula and Drusilla planned to have a boy child who would inherit the empire. When Caligula was afflicted with a serious illness, he named Drusilla as his successor. One aristocrat offered his life if the gods would save the emperor. Caligula took him at his word. The heads of those who predicted his death were piled on his sick bed, so he could draw strength from them.

Caligula's other two sisters, Livilla and Agrippina the Younger, fell victim to his paranoia. They were put on display in a tent erected in front of the palace where, for five days, they were forced to have sex with all comers, including cripples and lepers. Agrippina was pregnant at the time. An imperial commission kept a tally and recorded that an astonishing 7,000 sex acts took place.

After the death of Drusilla, Caligula lived in incest with Livilla and Agrippina, while prostituting them to his catamites. He married them off, but after their weddings he took them back to his house, warning their new husbands 'not to take liberties with my wife'. He also had sex with them openly in front of his own wife. Finally he had them banished.

The Equine Heir

The story that Caligula made his horse Incitatus a consul is probably without foundation, though his favourite mount was given a marble stall, an ivory manger with purple trappings and a jewelled necklace, and a house with furniture and servants. And the entire neighbourhood was ordered to keep silent so that the horse could sleep undisturbed. It is said that, after the death of Drusilla, Caligula attempted to conceive a fitting heir with Incitatus.

Eventually, the *spintriae* were allowed back into Rome to put on ever-more spectacular displays of public copulation, and dancers, singers, actors and prostitutes were summoned from the four corners of the empire. Meanwhile Caligula grew more cruel. Philosophers who criticized him had their mouths sewn up so they could not speak and their hands cut off so they could not write.

EXECUTIONS AS ENTERTAINMENT

Caligula ordered executions on a whim, or to fill the imperial coffers. He was forever thinking up more sadistic deaths for his victims. Parents were forced to watch the execution of their children. Torture, decapitation and dismemberment were provided as entertainment while he was eating. Caligula himself appeared in the arena with a razor-sharp sword, facing gladiators armed only with wooden daggers, and, to earn more money for the imperial coffers, Roman matrons and their sons and daughters were forced into prostitution. Caligula had them displayed naked in a brothel set up in his palace.

He had any man or woman he wanted, simply sending divorce papers to their spouses if necessary. His passion for Pyrallis, a common prostitute, was also notorious. He counted among his lovers a beautiful young pantomime actor, whom he was not ashamed to kiss in public, his brother-in-law and various hostages. He abducted the wife of Gaius Piso and raped her, then banished her when he suspected she was seeing Piso again. Later he married the wife of one of his generals, then abandoned her, giving orders that no other man was to make love to her.

The Death of Drusilla

At the age of 23, Drusilla suddenly died. The doctors diagnosed 'a surfeit of buggery'. She had just finished a marathon 24-hour session with Caligula and seven well-endowed studs freshly arrived from Caesariensis, modern-day Algeria. In grief, Caligula sodomized her dead body. Even after she was cremated, he tried to revive her by masturbating into her ashes.

Caligula declared Drusilla a god. Senators and philosophers who insisted that only outstanding figures, such as Julius Caesar and Augustus, could become gods were despatched to the arena where they were crucified upside down and burnt alive. Temples were consecrated to honour her throughout Rome and the empire, and coins were minted in her memory. A season of public mourning was announced when it was declared a capital offence to laugh, bathe or even dine with members of your own family. Meanwhile Caligula began making preparations to declare himself a god and join her.

Caesonia, reputedly the most lascivious woman in Rome, was often seen in his company. Although she was seven years older than him, her masculine looks appealed to the effeminate Caligula. He named the little girl he sired with her Drusilla and aimed to make her his heir.

Members of distant tribes known for their sexual dexterity – the Garamantes, Cietae and Quinquegentanei – were summoned to teach him the 'seven secrets of sexual self-annihilation'. He had himself buggered publicly by his favourite gladiator, who had his head cut off at the moment of orgasm so Caligula was bathed in blood.

Plied with drugs to enhance his sexual performance, Caligula often wore women's clothing or dressed as a god with a blond beard or as Venus or a triumphant general, wearing the breastplate of Alexander the Great, which he had stolen from his sarcophagus in Alexandria. One accused traitor was forced to publicly sodomize his own father, before strangling him. Other traitors were burnt to death with Caligula looking on in flowing women's robes.

Caligula humiliated those of rank around him. He would insist on sleeping with their wives and, afterwards, tell the husband publicly that his wife was no good in bed, or hire her out as a whore to any low-life who wanted her. However, he made the mistake of humiliating the tribune of the Praetorian Guard in this way. The Guard cut him down at the Palatine Games and Caligula was despatched with a sword thrust through his private parts.

NERO
LEARNT INIQUITY AT HIS MOTHER'S BREAST
AD 37-68

The fifth emperor of Rome, Nero, had an incestuous affair with his mother and then murdered her. He liked to dress in women's clothes and organized lavish orgies with vast pavilions full of naked prostitutes. Even upper-class women were forced into prostitution. He was married twice to women and twice to men – the first time as husband to a slave boy who was castrated, and the second time as wife to a slave who was not. He also donned a slave's dress so that he could attend brothels incognito. Eventually the Romans grew tired of him and he was forced to commit suicide.

Nero came from a dysfunctional family. His father, Gnaeus Domitius Ahenobus, was prosecuted by Augustus for the bloodthirsty games he put on. He ran over a child on the Appian Way for fun, killed one of his freedmen for not drinking as much as he was told and ripped out another man's eye in the forum. Under Tiberius he was charged with treason, adultery and incest with his sister, and was only saved by the accession of his brother-in-law, Caligula. He died when Nero was three, leaving the child to learn everything he needed to know about cruelty and perversion from his monstrous mother, Agrippina.

The granddaughter to Julia the Elder, Augustus's promiscuous daughter, Agrippina, was Caligula's much-abused sister. She urinated on her brother's grave when she returned from exile and fed his remains to wild dogs. She poisoned her second husband, Passienus Crispus, to become the fourth wife of Caligula's successor – and her uncle – Claudius. He named Nero co-heir beside his own son, seven-year-old Britannicus, whom Agrippina later murdered – though another story has it that Nero himself poisoned Britannicus, after using him as a catamite. Meanwhile, Agrippina was no more faithful to Claudius than his previous wife, the notorious Messalina, had been. Eventually, she poisoned him too.

INCESTUOUS PASSION

With no father around, Nero developed an incestuous passion for his own mother. Mother and son often rode together in the same litter and stains on his clothes afterwards seemed to indicate that something sexual had been going on. Nero married his cousin Octavia, after her fiancé had been forced to commit suicide. But among his concubines he included a prostitute who looked like Agrippina, and he had little time for the virtuous Octavia. Nero was

Fiddling While Rome Burns

Nero is popularly portrayed as the mad emperor who played the fiddle while Rome burned. This is not true. The violin was not invented until the 16th century and its bowed forerunner did not reach Europe from Central Asia until the tenth century. Nero, however, did play the lyre – but not while Rome burned in AD 64. In fact he directed the fire-fighting.

The story that he was singing and playing the lyre while the city burned was probably put around because he took advantage of the destruction to build an extravagant palace called the Golden House. He wanted to blame the Jews for starting the fire. However, his wife Poppaea liked the Jews at court so, instead, she suggested blaming the Christians. With typical cruelty, Nero had Christians tied to stakes, smeared with tar and set alight as torches to illuminate the gardens where those rendered homeless by the fire sought refuge.

just 17 when Claudius died, so his mother ruled as regent. To weaken her influence, Nero's tutor, Lucius Annaeus Seneca, furnished him with a mistress named Acte, whom he tried to marry though it was against the law to do so as she had once been a slave. Seneca also provided Nero with handsome male slaves to sleep with.

Nero disliked the brutality of the gladiatorial arena and became an admirer of all things Greek, beginning poetry competitions, theatrical performances and athletics as rival attractions. Even the Vestal Virgins were invited to watch the athletics, though the men competed naked. There was opposition to this.

GIVEN UP TO DEBAUCHERY

'These foreign pursuits were ruining our young men, who were giving themselves up to the indolent and shameful homosexual practices of the gymnasium,' lamented the orator Tacitus. 'In this the emperor and the Senate led the way, having not only given a free rein to vice, but even compelled Roman nobles, in the name of oratory and poetry, to degrade themselves on stage.

> 'AGRIPPINA RAGED WITH WOMANLY JEALOUSY THAT SHE HAD A FREEDWOMAN FOR A RIVAL AND A MAID FOR A DAUGHTER-IN-LAW. SHE COULD NOT WAIT FOR HER SON'S REPENTANCE OR SATIETY.'
> Tacitus

What was left for them was to strip themselves naked, put on boxing gloves, and practise fighting thus instead of with the weapons of a soldier ... Whole nights were now given up to debauchery, what was left for virtue? Every debauchee, in these promiscuous crowds, could practise by night the lusts he had conceived as fantasy during the day.'

Nero opened the Pons Milvius, a celebrated sexual resort close to the city, 'to allow full freedom to lust and debauchery of every sort there'. He also started the Juvenalia, a festival celebrating the arrival of puberty when the first down was shaved from a boy's face. This became an 'occasion for great licentiousness and debauchery, especially of a pederastic nature, and the fullest opportunity taken thereof, for gratifying such tastes'.

Secretly Nero went out in disguise to rob shops and murder people, dropping their bodies down the sewer. He would visit the taverns and brothels of the Subura, having sex with both women and boys. He also raped a Vestal Virgin.

Nero wanted others to share his vices. He held huge public feasts, inviting all the prostitutes and nude dancing girls in the city. When he cruised down the Tiber to Ostia or around the Gulf of Pozzuoli, temporary brothels were erected along the shore, staffed by married women. He built a huge bath complex near his summer residence at Baiae near Naples, which became another sex resort.

Nero himself practised every kind of perversion. 'As for his own body, it is known that he dishonoured it to such a degree,' wrote Suetonius, 'that after he had defiled every part of it with unnatural pollution, he at last devised a new kind of sport.' He had men, women and children tied to stakes naked. Then, dressed in skins, he would attack their private parts as if he were a wild animal. 'After working up sufficient excitement by this means, he was despatched – shall we say – by his freedman Doryphorus,' said Suetonius.

Gaius Ofonius Tigellinus

After AD 62, Nero's closest advisor was Gaius Ofonius Tigellinus, who had been exiled in AD 39 by Caligula for adultery with his sisters, Agrippina and Livilla, and a number of other Roman matrons. Tacitus gave a description of a feast and entertainment laid on by Tigellinus in Nero's honour.

AD 10–6

'The most notorious and profligate of these entertainments were those given in Rome by Tigellinus,' he wrote. 'A banquet set out upon a barge built for the purpose on a lake, and this barge was towed about by vessels picked out in gold and ivory and rowed by naked debauched youths who were assorted according to their age and proficiency in libidinous practices ... On the banks of the lake were brothels, filled with women of rank, and opposite them naked prostitutes, indulging in indecent gestures and lewd posturings. At nightfall, the nearby woods and houses re-echoed with songs, and were ablaze with lights, and Nero disgraced himself with every kind of abomination, natural and unnatural, leaving no further depths of debauchery into which he could sink.'

Nero tried to divorce Octavia, but could find no one to testify that they had committed adultery with her. She was banished to the island of Pandataria. When she complained of her treatment, her maids were tortured to death. He then had the husband of Poppaea Sabina murdered and took her as a lover. 'This woman had every quality – except virtue,' wrote Tacitus. 'She cared nothing for her reputation, sharing her affections between her husband and lovers, and transferring her favours when she saw advantage in it.'

Nero's mother did not approve, so he married Poppaea off to his friend Otho while continuing the affair. But Agrippina continued interfering, so he stripped her of her honours and privileges, and banished her to her riverside estate. Even this did not guarantee her safety. One night after she had dined with him at Baiae, he offered her one of his boats to take her home. He was seen kissing her breasts before she got on board. The boat had been rigged to sink, but Agrippina did not drown, managing to swim ashore. So Nero sent a military tribune to kill her. He ordered that the first stab should be to her womb – that is, 'the place where the emperor first entered the world'. Despite this, it was announced that she had committed suicide. Nero could not wait to examine her corpse, 'handling every part of it, finding fault with some, commending others'.

In AD 62, Nero had Octavia murdered. Her severed head was sent to Poppaea. Just 12 days later Nero and Poppaea married. As empress, Poppaea required the milk of 500 wild asses for her daily bath. Later she had Seneca killed because he favoured Nero's mistress Acte over her.

DOUBLE WEDDING

When Poppaea died in AD 65, Nero replaced her with a young boy named Sporus who looked like her. He had him castrated and had a slit made in his perineum so he could use him as a wife. On a trip to Greece, they underwent a wedding ceremony. Nero also married Doryphorus – but this time Nero dressed as the wife.

'The dowry, the marriage bed, the nuptial torch, were all there. Everything was in public and exposed to view – even those things which are usually performed in darkness when the bride is a woman,' said Suetonius. And on the wedding night Nero 'imitated the moans and cries of a virgin being deflowered'.

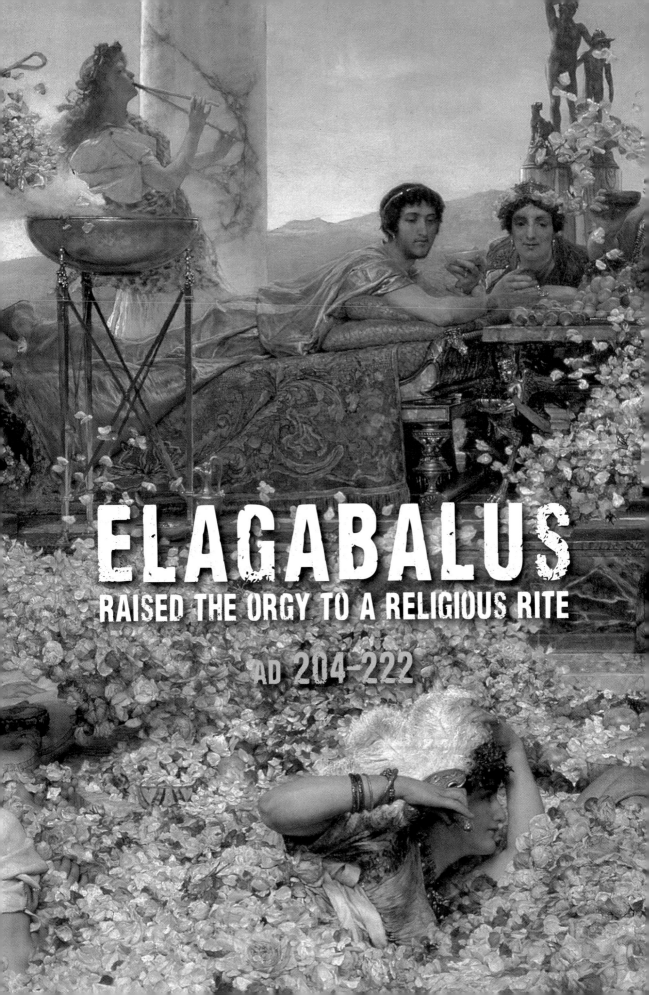

ELAGABALUS
RAISED THE ORGY TO A RELIGIOUS RITE

AD 204–222

In AD 218, the 14-year-old Elagabalus became the 28th emperor of Rome. Born in Syria, he was a follower of the sun god Elah-Gabal whose rites involved 'a chorus of Syrian damsels performing lascivious dances to the sound of barbarian music'. He organized lavish orgies with his concubines and catamites, and shaved the genitals of his lovers of both sexes with the razor he used for his own beard. He was eventually murdered after violating the Vestal Virgins.

Elagabalus, it was said, was 'a prince who imbibed pleasure through all the cavities of his body'. He was a member of the family of the hereditary priest of the sun god Elah-Gabal – giving him the name Elagabalus in Latin and Heliogabalus in Greek. In the name of that god, he worshipped the phallus, symbolically and in everyday life.

The rites of his religion, Sol Invicta, involved him 'dancing indolently to the kiss of flutes', played in the temple by scantily clad – if not naked – girls. However, as a priest of the sun god, he was constrained to act as effeminately as possible. He was said to be as beautiful as the young Bacchus and wore semi-transparent clothes that revealed more than they obscured. He borrowed these translucent garments from his mother, who had used them to delight her lovers – of whom, it was said, he was one.

In the temple there was a phallus-shaped stone, probably a meteorite, worshipped by Elagabalus. Roman soldiers came to see the spectacle. 'When he did sacrifice and danced in the foreign way around the altar to the sound of flutes, pipes and other instruments,' said the historian Herodian, 'he took the eyes of all men – especially of soldiers, who knew that he was of royal birth. His youthful beauty fascinated those who saw him ... The soldiers used to come to the city often and, visiting the temple to attend service there, took pleasure in watching the young man.'

Some thought he was Eros, others that he was the son of the current emperor, Caracalla. His grandmother, Julia Maesa, had stayed in Rome during Caracalla's reign. During that period she had amassed great wealth and she might easily have persuaded her daughter, Julia Soemias, to accommodate her cousin Caracalla. Julia Soemias was famous for 'granting her favours

> 'IT IS STATED THAT THE BEAUTY OF ELAGABALUS AND THE UNRESTRAINED EXERCISE OF HIS ALL-PERVADING PASSION FOR PEDERASTY SO ENDEARED HIM TO THE SOLDIERS.'
>
> Charles Reginald Dawes

indiscriminately for the satisfaction of her own lust'. The Roman writer Aelius Lampridius suggested that Elagabalus – whose birth name was Varius Avitus Bassianus – had been named Varius because his mother 'lived like a whore and practised baseness of all kinds, and he was conceived by the seed of "various" gentlemen, as happens with a whore'.

Julia Soemias went along with the story that Caracalla was Elagabalus's father. There may even have been some truth in this. Caracalla famously had a Vestal Virgin burned to death after he had tried to rape her. She protested the sentence on the grounds that he had failed to rape her and was unable to perform because Julia Soemias had worn him out. Julia Maesa was enormously wealthy and showered gold on all who believed Elagabalus was the son of Caracalla.

The Romans loved Elagabalus. It was said: 'He charmed and fascinated all those in any way susceptible who came into contact with him ... The soft feminine delicacy and grace of his form and features, and his girlish beauty, is admitted by all, even his severest detractors.' At the age of 15, while still in Syria, he was proclaimed emperor of Rome.

NO RIVAL

Elagabalus headed for Rome, carrying his black stone phallus with him. At Nicomedia he murdered his mother's lover Gannys, perhaps out of jealousy – though, in bed, it was said he was no rival for Elagabalus. From then on, Elagabalus's mother became his pander.

Vestal Virgins

The Vestal Virgins were girls from respectable families who served as priestesses in the Temple of Vesta, goddess of the hearth. Their job was to tend the sacred fire, bring water from the sacred spring – Vesta eschewed water from the city's water supply – and prepare food. Girls were selected by the chief priest or *pontifex maximus* – literally 'the great bridge builder', a title later adopted by the popes. They were chosen between the ages of six and ten and served for 30 years. Those who violated their vow of chastity were punished by being scourged and buried alive.

The cult of Vesta pre-dated Rome. Indeed, the founders of Rome, Romulus and Remus, were said to have been the sons of the Vestal Virgin Rhea Sylvia, who had been raped by Mars. In disgrace, she was ordered to drown the twins in the River Tiber. However, they survived and were washed ashore at the site of Rome, where they were suckled by a wolf. The Latin for she-wolf is *lupa*, though *lupa* also means a prostitute. Misfortunes that befell the city of Rome were blamed on the sexual misbehaviour of the Vestal Virgins.

When he entered Rome, Elagabalus was wearing a see-through purple robe, purple being the imperial colour. He was covered in jewellery and his face was made up with pencilled eyebrows and painted cheeks. A full-length portrait of him in this outfit also hung in the Senate.

While Julia Maesa got on with wielding power, Elagabalus was otherwise occupied. According to his biographer Aelius Lampridius, he 'devised different kinds of voluptuousness, excelling in this respect even the inventors of the spintrian postures familiar to the ancient emperors, for he certainly knew the refinements of Tiberius, Caligula and Nero'. 'Spintrian' is defined by Thomas Blount's *Glossographia* of 1656 as 'pertaining to those that seek out, or invent, new and monstrous actions of lust'.

Wearing a blond wig, Elagabalus prostituted himself in taverns and brothels. He propositioned clients from the palace and 'provided brothels at his house for his friends, clients and slaves', according to Aelius Lampridius.

On stage he played Aphrodite, the Greek goddess of sexual love and beauty, in the *Judgement of Paris*, where the Trojan hero Paris is charged by Zeus to determine which of the three goddesses, Hera, Athena or Aphrodite, was the most beautiful. During the action, he would drop his clothes and kneel, naked, 'with his buttocks projecting and thrust back on the front of his debaucher'. His body was smooth, depilated, with the hair removed from every part. He insisted his lovers should also be hairless, afterwards using the same razor to shave his own face.

His jewel-encrusted carriage was drawn around town by hand-picked teams of naked young women while he whipped their straining buttocks, and the carriage was stopped if he saw a

The Prostitution of Elagabalus

The Roman writer Cassius Dio, who lived in the reign of Elagabalus, wrote: 'At night he would enter some low tavern, where, with false hair, he fulfilled the functions of a tavern-girl. He resorted to the famous lupanars where, after having evicted the courtesans, he gave himself up to prostitution, judging his own beauty by how much gold he took home. Finally, he established an apartment in the palace where he abandoned himself to incontinence, standing quite naked at the door of the chamber, like the prostitutes, drawing the curtain which was hung on rings of gold, and inviting passers-by with the soft and effeminate voice of the courtesans. He had men there charged to let themselves be enticed. And, as for other things, he had for that purpose a host of emissaries whose occupation it was to seek out those who by their lasciviousness and sexual power could give him most pleasure. He drew money from them and, glorifying in his gains, was constantly in discussion with his companions in debauchery, pretending to have more lovers and to have earned more money than they had.'

well-endowed young boy. Gold dust was sprinkled before him when he walked. He emptied his bowels into a golden bowl and urinated into a pot made of onyx. Men with large penises and 'amorous strength' were given senior positions in his administration. The empire was scoured for men with big penises; Elagabalus paid enormous finders' fees.

When Zoticus, the son of a cook from Smyrna, was found and 'surpassed all the world in the largeness of his private parts', he was brought to Rome where he bowed low before Elagabalus and said: 'Hail, emperor, my master.' Elagabalus replied girlishly: 'Do not call me master. I am your mistress.'

'PUSH AWAY COOK-BOY'

Zoticus and Elagabalus were married and the emperor 'submitted to the carnal act' while the bridesmaids – or rather bridesmen – cried out 'Push away cook-boy', in reference to his father's profession. At least, that is Aelius Lampridius's version. Cassius Dio says that a jealous lover slipped Zoticus a potion that prevented him from getting an erection, and he was banished from Rome.

Then Elagabalus fell in love with a fair-haired charioteer named Hierocles. Aelius Lampridius said Elagabalus proclaimed his love for all to see by kissing Hierocles' private parts in public in a way 'which it is indecent even to mention'. They married and Hierocles was recognized as the 'husband' of the emperor. Elagabalus was then said 'to more faithfully imitate the most libertine of women; he committed adultery, for which he was beaten and punished by his husband'. He arranged to be caught in acts of infidelity – even with Hierocles' favourite brother – so that he would be beaten and would often appear in public with bruises and black eyes.

Elagabalus also married several women, largely for political reasons. However, one of them was a Vestal Virgin, which outraged the Romans.

In his religious rites, he began sacrificing children – 'boys that were noble and good-looking and had fathers and mothers still living'. According to Lampridius, 'he inspected the children's innards and tortured the victims according to his own native ritual'. Followers of Sol Invicta circumcised themselves and sometimes castrated themselves, throwing their severed sexual organs into the temple. Elagabalus once prepared himself for this rite, but thought better of it.

POPE ALEXANDER VI

VICE IN THE VATICAN

1431–1503

A scion of Spain's powerful Borgia family, Rodrigo Borgia did not think that being a Catholic priest should prevent you from having a fulfilling sex life. By the time he was a cardinal, he had numerous mistresses and children. When he became pope, he staged 'whores' races' in the papal apartment. He also committed incest with his daughter, Lucrezia. While she also slept with her brother, there is no evidence that she poisoned anyone, contrary to popular belief.

By the time Rodrigo Borgia left Spain, he had at least six illegitimate children by assorted mistresses. When he was studying law in Bologna, his tutor Gaspare de Verona said: 'He is handsome; with a most cheerful countenance and genial bearing. He is gifted with a honeyed and choice eloquence. Beautiful women are attracted to love him and are excited by him in a quite remarkable way, more powerfully than an iron is attracted by a magnet.'

In 1456 his uncle, Pope Calistus III (1455–58), appointed Rodrigo Borgia cardinal and installed him as archbishop of Valencia. Now he added wealth to his attractions. He seduced a widow, ravished her two daughters and 'initiated them into the most hideous voluptuousness'. One of them had three children by him; one of their great-great-grandchildren went on to become Pope Innocent X (1644–55).

PAPAL CONDEMNATION

While staying with the Marchesa of Mantua, Rodrigo entertained himself with the beautiful wife of a dim-witted nobleman. Pius II (1458–64) condemned this. 'You do not abstain from hunting or games, or from intercourse with women,' he wrote in rebuke. Rodrigo responded by staging an orgy. The pope then condemned him for wearing his cardinal's robes to such a scandalous Bacchanalia. In Mantua, Rodrigo also met Roman beauty Vannozza Catanei, who bore him at least four children – Cesare, Juan, Lucrezia and Jofré.

Lucrezia was sexually available to both Rodrigo and Cesare, among others. It is still a matter of debate whether her first child was sired by her father or by her brother. Cesare and Juan used to compete for their father's favour by supplying beautiful women for his private harem. At one point, Juan outshone Cesare by supplying a Spanish beauty who moved Rodrigo to ecstasy. In jealousy, Cesare stabbed his brother and threw his body in the Tiber. Rodrigo was so upset that he mended his ways, but not for long.

It is said that Rodrigo and Cesare imprisoned and raped the most beautiful young man in Italy. His body was later found in the Tiber with a stone tied around his neck. But normally Rodrigo preferred women. In 1480, he seduced 16-year-old Giulia Farnese, although she was already married. Romans called her, sarcastically, the 'bride of Christ'. He later made her brother a cardinal – nicknamed 'cardinal petticoat' – and he went on to become Pope Paul III (1534–49).

When Pius II died, Rodrigo was disappointed not to be made pope. But under Sixtus IV (1471–84) his amorous

> **'IN ORDER THAT YOUR LUSTS MIGHT BE ALL THE MORE UNRESTRAINED, THE HUSBANDS, FATHERS, BROTHERS, KINSMEN OF THE YOUNG GIRLS WERE NOT INVITED.'**
>
> Pope Pius II

The Avignon Papacy

Between 1309 and 1377, popes resided in Avignon in southern France. Away from Rome, the papacy went through a particularly louche period.

• Clement V (1305–14) 'removed the papal see to Avignon so that he might perpetrate his wickedness in greater privacy', and conducted church business through his mistress.

• John XXII (1316–34) sold indulgences, doing a particularly brisk trade in incest and sodomy. He also introduced the *cullagium*, an annual sex tax a clergyman had to pay if he wanted to keep a concubine.

• Benedict XII (1334–42) deflowered a 14-year-old when he was an inquisitor and continued having sex with her after she married. He offered the poet Petrarch a cardinal's hat if he could sleep with his sister.

• Clement VI (1342–52) 'swept along in a flood of the most obscene pleasure, an incredible storm of debauchery, the most horrid and unprecedented shipwreck of chastity', according to Petrarch.

• Urban V (1362–70) tried to return to Rome, taking his children with him.

• Gregory XI (1370–78) succeeded in taking the papal see back to Rome. When he left Avignon, his mother tore open her robe to show him the breasts that had suckled him and begged him not to go.

activities went unnoticed. Rome turned into one giant brothel with an estimated 50,000 prostitutes working in the city. Rodrigo missed out again when Sixtus died, and when his successor Innocent VIII (1484–92) died, Rodrigo found himself one vote short in the conclave to elect the new pope. The clinching vote belonged to a Venetian monk, who wanted 5,000 crowns and one night with 12-year-old Lucrezia. The deal was done and Rodrigo became Pope Alexander VI.

CARNAL TREATS

As pope, Rodrigo laid on entertainments featuring naked dancers. During festivals, he had an average of 25 courtesans a night laid on for his amusement. John Burchard, bishop of Ostia, described a supper that Cesare Borgia put on for his father and sister in the papal apartments: 'Fifty reputable whores, not common but the kind called courtesans, supped and after supper they danced about with the servants and others in that place, first in their clothes and then nude ... candelabra with lighted candles were set on the floor and chestnuts were strewn about and the naked courtesans on hands and knees gathered them up, wriggling in and out among the candelabra ... Then all those present in the hall were carnally treated in public'. Rodrigo, Cesare and Lucrezia then handed out prizes to the men who had copulated the most times with the prostitutes.

Sometimes Rodrigo's playmates even interrupted Mass. On one occasion, he brought giggling women up to the altar and the sanctified Host was trampled under foot. Even when he travelled, his retinue would include scantily clad dancing girls – to the outrage of the rest of Christendom.

Rodrigo appointed his son Cesare an archbishop and cardinal. Skilfully skirting the stipulation that a cardinal must be legitimate, he issued two papal bills. One certified that Cesare was the legitimate son of Vannozza Catanei and her 'husband' and was made public. The other acknowledged that Cesare was Rodrigo's son and was kept private.

Rodrigo also encouraged sexual misbehaviour in others. He gave the blessing at the funeral of one 15-year-old Florentine lad who had died, it was said, of sexual excess. He had had sexual intercourse eleven times in one night – in another account, seven times in one hour. Alexander also sold indulgences, pardoning sins yet to be committed. One nobleman paid 24,000 gold pieces for permission to commit incest with his sister. Peter Mendoza, cardinal of Valencia, bought permission to call his catamite his natural son.

When Lucrezia married, Rodrigo outdid the bride at the wedding. He wore a gold Turkish robe whose train was carried by an African slave girl. He amused himself by throwing confetti down the low-cut bodices of the ladies' dresses. Then, when the moment came for the marriage to be consummated, Rodrigo accompanied the couple to the bridal chamber.

'There such shocking and hideous scenes took place as no language can convey or describe,' wrote one chronicler. 'The Pope played the part of matron for his daughter; Lucrezia, that Messalina who, even while a child, had been by her father and brothers initiated into the most hideous debauchery, played, in this instance, the part of an innocent in order to prolong the obscenities of the comedy; and the "marriage" took place in the presence of the pontifical family.'

NON-CONSUMMATION

Even after she married, according to Burchard, Lucrezia remained in the papal apartments. When Giulia Farnese took her to visit her husband, Rodrigo was beside

Papal Misbehaviour

Alexander VI was not the only pope to misbehave. Many have failed to be celibate. The first pope, St Peter, had a daughter. Pius II wrote pornography and had a very active sex life before he became pope. Leo X (1513–21) was an ostentatious homosexual. There was a period in the ninth, tenth and early eleventh centuries called the 'Papal Pornocracy', when a mother and daughter alternately put their lovers and children on the papal throne. Popes often ran the brothels in Rome, making extra cash from the pilgrims who flocked there.

But possibly the worst pope of all was John XXIII (1410–15), later reclassified as an antipope. He began his career as a pirate but then realized there was more money in the church. When he was papal legate to Bologna, he had a palace with a hundred concubines in it. When he became pope, there was a schism and the Catholic Church had more popes than it needed. He was taken to the Council of Constant in 1414. It is said that every prostitute in Europe attended – as all the clergymen were there, the city was full of single men with money.

John was charged with 54 capital offences. He admitted four – murder, incest, adultery and, of all things for a pope, atheism. He was fined, deposed and jailed. But he bribed his way out of jail and went on to become a cardinal again.

himself with jealousy – doubly so as the two of them had left him. He wrote letters that threatened them with eternal damnation if they did not return. When they did, he was soon back to his normal self, sleeping with three other women – 'one of them a nun from Valencia, another a Castilian, a third a very beautiful girl from Venice, fifteen or sixteen years of age', as Ludovico Sforza told the Milan Senate.

Ludovico was the uncle of Lucrezia's first husband; the marriage was annulled by Rodrigo on the grounds of non-consummation. As part of the procedure, a papal commission had to declare that Lucrezia was a virgin – 'a conclusion that set all of Italy laughing,' said a chronicler. 'It was common knowledge that she was the biggest whore there ever was in Rome.' When the divorce was finally granted, she was pregnant with the miraculous papal child known as the *Infans Romans*.

MICHELANGELO

THE LAST JUDGEMENT

1475–1547

Throughout his life the Renaissance master Michelangelo was surrounded by nude models. He thought that nothing was more beautiful than a young man naked and his sculpture and painting gave him a unique opportunity to indulge his passion. No other artist, gay or straight, male or female, concentrated so much on the male nude. Following the convention of the time, the genitals of his nudes are undeveloped, boyish, but he imbued a sensual, loving quality to their pert buttocks. However, his notebooks reveal a darker passion.

Michelangelo Buonarroti was the greatest artist of the human body. As a study of the male nude, his *David* is beyond comparison. However, his work on the female nude was not rendered with the same ardour. Despite his exquisite draughtsmanship, he simply could not portray breasts. However, the more intimate parts of a woman's anatomy were not required in his largely religious work, which was just as well. He never had a female model as he could not bear to look at a woman's naked body.

While Florentine art of the Renaissance embraced the ideals of classical Greece, homosexuality was frowned upon. In 1502, when Michelangelo was 27, it was outlawed. Four years later, the laws were strengthened when the penalty for procuring was the amputation of a hand. Fathers who allowed their sons to engage in homosexual practices were punished and houses where homosexual acts took place were burnt down. Consequently, Michelangelo's homosexual impulses had to be sublimated into his art. He regularly hints at masturbation, often mutual male masturbation. Psychoanalysts say that Michelangelo's work reveals an urge to be sodomized, that he feels that sex with a woman will be punished by castration, and that being sodomized by a young male god was the route to immortality.

> 'IF CAPTURE AND DEFEAT MUST BE MY JOY, IT IS NO WONDER THAT, ALONE AND NAKED, I REMAIN PRISONER OF A KNIGHT-AT-ARMS.'
>
> Michelangelo Buonarroti

'GREAT SODOMITE'

Michelangelo spent much of his life in Rome, where attitudes to homosexuality were much looser. His patron, Pope Julius II (1503–13), was known as a 'great sodomite', despite the fact that, as a cardinal, he had had three daughters and many mistresses. However, after contracting syphilis from one of them, he turned his attention entirely to boys. Julius was succeeded by Leo X, a Medici who did little to hide his own homosexual proclivities. Nevertheless, Michelangelo was blackmailed over his love of men by the satirist and 'Scourge of Princes' Pietro Aretino, whom he bought off with a few of his drawings.

In 1520, when Michelangelo was 45, he became attached to Gherardo Perini. He wrote to him often and gave him drawings. In February 1522, Michelangelo wrote to Perini asking him to come over, so that he would not have to spend another night alone drawing. What would happen if Perini did not show up was made clear. The letter is decorated with a picture of a small boy with his penis in his hand, an image that Michelangelo later used in the work *A Children's Bacchanal*, which he gave to another lover.

In the autumn of 1522, 16-year-old Antonio Mini moved into Michelangelo's house. They lived together for nine years until, in 1531, Mini left for France. As a parting gift, Michelangelo gave him the painting *Leda and the Swan*, which shows a naked Leda kissing a swan that lies between her legs. The swan's neck is extremely phallic and Leda is plainly in sexual ecstasy. This is easily the most erotic image Michelangelo ever created.

There had been other apprentices who enjoyed Michelangelo's special favours. Piero d'Argento left him in 1509, but remained in regular communication. Silvio Falcone was dismissed in 1517, but 15 years later he was still writing to Michelangelo, asking to be allowed to repay 'the love you bore me when I was in your service'. But neither of these boys was allowed to share in Michelangelo's personal art collection the way Mini did.

While Mini was still in residence, Michelangelo met Andrea Quaratesi, the teenage offspring of a Florentine banking family. The only surviving portrait that Michelangelo completed is of Quaratesi. In a scribbled note Michelangelo asks Quaratesi to 'love me' and calls him his 'great consolation'. Quaratesi is also depicted on an exercise sheet. From his figure it is estimated that he was about 14. Next to him Michelangelo drew a screaming satyr and a man defecating.

Misbehaving Renaissance Artists

In the Renaissance artists began painting and sculpting the naked human body again, so there was temptation everywhere.
• Raphael painted his mistress Margherita Luiti nude in the Mona Lisa pose. He called her *La Fornarina*, which means 'baker's daughter' – *fornicarina* means affectionately 'little prostitute'.
• Caravaggio shared a rent boy with his married friend Onorio Longhi.
• Benvenuto Cellini was sentenced to four years' imprisonment for sodomy in 1557. It was not his first offence.
• Botticelli, who painted *The Birth of Venus*, was also charged with sodomy.
• Titian used Venetian prostitutes and mistresses interchangeably as his models.
• Giovanni Antonio Bazzi slept with his apprentices and was known as *Il Sodoma*.

THE RAPE OF GANYMEDE

Humans engaged in sexual relations with birds appear as a motif throughout Michelangelo's work, not just in *Leda and the Swan*. In *The Rape of Ganymede*, he shows a naked youth being sexually assaulted by Zeus in the form of an eagle. The full-frontal Ganymede is shown in ecstasy while the eagle's clawed feet spread his legs. The eagle is plainly taking him from behind and its penis emerges through what appears to be a vaginal cleft in the boy's scrotum.

In the *Punishment of Tityus*, a naked man lies supine, overpowered by a huge bird. In Michelangelo's day, the word 'bird' (*uccello*) was slang for the penis, as it was in the late 19th and early 20th centuries in the United States. A 'bird' or 'young thrush', in Florentine slang, was also a boy who might be bagged and plucked.

In 1533, Michelangelo began a relationship with a young Florentine boy named Febo di Poggio. This relationship eventually forced him to leave Florence for good. He wrote di Poggio letters assuring him of his love. There were also passionate love poems to Febo:

Leonardo da Vinci

1452–1519

Leonardo da Vinci was Michelangelo's contemporary and great rival. It has often been assumed that Leonardo was also gay because he did not marry. Artists were not well paid during the Renaissance and few could afford a wife. However, in 1476 Leonardo was charged with sodomy. At the time, accusations could be made anonymously simply by dropping the allegations in a barrel. When the case came to court, the charges were dropped because there was no evidence or statements from witnesses. One of Leonardo's co-defendants was a Medici and the charge seems to have been a political smear. Making unfounded allegations of sodomy was a common method of defamation. The rapacious Pietro Aretino – who wrote a Renaissance textbook on sexual positions – was accused of sodomy and Benvenuto Cellini – who was no shrinking violet when it came to women – was convicted, twice.

Leonardo surrounded himself with pretty young boys. But he was an artist. He needed apprentices to run his studio and the male nude was in vogue at the time. As an apprentice, Leonardo had been a nude model himself. One of his pupils was Giovanni Antonio Bazzi, known at *Il Sodoma*.

As a youth, Leonardo wrote songs, played the lute and was Renaissance Florence's version of a rock star. By all accounts Leonardo was something of a ladies' man. He always dressed in the latest fashions and tended his hair. He scarcely concealed his interest in the opposite sex. Unlike Michelangelo he was skilled in portraying breasts, even when they are under fabric, and there are often breast-shaped hills in the background of his pictures. His anatomical studies explore every detail of the female sexual organs. His painting of *Leda and the Swan* is the first in the Western canon in which a female nude makes no attempt to hide her pubis.

In his notebooks he wrote a short essay on how to seduce women and mentions, in passing, his acquaintance with prostitutes. Brothel records from the period show that he was a regular user of girls and had his favourites.

Leonardo's most famous painting is *Mona Lisa*, who is portrayed with a very distinct cleavage. His studio produced a number of nude *Mona Lisas*, thought to have been copies from a Leonardo original. The model in the nudes from Leonardo's studio is plainly the same woman who posed for *Leda and the Swan*. From her hairstyle it can be deduced that she was a prostitute. Her working name was *La Cremona* – she probably came from Cremona in Lombardy. He used her regularly. Leonardo's household accounts show that she travelled around Italy with him. When Leonardo died in France in 1519, he left a very expensive fur coat to a woman named *La Matura*, who may have been the same woman.

I truly should, so happy was my lot.
While Phoebus was inflaming all the hill,
Have risen from the earth while I was able,
With his feathers, and made my dying sweet.

Phoebus was, of course, Febo and *poggio* in Italian means a hillock or a knoll. In the context of homosexual love, it is plain which hillock can be inflamed. And here we have feathers again. In Rome, Michelangelo fell for a handsome young aristocrat named Tommaso de' Cavalieri. He was 23, whereas Michelangelo was 57. Again Michelangelo bombarded his lover with love letters, poetry and drawings, including *A Children's Bacchanal*, *The Rape of Ganymede* and the *Punishment of Tityus*. They lived together for six months.

Ten years later, he was still writing to Tommaso – and his poems were still full of birds descending from the skies to pluck up the hearts of mortal men.

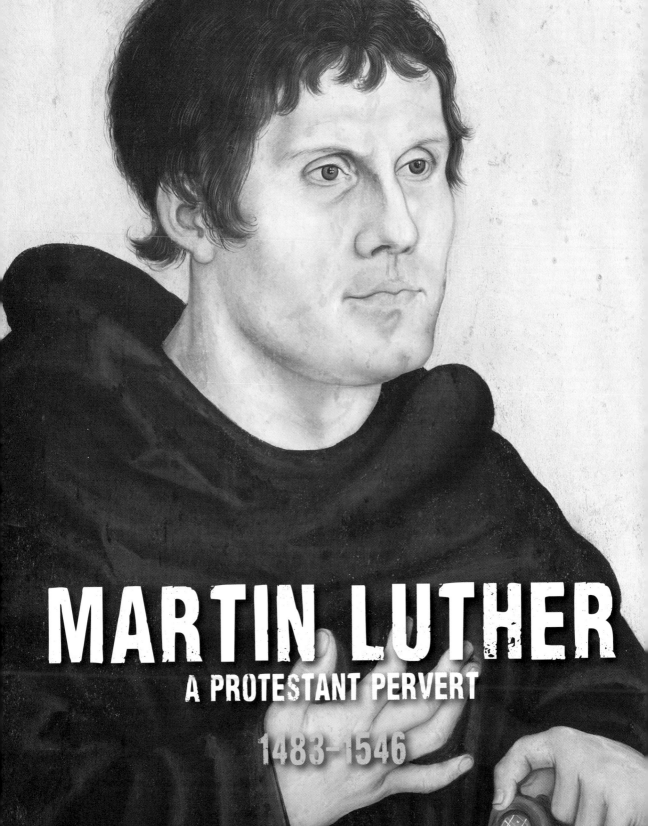

MARTIN LUTHER
A PROTESTANT PERVERT
1483-1546

Martin Luther was not cut out to be a monk and condemned vows of celibacy long before he broke with the Catholic Church and married a runaway nun. He was not the ideal husband as he was obsessed with filth – of the excremental kind. Before his marriage, he slept in a dirty, mildewed bed. Then he and his wife moved into a former monastery known as 'The Black Cloister'.

Progenitor of the Reformation, Martin Luther came from a poor background. His father was a copper miner who often beat him. In their impoverished circumstances the entire family slept together – presumably presenting the impressionable youngster with opportunities to observe sex acts at first hand. No wonder he considered sex an entirely natural human function. However, the conditions can hardly have been hygienic.

The family's finances improved while Luther was growing up. His father became a leaseholder of mines and smelters, and one of four citizen representatives on the local council. Martin enrolled in Erfurt University to study law, then entered the house of Augustinian Hermits in Erfurt, much to the chagrin of his parents. He later attributed his decision to change professions to a near miss by a lightning strike during a thunderstorm when he was returning to university on horseback after a trip home. He told his father he was terrified and cried out, 'Help, Saint Anna, and I will become a monk!' In his book *De votis monasticis* – 'Concerning Monastic Vows' – Luther said: 'Not freely or desirously did I become a monk, but walled around with terror and agony of sudden death, I vowed a constrained and necessary vow.'

TEMPTATIONS OF THE FLESH

As a monk, Luther found that he had to wrestle with the 'temptations of the flesh', resulting in frequent nocturnal pollutions. But this did not encourage him to change his bed sheets, which he kept on his bed for more than a year at a time. Apparently he liked the smell of his own sweat that permeated them.

Johann von Staupitz, the Vicar-General of the Augustinian Order in Germany, realized that the young Luther needed worldly distractions, so sent him back to university to study theology. In 1510, Luther was chosen as one of two monks to visit Rome. What he saw there shocked him. The syphilitic Julius II then occupied the papal chair. On 2 July 1510, he issued a papal act establishing a brothel where young women could ply their trade under the aegis of the church. It provided much-needed money for religious orders. Under the later popes, Leo X and Clement VII (1523–34), prostitutes who worked there had to leave a quarter of their goods and chattels to the nuns of Sainte-Marie-Madeleine after they died. The church

Coprophagia

Plenty of religious fanatics have been interested in filth. The followers of the Moabite good Baal-Phegor were trained to eat faeces. Ascetics in the early Christian church also ate excrement as a method of self-mortification. In *Sex in History*, the author G. Rattray Taylor mentions the 17th-century ecstatic St Marguerite Marie Alacoque who 'dwelt on these ideas with irresistible compulsion. In her diaries she describes how once, when she wished to clean up the vomit of a sick patient, she "could not resist" doing so with her tongue, an action which caused her so much pleasure she wished she could do the same every day.'

was so worldly that the queen of France sent two young noblemen to the cardinal of Nantz to be 'instructed'. Julius himself seemed to prefer Germans. His conquest of one was celebrated in verse:

To Rome, a German came of fair aspect,
But he returned a woman in effect.

What Julius made of Luther is not recorded, but Luther was certainly disillusioned with the pope. Back in Germany, he began planning how to reform the church and contemplated *Anfechtung* – 'temptation'. In 1517, he nailed his 59 theses to the door of Castle Church in Wittenberg. Leo X, who had become pope in 1513, dismissed him as a 'drunken German' and excommunicated him.

INDULGENCES

What concerned Luther particularly was the sale of indulgences. These offered the full or partial remission of temporal punishment for sins, which meant that the sinner would spend less time waiting in purgatory before getting to heaven. They had been granted since the sixth century, but by the time of Alexander VI, the Borgia pope, they had become a lucrative business, with wealthy Christians buying indulgences as a licence to commit specific sins. Leo X famously used the sale of indulgences to finance the reconstruction of St Peter's Basilica.

Luther soon garnered a following for his Reformation because it gave monks and clerics the opportunity to renounce their vow of celibacy. In 1519, he confessed in a sermon that his own sexual desires were overpowering. He felt no guilt about this though; he maintained that sex was a natural function ordained by God.

Although he was tormented with lust, Luther did not plan to marry: 'I shall never take a wife, as I feel at present. Not that I am insensible to my flesh or sex (for I am neither wood nor stone); but my mind is averse to wedlock because I daily expect the death of a heretic,' he wrote on 30 November 1524.

> **'SUDDENLY, AND WHILE I WAS OCCUPIED WITH FAR DIFFERENT THOUGHTS, THE LORD HAS PLUNGED ME INTO MARRIAGE.'**
> Martin Luther

However, in April 1523, he helped 12 nuns to escape from the Nimbschen Cistercian convent, arranging for them to be smuggled out of the nunnery in herring barrels. One of them was 24-year-old Katharina von Bora. Luther married her on 13 June 1525, less than seven months after he had said he would not wed. Women, he said, though emotionally weaker than men, craved sex more. He seems to have done his duty, despite himself. After he married, he recorded that he was often tempted by the devil when he touched 'specific parts' of Katharina's body. The devil, he said, lost his greatest battles 'right in bed, next to Katie'. Nevertheless, though he was already 42 and not in the best of health, they had six children, four of whom survived into adulthood.

Luther's lifelong battle with the devil manifested itself in coprophilia. He regularly wrote home detailing his defecations and was known to cry out to the devil: 'I have shit my pants, and you can hang them around your neck and wipe your mouth with it.' He also claimed that he could blow away an evil spirit 'with a single fart'.

Leo X

1475–1521

Although Leo X was never ordained as a priest, he was tonsured at the age of 7 and became a cardinal at 13. A member of the wealthy Florentine Medici family, he 'looked upon the papal court as a centre of amusement', according to the *Catholic Encyclopædia*. Although he had a number of illegitimate children, the Romans were surprised to find that he did not bring a mistress with him when he was elected pope. Florentine statesman Francesco Guicciardini reported that the new pope was excessively devoted to the flesh, 'especially those pleasures which cannot, with delicacy, be mentioned'. Former monk Joseph McCabe described him as 'a coarse, frivolous, cynical voluptuary, probably addicted to homosexual vice'.

Plainly Leo had been practising sodomy for many years. When he was elected, he was suffering from chronic ulcers on his backside and had to be carried to the conclave on a stretcher. His backside was almost his downfall. Leo had foolishly made one of his lovers, Alfonso Petrucci, a cardinal. Unfortunately Petrucci fancied being pope himself and, as a cardinal, was just one step away. He bribed a Florentine doctor named Battista de Vercelli to insert poison in Leo's rectum when he was operating on his piles. However, Leo's secret police intercepted a note outlining the plot. Under torture, Vercelli confessed and was hanged,

drawn and quartered. Petrucci fled, but Leo sent the Spanish ambassador to guarantee him safe conduct if he returned to Rome. Foolishly, Petrucci took up the offer and was thrown into the infamous Sammarocco dungeon under the Castel Sant'Angelo. When the Spanish ambassador complained that the guarantee he had given had been violated, Leo replied: 'No faith need be kept with a poisoner.'

Petrucci was racked daily until he confessed. 'Eight times I, Cardinal Petrucci, went to a consistory with a stiletto beneath my robes, waiting for the opportunity to kill de'Medici,' his confession said. He was sentenced to death, but the pope would not allow a Christian to lay a finger on a prince of the church. So Petrucci was strangled by a Moor. As befitting his station, a silken cord in cardinal's crimson was used to choke the life out of him.

While it is fairly certain that Martin Luther disapproved of sodomy, it was the sale of papal indulgences that really exercised him. Rome boasted some 7,000 registered prostitutes – for a population of just 50,000 – but 3the papal brothels were not bringing in enough cash, especially for Leo's ambitious building works, so he increased the sale of indulgences. He was also happy to sell cardinal's hats to atheists, which fetched anywhere between 24,000 and 70,000 ducats.

Although Luther himself seems to have been faithful to Katharina, he was not against sex outside marriage. If a married man needed another woman to satisfy his sexual needs, he said, he should feel free to take a mistress. Even bigamy was preferable to divorce in his eyes. He also maintained that if a man was impotent, he should find an able sexual partner for his wife. It is not recorded whether he was as good as his word when he became increasingly frail after 1531, when Katie was still only 32. Other than in his views on sex, Luther was conservative when it came to marriage. A man, he thought, should rule his wife. Her only role was to love, honour and obey. And wives should stay at home. 'The way they are made indicates this,' he said, 'for they have broad hips and a wide fundament to sit upon.'

Luther was more than content with Katharina. He wrote in 1526, after 14 months of marriage: 'My Katie is in all things so obliging and pleasing to me that I would not exchange my poverty for the riches of Croesus.'

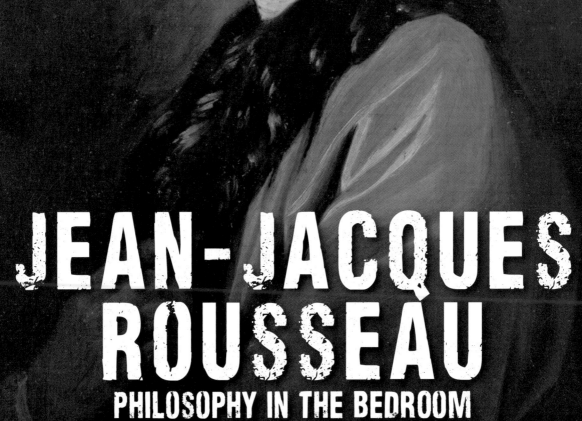

JEAN-JACQUES
ROUSSEAU
PHILOSOPHY IN THE BEDROOM

1712-1778

Writer, philosopher and political theorist, Jean-Jacques Rousseau inspired the French Revolution and the Romantic generation. The sexually ambivalent writer George Sand called him 'St Rousseau', while Voltaire and David Hume called him 'a monster'. His greatest epigram, 'Man was born free, but he is everywhere in chains' – the first sentence of his influential *Social Contract* – barely conceals his masochistic yearnings. He became more famous after his death through his *Confessions*. And he had much to confess.

At the tender age of 11, Rousseau received a sound thrashing for some minor infraction at the hands of his 40-year-old schoolteacher Mademoiselle Lambertier, though he later claimed that he was 8 and she was 30. She quickly realized the effect it had on him and refused to spank him again, no matter how bad he had been. However, for the rest of his life he went into 'erotic frenzies' over the prospect of being spanked.

When he was young Rousseau managed to indulge this impulse with 11-year-old Mademoiselle Goton. She would 'play school mistress' with him and – if he 'begged on bended knees' – spank him. The young girl would treat him as a child and 'allowed herself to take the greatest liberties with me, without permitting me to take a single one with her'. This Rousseau found thoroughly satisfying. The two deviant children were soon separated.

With this primary sexual impulse thwarted, his erotic frenzy had to exhibit itself in different ways. He would hide in dark alleys and moon at passing women on the off-chance that they would spank his bare behind. This was none too successful. In his *Confessions*, he related how he once flashed at some girls who were on their way to fetch water from a well. But they found the sight 'more laughable than seductive'. He was then pursued by a mob of outraged men and women wielding broom handles. He recorded that he managed to talk himself out of trouble.

EMOTIONALLY ATTACHED

Forced to flee Calvinist Geneva when he was 16, Rousseau took up with the buxom 29-year-old Françoise-Louise de Warens. Separated from her Protestant husband, she was paid by the king of Piedmont to convert young male Protestants to Catholicism. Rousseau stayed at her house in Chambéry, Savoy, where she lived with her young lover, Claude Anet, the former gardener at her husband's home. She encouraged Rousseau to study philosophy and they grew emotionally attached. She called him 'Little Cat', while he called her *maman* – 'mother'. His own mother had died when he was born.

When Rousseau turned 21, Madame de Warens formally proposed that he become her lover, alongside Anet. She gave him a week to consider the proposal. He accepted, though he said he felt more like a son than a lover. 'I love her too much to desire her,' he said.

> 'WHO WOULD BELIEVE THAT THIS CHILDHOOD PUNISHMENT, SUFFERED AT THE AGE OF EIGHT AT THE HANDS OF A SPINSTER OF THIRTY, WAS TO DETERMINE MY TASTES, MY DESIRES, MY PASSIONS.'
> Jean-Jacques Rousseau

41

He found her cold in bed and did not enjoy the experience. 'Twice or three times, as I pressed her passionately to me, I soaked her breast with my tears,' he said. 'It was as if I was committing incest.' However, he did become erotically attached to her in the most bizarre way. He would wander through her house, kissing the bed curtains, the armchair where she sat – even the floor where she had walked.

In 1734, Anet died. For the next three years, Rousseau had Madame de Warens and her soft furnishings to himself. Then she took another young lover, who also moved into the house. This second *ménage à trois* was too much for Rousseau, who left to take a job as a tutor in Lyons. He moved to Paris, and then between 1743 and 1744 he worked as secretary to the Comte de Montaigue, the French ambassador to Venice.

A SECRET DEFECT

At that time Venice was the pleasure capital of Europe and Rousseau found himself surrounded by prostitutes, whom he affected to loathe. However, he did use them. One local favourite was a woman named Zulietta. She was so beautiful that Rousseau believed her to be some sort of goddess. When he first visited her and was about to 'pluck her fruit', he was overwhelmed with emotion and began to cry. It offended him emotionally, aesthetically and philosophically that such an elevated beauty should be a lowly prostitute. There must be some 'secret defect in her', he reasoned, 'that would make her repulsive'. Then, when she had dried his tears and he was ready to enter her again, he found her fatal flaw. 'I perceived that she had a malformed nipple,' he said. 'I beat my brow, looked hard and made certain that this nipple did not match the other one.'

This may just have been the product of his tortured imagination, of course. Three years earlier, Casanova had been with Zulietta and mentioned nothing about a misshapen nipple. Casanova was meticulously observant about his lovers and in his autobiography, *My Life,* he found her faultless. But the supposed malformation set Rousseau's mind racing. He wondered if there was some reason for it.

'I was struck by the thought that it resulted from some remarkable imperfection of Nature,' he wrote. 'I saw clear as day that I held in my arms some kind of monster rejected by Nature, man and love.' Rousseau was no diplomat. He pointed out the malformed nipple to its owner. Zulietta curtly told him that, in future, he should leave women alone and devote himself to mathematics.

Returning to Paris, Rousseau became infatuated with the chambermaid in his hotel. Her name was Thérèse le Vasseur. She was 24; he was 33. By this time, Rousseau was making his way as an intellectual. While Thérèse was beautiful, kind, a good cook and devoted to him, she was uneducated. She never learnt to spell, count money, tell the time or even remember the months

> ## Types of Flagellants
>
> According to *Venus Schoolmistress; or Birchen Sports*, which was first published in 1788, male flagellants were divided into three types:
> 1. Those who liked to receive more or less severe chastisement from the hand of a woman who took pleasure in wielding the rod with power and skill.
> 2. Those who like to apply the rod to a female.
> 3. Those who like to watch. Female flagellants could be categorized in exactly the same way. It was thought that the book was written by the famous London madam Mary Wilson.

George Sand

1804–1876

The novelist and proto-feminist George Sand was an ardent admirer of Rousseau. Having changed her name from Amandine-Aurore-Lucile Dudevant, she took to wearing men's clothes and smoking cigars. There were rumours of lesbian affairs and perhaps even an incestuous liaison with her son. She took numerous male lovers, but these relationships were largely unsuccessful. Dramatist Prosper Mérimée found her frigid. Though she kissed and bit writer Jules Sandeau, he described her as a 'graveyard'. Famously she fell for the tubercular Polish composer Frédéric Chopin, who was six years younger than her. She complained of his spinsterish attitude to sex. 'Can you ever have love without a single kiss, and kisses without voluptuousness?' she asked. She stopped sleeping with Chopin long before their nine-year affair came to an end. He responded by seeking consolation with her 18-year-old daughter.

Sand fell desperately in love with Michel de Bourges, who was bald, ugly and married, but made her 'tremble with desire'. She called the painter Charles Marchal her 'fat baby'. And her name was linked with Gustave Planche, who was not known for his attention to personal hygiene. He challenged a literary critic who had panned Sand's novel *Lélia* to a duel. No one was hurt, but the sales of *Lélia* went through the roof.

There was one woman in her life, though. She wrote to the actress Marie Dorval: 'In the theatre or in your bed, I simply must come and kiss you, my lady, or I shall do something crazy.'

of the year. Although Rousseau himself was only the son of a lowly watchmaker, he considered her beneath him. 'I shall never leave you, but I will never marry you,' he told her.

Rousseau was extraordinarily cruel to her, forcing her to give up their five illegitimate children to the foundling hospital on the flimsy pretext that, as they were not married, he was protecting her reputation. They did finally marry, but only after 23 years together.

Rousseau complained that, like his other lovers, Thérèse was cold in bed. However, James Boswell reported that, in her only infidelity, Thérèse 'mated' most satisfactorily 13 times. According to Boswell, a great admirer of Rousseau, Thérèse considered him 'vigorous' in bed, while Rousseau lacked 'art' when it came to lovemaking.

Rousseau was not above bizarre amorous adventures. One female friend sent him 'an under-petticoat which she had worn and out of which she wanted me to make myself a waistcoat'. This sent him into raptures. 'It was as if she had stripped herself to clothe me,' he said. 'In my emotion I kissed the note and the petticoat twenty times in tears.'

When he was 44 Rousseau fell in love, he claimed for the one and only time. The object of his affection was the matronly Sophie d'Houdetot. She was encumbered with both a husband and a lover, who was fortunately away a great deal. Again, Rousseau claimed that he 'loved her too much to possess her'. But he seems nonetheless to have made an effort. 'The continuance over three months of ceaseless stimulation and privation threw me into an exhaustion from which I did not recover for several years and brought on a rupture that I shall carry to the grave,' he lamented, 'such was the sole amorous gratification.' Rousseau used this affair and his relationship with Madame de Warens as the basis for his epistolary novel *Julie: or, the New Héloïse*.

Many of Rousseau's kinks have been traced to the bladder ailment he suffered from for most of his life. Thérèse had to insert a catheter into his penis so he could urinate. Sex became so painful that he gave it up for the final 23 years of his life, and resorted to masturbation for gratification.

JAMES BOSWELL

'FAIRLY LOST IN SUPREME RAPTURE'

1740–1795

James Boswell is most famous for his biography of Dr Johnson. He was also a compulsive diarist, detailing in particular his sexual adventures. The compulsion to write, hypergraphia, is associated with fronto-temporal dementia, a degeneration of the front of the brain. This can also result in the disinhibition and hypersexuality exhibited by Boswell. The dementia could have been caused by bouts of sexually transmitted disease that he suffered throughout his life.

Born in Calvinist Scotland, Boswell was terrified by sin and hellfire as a youth. But his sex drive was strong. He masturbated against tree trunks, which he considered a small sin. By the time he was 13 he was petrified by a larger sin, fornication. For a time, he considered self-castration as a possible cure. He also toyed with the idea of becoming a Catholic after falling in love with a Catholic actress. Then he found that his black hair and dark eyes were inordinately attractive to women.

Boswell first experienced the 'melting and transporting rites of love' with a prostitute named Sally Forrester. After that, he went with countless prostitutes, who gave him regular doses of gonorrhoea and other infections.

LIFE OF A LIBERTINE

At the age of 20, Boswell ran away to London where he lived the life of a libertine for three months. His father forced him to return to Scotland and he completed his legal studies. Back in London in 1762, he planned a 'winter's safe copulation' with Mrs Anne Lewis, his first real mistress. They consummated their passion in the Black Lion Inn, where he records climaxing five times in a single night. The whole experience cost him 18 shillings.

There was another cost though. Six days later he recorded: 'Too, too plain was Signor Gonorrhoea.'

Boswell reported a similar feat with an actress named Louisa. 'Five times was I fairly lost in supreme rapture,' he wrote. 'Louisa was madly fond of me; she declared I was a prodigy and asked me if this was not extraordinary for human nature.'

Though he sometimes used a condom for protection, Boswell regularly contracted venereal diseases. During his third case at the age of 22, he described his terror at this punishment for his undeniable sins as 'an unaccountable alarm of unexpected evil'. He also suffered from an inflamed prostate gland, inflammation of the epididymis gland behind the testicles and crab lice. In an attempt to cure his condition, Boswell downed all manner of concoctions. He also underwent bloodletting, cauterization of the sores and irrigation of the urinary tract.

In 1765, Boswell began a tour of the Continent. In Berlin, he seduced a soldier's wife who was pregnant and came to his room selling chocolate. He recorded that it was 'in a minute – over'. In Siena he began a short-lived affair with the high-born Girolama Piccolomini. His infatuation

> 'A LITTLE HEAT IN THE MEMBERS OF MY BODY SACRED TO CUPID, VERY LIKE A SYMPTOM OF THAT DISTEMPER WHICH VENUS, WHEN CROSS, TAKES IT INTO HER HEAD TO PLAGUE HER VOTARIES.'
>
> James Boswell

was reciprocated. However, when Boswell's valet took love letters to Girolama, he was often also carrying other letters for other signorine. In Holland, Boswell pursued vivacious young Dutchwoman Isabella van Tuyll, who wrote under the name Belle van Zuylen. She was his social and intellectual superior, and refused his repeated proposals of marriage. He returned to England with Rousseau's mistress Thérèse le Vasseur, having a brief affair with her on the way.

Boswell made an effort to find himself a rich wife, but the result was all too predictable. While toasting one prospect he was courting, he said, 'I got myself quite intoxicated, went to a Bawdy-house and passed a whole night in the arms of a Whore.' Nevertheless it was worth it. Writing to a friend in 1767, he said: 'She indeed was a fine strong spirited Girl, a Whore worthy of Boswell if Boswell must have a whore.'

Two years later, Boswell married his penniless first cousin. They had seven children, five of whom survived into adulthood. Boswell had at least two illegitimate children as well – a son with Peggy Doag, a servant girl, who died in infancy, and a daughter with Mrs Dodds, a lady 'admirably formed for amorous dalliance' though 'ill-bred ... quite a rompish girl'.

'The French Pox'

Eighteenth-century London boasted numerous cures for syphilis, which was fortunate since the disease was extremely prevalent. Boswell was particularly enthusiastic about the ubiquitous Balm of Gilead. Boswell also caught gonorrhoea some 19 times and underwent blood-letting, purges and special diets. His favourite treatment was Kennedy's Lisbon Diet Drink, a concoction of liquorice, sarsaparilla, sassafras and guaic wood advertised as a cure for scurvy and leprosy as well as gonorrhoea. He downed two bottles a day at half-a-guinea a time.

There was also *Aqua Mirabilis*, which was made from dried horse droppings mixed with vegetable oil. It was claimed that it could cure palsy, dropsy and the plague along with all manner of venereal diseases. For those caught out 'too often sporting in the Garden of Venus', as one handbill put it, there were also Bateman's Drops and Velno's Vegetable Cure, though detractors warned that this made your limbs turn into plants. Restorative Electuary was 'a sovereign remedy for venereal complaints', while Leake's Genuine Pills were 'much used for curing venereal disease in a short time'.

DECIPHERING THE CODE

While married, Boswell recorded his sexual indiscretions in his diaries in a code using Greek letters. Unfortunately his wife was an educated woman and could decipher the code. After his infidelities there would be tearful apologies, and he would beg her forgiveness before again promising her, and himself, that he would reform. However, this was not genuine. He claimed that 'licentious love' made him 'humane, polite, generous' – though only generous in compliments, not with cash. He often tried to trick prostitutes out of their money. Unsurprisingly his wife eventually became 'averse to hymeneal rites'. He told her, in that case, he must take a concubine and she agreed.

When his wife died of tuberculosis in 1789, Boswell comforted himself with more prostitutes. Despite being a devout Christian, even in church he found himself planning to have other women and the litany of sexual indulgence continued. Boswell enjoyed 'free-hearted ladies of all kinds: from the splendid Madam at 50 guineas a night down to the civil nymph with white-thread stockings who tramps down the Strand and will resign her engaging person to your honour for a pint of wine and a shilling'. In those days, it took an ordinary working man three hours to earn a shilling and it was enough to pay the rent of a cheap lodging in a garret for a week.

However, with cheap whores there were hidden costs. One woman with whom Boswell enjoyed a brief coupling in Whitehall Gardens used the opportunity to steal a handkerchief from his pocket, leaving him 'shocked to think that I had been intimately united with a low, abandoned, perjured, pilfering creature'. On the other hand there were pleasures to be had for free. One day in Covent Garden, Boswell 'met two very pretty little girls who asked me to take them with me'. He explained that he had no money to pay them. Nevertheless they went with him to a private room in the Shakespeare Head where he had sex with both of them.

Boswell was not above cheating the women with whom he had sex. One poor girl complained that sixpence was not adequate compensation for the services she was providing; when a crowd gathered, he insisted that he was an army veteran on half-pay and could afford no more. He then forced himself on her and 'abused her blackguard style' – that is, he raped her. But Boswell's greatest thrill seems to have come from the location of his encounters. He loved to have sex in public parks and on the corners of dark streets. One day he met 'a strong, jolly young damsel' outside St James's Palace and had her on Westminster Bridge with the Thames gurgling below. 'The whim of doing it there with the Thames rolling below us amused me very much,' he wrote. A few weeks later, Boswell picked up 'a fresh, agreeable young girl called Alice Gibbs' in Downing Street. It seems he was an exhibitionist both in the street and on the page.

Generally, he boasted that he performed 'most manfully' and, on one occasion, bragged of dipping 'my machine into the Canal'. He recorded only five instances of impotence, usually with his wife. Boswell died at the age of 54 from complications arising from gonorrhoea.

'Walter'

Another extreme example of sexual hypergraphia came from the pen of the anonymous Victorian writer 'Walter', who published 11 volumes of his erotic adventures – over 4,000 pages – in Amsterdam between 1888 and 1894. Running to over one million words, this massive sexual memoir was called *My Secret Life*. Only 20 to 25 sets were printed originally. They sold at £60 per set, the equivalent of over £4,000 at today's prices.

'Walter' recalls sexual encounters with hundreds of women. Most of them were prostitutes, though some were servant girls or working-class women of whom a Victorian gentleman could easily take advantage. 'Walter' had sex with men and women, experienced flagellation and exhibited myriad sexual fetishes. He was also caught up in the defloration mania of the time, seeking out ever younger girls to deflower. On one occasion, he records his repeated rape of a ten-year-old girl. Today, he would be considered a paedophile.

There are other shocking outbursts of violence in *My Secret Life* that reveal a darker secret. The book *Jack the Ripper's Secret Confession*, published in 2010, puts forward the theory that 'Walter' was, in fact, Jack the Ripper and shows that it is possible to identify the Ripper's victims from its pages. It has yet to be ascertained with any certainty just who 'Walter' was. However, like Boswell, he suffered the compulsion to record every detail of his sexual encounters.

MARQUIS DE SADE

THE MASTER OF PAIN

1740–1814

Possibly the most famous pervert of all time, the Marquis de Sade, a dissolute French nobleman, gave his name to 'sadism'. This is defined by the *Oxford English Dictionary* as 'Enthusiasm for inflicting pain, suffering, or humiliation on others; specifically a psychological disorder characterized by sexual fantasies, urges, or behaviour involving the subjection of another person to pain, humiliation, bondage, etc.' It was a perversion that de Sade made his own, indulging it whenever possible during his life and advocating it in his literary output.

Born into an aristocratic family, the four-year-old Marquis beat up his cousin over a toy and was sent to live with his grandmother. She had five daughters, one of whom was a notoriously promiscuous beauty. The other four were nuns, but nonetheless worldly. For fear that they might corrupt the boy, the young Marquis was placed in the care of the Abbé de Sade. A friend of Voltaire, the Abbé filled his house with a number of female companions, including a local prostitute. He also maintained a noted library of erotica.

At the age of ten, de Sade was sent to a Jesuit public school where sodomy and corporal punishment were practised. The beatings took place in front of the whole student body. At 15, he enrolled in the King's Light Cavalry and fought in the Seven Years War. A captain at 18, he was stationed in Germany where he could give his sexual appetite full rein.

The Marquis's growing reputation for licentious behaviour limited his choice of bride. However, his father found Renée-Pelagie de Montreuil, the daughter of a local magistrate, who came with a good dowry. Meanwhile, the Marquis was having an affair with a woman in Provence, in southern France, and had contracted gonorrhoea. The newlyweds went to live with de Sade's in-laws. Within months of the wedding, he began an affair with an actress, La Beauvoisin. Then he was arrested for abusing prostitutes whom he took to a 'little house' he kept in the Parisian suburb of Arcueil. One of the prostitutes, Jeanne Testard, complained that he had harangued her in a blasphemous fashion,

The 120 Days of Sodom

In 1785, the Marquis de Sade wrote *Les 120 journées de Sodome ou l'école du libertinage – The 120 Days of Sodom* or the *'School of Licentiousness'*. In it, four wealthy male libertines decide to enjoy the ultimate orgy. They lock themselves away in a remote castle for four months. With them are eight men, chosen for the size of their penises. Four are accomplices; the other four become victims. There are also eight beautiful teenage girls and eight boys aged between 12 and 15, who have been kidnapped. They are virgins who are to be deflowered during the course of the orgy. In addition, there are the daughters of the four protagonists, whom they have been abusing for some time. And, for contrast, there are four ugly old women.

There are also four female brothel keepers who tell them the stories of their lives and adventures, which are then used as inspiration for the action. This begins with straightforward sexual abuse, veers through the spectrum of perversions and ends with torture and murder. The work was not published until the 20th century, and even then, because of its themes of sexual violence, cruelty and child abuse, it has frequently been banned.

> ## 'I WANTED ONLY TO TRY TO LIVE IN ACCORD WITH THE PROMPTINGS WHICH CAME FROM MY TRUE SELF. WHY WAS THAT SO VERY DIFFICULT?'
> Marquis de Sade

masturbated into a chalice, called God a 'motherfucker and put two communion wafers inside her vagina, before entering it himself, while screaming: "If thou art God, avenge thyself."' She was then forced to beat him with a red-hot cat-o'-nine-tails. When she refused to pick a whip and allow him to beat her, he masturbated over two crucifixes, held her at sword-point and forced her to repeat his blasphemies. On the orders of the king, de Sade was imprisoned in the dungeon beneath the fortress of Vincennes.

His father-in-law used his influence to get him released after three weeks, whereupon de Sade took up with an 18-year-old beauty named Colet. She was so well practised in her art that she could earn 720 livres in an evening. Then he took the actress La Beauvoisin to the family's country estate, Lacoste, where they partied with the Abbé. When de Sade's father died in 1767, he renovated Lacoste, adding a secret room in which he kept his library of pornography. Meanwhile his wife gave birth to their first son and de Sade embarked on fresh affairs.

On Easter Sunday 1768, de Sade took Rose Kellor, a widowed unemployed cook whom he had found begging, to his house in Arceuil, promising to find her work in domestic service. When they got there, he ordered her to strip. When she refused to take off her skirt, he tore it off her and whipped her naked buttocks until he reached orgasm.

De Sade was imprisoned once again. This time his wife joined her father in efforts to get his sentence reduced to four months. On his release, he began organizing orgies at Lacoste. On 27 July 1772, four prostitutes were brought from Marseilles. The Marquis would either whip a prostitute while masturbating his valet Latour, make love to a prostitute while being sodomized by Latour, or sodomize a prostitute while she was performing fellatio on Latour. Meanwhile he fed the women sweets laced with the aphrodisiac Spanish fly.

When he asked to be allowed to whip the young women with a particularly violent-looking implement that was already covered with his own blood, they grew afraid and left. Latour and de Sade then found another young woman named Marguerite Coste. She, too, was given candies laced with Spanish fly, but refused to allow de Sade to sodomize her. Then she vomited the candies and was taken to the doctor, who reported what had happened. With further evidence provided by the prostitutes, the authorities issued an arrest warrant but, forewarned, Latour and de Sade fled the country, accompanied by the Marquis's ravishing young sister-in-law with whom it is assumed he was having an affair. Nevertheless, he was arrested in Sardinia and imprisoned in the Fortress of Miolans. But the following year, he escaped.

SIX WEEKS OF ORGIES

Returning to Lacoste, de Sade and his wife – and now accomplice – Pelagie hired six teenage girls. For six weeks, he orchestrated orgies that featured bondage, flagellation, fellatio, masturbation and sodomy – both heterosexual and homosexual. After the girls' parents began to ask where they were, the Marquis was arrested and returned to the dungeon at Vincennes.

Later transferred to the Bastille, he was imprisoned for 13 years until freed by the French Revolution in 1789. He spent his time using his fevered imagination to write *The 120 Days of*

John Coutts

The lexicon of modern sadism – with its dominatrixes, leather basques, high-laced spike-heeled boots, hooded gimps, bondage and amputees – was developed by John Coutts in the middle of the 20th century. Born in Singapore in 1902, he moved to Australia in the 1920s where he came across the catalogue of the MacNaught shoe store in King Street, Sydney. It featured photographs of thigh boots and extreme lace-up shoes. He also subscribed to the specialist magazine *London Life*, which featured women in tight corsets or otherwise constrained.

In 1935, he began to draw his own sexual fantasies. Then in the early 1940s, he started photographing his wife Holly Anna Faram posed as a dominatrix clad in leather, sporting boots from MacNaught's or naked and tied to a tree. In 1946, he set sail for Canada where he produced a magazine called *Bizarre* under the name John Willie. It carried photographs of Holly, stories of bondage and a cartoon strip drawn by Coutts himself called 'The Adventures of Sweet Gwendoline', which featured two leather-corseted lesbians.

By the mid-1950s, when Coutts moved to Greenwich Village in New York, *Bizarre* had a cult following. He came up with more titles featuring leather-clad mistresses whipping both men and women. As the 1950s drew to a close, more pornographic magazines were springing up that featured glamour photography. Coutts teamed up with photographer Irving Kraw and model Betty Page to portray his sadomasochistic fantasies. He also branched out into true crime magazines, which often had attractive young women tied up or otherwise in peril on their covers.

In California, these images played on the mind of a mild-mannered mummy's boy named Harvey Glatman. Born in the Bronx in 1928 and brought up in Denver, Colorado, Glatman had been obsessed with rope since the age of 12. After a series of petty crimes, in 1957 his mother gave him the money to set up as a TV repairman in Los Angeles. He also claimed to be a freelance photographer.

On 1 August 1957, 19-year-old model Judy Dull visited Glatman's makeshift studio. A blonde, he declared her the girl of his dreams. He tied her up, saying that he was taking cover shots for a true crime magazine. Once she was helpless, he undressed her and raped her twice. Afterwards he said he would take her to some remote spot in the desert and release her. She promised not to cry out if he did not hurt her. Out in the Nevada desert, he got her to pose for more erotic photographs. In some of them, she had a noose around her neck. Finally, he tightened the rope and killed her.

Glatman killed two more women in the same fashion. But on the way out to the desert a fourth time, his victim fought back. They were struggling when a police officer drove by. Glatman confessed and ended his life in the gas chamber.

Coutts, who already had a drink problem, was horrified when he found out about Glatman, feeling that his fantasies were responsible for the death of three women. His magazine folded, he went bankrupt and his health failed. Coutts died of a brain tumour, penniless, in 1961.

Sodom, Justine and *Philosophy in the Boudoir*. When he was released, he took up with a young actress named Quesnet and got involved in Revolutionary politics. To restore his fortunes, he put on plays and began publishing some of his prose work anonymously.

In 1801, Napoleon ordered his arrest. He was imprisoned without trial in Sainte-Pélagie prison. Following allegations of attempts to seduce younger prisoners there, his family had him declared insane. He was taken to the asylum at Charenton where he caused new scandals, staging his plays with inmates as actors. Although now in his seventies, he began an affair with the 13-year-old daughter of an employee at the asylum that lasted until he died. His will specified that 'the traces of my grave disappear from the face of the earth, as I flatter myself that my memory will be effaced from the mind of men'. In this aim he was to be disappointed.

EMMA HAMILTON

POSING *AU NATUREL*

1761–1815

The mistress of Nelson and the wife of the British envoy to Naples, Emma Hamilton was a great beauty and one of those women who found it hard to keep her clothes on. She posed nude for great artists, quack doctors and just for fun. Her naked perfection was admired by all those who saw it and she knew full well what effect it had upon men.

Born Emily Lyon, the daughter of a blacksmith in Cheshire, she lost her virginity when one of her male relatives was press-ganged. She went to the ship's captain, John Willet Payne, to ask for her relative's freedom. He granted it for a price – her own body – and she became Payne's mistress.

She posed nude as an example of perfect health and beauty in Dr James Graham's Temple of Health. The doctor's hour-long talks were illustrated by a series of attractive young women – referred to merely as a 'Hebe Vestina' or the 'Goddess of Youth and Health' – who appeared in various states of undress. In his *Reminiscences*, Henry Angelo, court fencing master to George IV, recalled seeing the 'female who was lectured upon, who had no more clothing than Venus when she rose from the sea'. Emma herself was said to have 'a perfect figure, fine regular features, and an indescribable charm and attractiveness about her face and expression'.

The painter Thomas Gainsborough's windows overlooked the Temple of Health and he used Emma as the model for the naked nymph in his picture *Musidor*. She went on to model nude and in flimsy clothing in classical works for Joshua Reynolds, George Romney and other artists. She may have been a prostitute too. Later she was taken up by Sir Harry Featherstonehaugh, who moved her into a cottage on his estate at Uppark in Sussex, where she would dance naked on the dining-room table.

PLEASURE GARDENS

When Featherstonehaugh tired of her, Emma moved in with a friend of his called Charles Grenville, who showed her off at the Ranelagh pleasure gardens. However, Grenville was short of money and, when his childless uncle, the British envoy to Naples Sir William Hamilton, took a shine to her, he suggested that Sir William took Emma 'under his protection' in return for making Grenville his heir.

Emma headed off to Naples where she became the learned Hamilton's mistress. In his *Travels in Italy*, Johann Wolfgang von Goethe wrote that Hamilton had reached an age where he found that, 'after his long study of art and nature, the summit of all joy in nature and art is a beautiful young girl'. Though 40 years Emma's senior, Hamilton was a vigorous old roué who paid to watch youths of both sexes swimming naked in the sea. Emma became famous in Neapolitan society for her 'attitudes'. She would adopt the classical poses found on the antique Greek vases Sir William collected. It is said that she wore classical Greek dress for this – or rather, a flimsy loose-fitting version of the type she wore when posing for George Romney and run up by her dressmaker. However, at least one surviving engraving shows her naked.

'HER FEATURES, LIKE THE LANGUAGE OF SHAKESPEARE, COULD EXHIBIT ALL THE FEELINGS OF NATURE AND ALL THE GRADATION OF EVERY PASSION.'
William Hayley

Her 'attitudes' became a sensation across Europe. With little change of dress, she posed as various classical figures from Medea to Queen Cleopatra, and her performances charmed aristocrats, artists such as Élisabeth-Louise Vigée-Le Brun, writers – including the great Goethe – along with kings and queens. They set off new dance trends across Europe and started a fashion for a draped Grecian style of dress. Her nude performances also started a trend, spawning the *poses plastiques* in which attractive young people, adopting the poses of classical statues, appeared on stage nude. In Italy it was also rumoured that Emma had a lesbian affair with the promiscuous Queen Caroline of Naples at her famously debauched court. In September 1791, while visiting London, she married Hamilton, signing the register in Marylebone parish church 'Amy Lyon'. This did not prevent her from taking other lovers, including Lord Bristol and the bishop of Derry.

Nelson first set eyes on Lady Hamilton in Naples in September 1793 and was immediately smitten. Although married, Nelson had picked up louche ways in the West Indies under the tutelage of the duke of Clarence, the future William IV, then an admiral, who outraged Georgian London when he returned from the Caribbean with a black concubine called 'Wowski'. Nelson also followed the tradition among naval officers serving in the Mediterranean leaving his marriage vows at Gibraltar.

MÉNAGE À TROIS

When Nelson returned to Naples in 1798 after the Battle of the Nile, he was greeted as a national hero after his victory in Egypt had saved the Kingdom of the Two Sicilies – Naples and Sicily – from invasion by the French. It was then that Nelson and Emma became very intimate: 'they made excursions in disguise, through the streets of Naples, visiting public places where they enjoyed themselves with the girls', according to her biography. Nelson travelled back to England overland with Emma and her husband, though it was plain they were lovers. Nelson left his wife and lived in a *ménage à trois* with the Hamiltons at 23 Piccadilly in London. This caused an enormous scandal and all three were ostracized by the court. Emma then fell pregnant by Nelson and gave birth to their daughter Horatia.

Hamilton tolerated being mocked as a cuckold until just before his death, when he complained that 'the whole of the attention of my wife is given to Lord N'. Before Nelson left for Trafalgar, he and Emma took communion in the local parish church and exchanged rings in what he considered to be a marriage in the eyes of God.

Striptease

The *pose plastique* tradition continued into the 20th century in Britain. In the 1930s, British law prohibited the display of naked girls moving. To get round this, the Windmill Theatre put on stationary *tableaux vivants* featuring nude girls. Famously, the theatre with its nude shows remained open throughout the Second World War, despite the bombing of London, boasting 'We never close'. Later they put on fan dancing, with nude girls hiding their bodies behind two large fans. At the end of the act, they removed the fans and posed naked for a moment while standing still.

By the 1960s, clubs were opening that featured striptease as they were beyond the control of the Lord Chamberlain, whose office regulated what appeared on stage. In 1968, the Lord Chamberlain relinquished control of live performances and it was possible to put on American-style striptease shows in public venues, including pubs and theatres.

The Celestial Bed

The main attraction of Dr Graham's Temple of Health – besides the nude Emma Hamilton – was the 'Celestial Bed'. This was made by a renowned tinsmith named Denton and was said to have cost Graham £10,000. It was in a separate room that could be reached by a private entrance. Graham himself left a description: 'The Grand Celestial Bed, whose magical influences are now celebrated from pole to pole and from the rising to the setting of the sun, is twelve feet long and nine feet wide, supported by forty pillars of brilliant glass of the most exquisite workmanship, in richly variegated colours.

'The super-celestial dome of the bed, which contains the odoriferous, balmy and ethereal spices, odours and essences, which is the grand reservoir of those reviving invigorating influences which are exhaled by the breath of music and by the exhilarating forces of electrical fire, is covered on the other side with brilliant panes of looking glass.

'On the utmost summit of the dome are placed two exquisite figures of Cupid and Psyche, with a figure of Hymen [the Greek god of marriage] behind, with his torch flaming with electrical fire in one hand and with the other, supporting the celestial crown, sparkling over a pair of living turtle doves, on a little bed of roses.

'The other elegant group of figures which sport on the top of the dome, having each of them musical instruments in their hands, which by the most expensive mechanism breathe forth sound corresponding to their instruments, flutes, guitars, violins, clarinets, trumpets, horns, oboes, kettle drums, etc. The post or pillars too, which support the grand dome are groups of musical instruments, golden pipes, etc., which in sweet concert breathe forth celestial sound, lulling the visions of Elysian joys.

'At the head of the bed appears sparkling with electrical fire a great first commandment: "BE FRUITFUL, MULTIPLY AND REPLENISH THE EARTH". Under that is an elegant sweet-toned organ in front of which is a fine landscape of moving figures, priest and bride's procession entering the Temple of Hymen.

'In the Celestial Bed no feather bed is employed but sometimes mattresses filled with sweet new wheat or oat straw mingled with balm, rose leaves, lavender flowers and oriental spices. The sheets are of the richest and softest silk, stained of various colours suited to the complexion. Pale green, rose colour, sky blue, white and purple, and are sweetly perfumed in oriental manner with the Tudor rose, or with rich gums or balsams.

'The chief principle of my Celestial Bed is produced by artificial lodestones. About 15 cwt of compound magnets are continually pouring forth in an ever-flowing circle.

'The bed is constructed with a double frame, which moves on an axis or pivot and can be converted into an inclined plane.

'Sometimes the mattresses are filled with the strongest, most springy hair, produced at vast expense from the tails of English stallions which are elastic to the highest degree'.

The bed, of course, was not for fornication, which Dr Graham condemned as robustly as masturbation. He even condemned a married couple sleeping together in the same bed, which he called 'matrimonial whoredom'. The bed was merely an aid for women to get pregnant.

After Nelson's death Emma's extravagance mired her in debt and in 1813 she found herself in the King's Bench debtors' prison in Southwark. With money from Nelson's brother, she got out of prison and took Horatia to live in Calais, where she drank herself to death. There is a memorial to her in the Parc Richelieu in the centre of Calais. Horatia was taken in by Nelson's sister and later married. She acknowledged that Nelson was her father but, until her death, denied that Emma was her mother. This allowed Victorian historians to make out that Lady Hamilton had had a merely platonic relationship with Nelson. The truth came out on the centenary of Trafalgar with the publication in 1905 of Walter Sichel's *Emma, Lady Hamilton*.

PAULINE BONAPARTE

THE IMPERIAL EXHIBITIONIST

1780-1825

Thanks to the meteoric career of her brother Napoleon, Pauline Bonaparte was transformed from peasant into princess. Famously beautiful and notoriously promiscuous, she showed off her body on every possible occasion. Her bath-time was a public event. She invited visitors to her boudoir while she dressed in clothes that left little to the imagination. But then, she had plenty to be proud of. 'With the finest and most regular features imaginable, she combined a most shapely figure, admired (alas!) too often,' wrote Countess Anna Potocka.

Pauline was the beauty of the Bonaparte family and her lush figure attracted legions of admirers from an early age. At the age of 15, she fell in love with the 40-year-old philanderer Louis Fréron, known as the 'king of the dandies'. Her mother disapproved and he was sent away.

Meanwhile Pauline made a habit of flirting with her brother's staff officers. Napoleon caught her *in flagrante delicto* in his office with Victor Emmanuel Leclerc. They married. As a wedding present Napoleon promoted Leclerc to brigadier general. In 1801, there was a slave rebellion in the French colony of Saint-Domingue on Hispaniola. Leclerc was sent to put down the uprising but Pauline did not want to leave Paris and her several lovers. One of them wrote later: 'Before she left for Saint-Domingue, there were no fewer than five of us in the same house sharing Pauline's favours. She was the greatest tramp and the most desirable.'

When Pauline heard of the posting, she locked herself in her bedroom for three days and only consented to go when Napoleon promised to send her regular shipments of Parisian gowns. In Haiti, Pauline organized balls and continued her promiscuous ways, largely with low-ranking soldiers and officers. Leclerc succeeded in putting down the rebellion but died of yellow fever. Pauline cut off her hair and placed it in the coffin with her husband's body.

NAKED AS A BABE

Returning to Paris, her grief was short-lived. She attended balls in dresses made of the sheerest of fabrics in order to show off her body. At the time, most French women did not bathe frequently, but since her body was constantly on display, Pauline made a fetish out of cleanliness. She bathed every morning in a bath filled with milk mixed with hot water. This was supposed to keep the skin soft, supple and white. After she had undressed, she would be carried, naked, to her bath by a black servant named Paul. When onlookers were scandalized, she said: 'But why not? A negro is not a man. Or are you shocked

Nude Entertainment

One of the earliest exponents of nude entertainment was Theodora, the wife of the sixth-century Byzantine emperor Justinian. Before they married, she performed naked on stage. The writer Procopius said: 'Often in the theatre too, in full view of all the people, she would throw off her clothes and stand naked in their midst, having only a ribbon around her private parts and groin – not because she was ashamed to expose these parts to the public too, but because no one is allowed to appear completely naked and a ribbon covering the vulva is compulsory'.

With this minimum covering she would lie face upwards on the stage and spread herself out. Then servants, who had been especially hired for the task, would sprinkle grains of barley over her private parts, and geese trained for the purpose would peck them off with their beaks and swallow them.

because he is not married?' Subsequently she married Paul off to one of her kitchen maids, but he continued to carry her, naked, to her bath.

While bathing, she would entertain male guests. Men were also invited to her boudoir where she rouged her nipples, selected her perfume, chose her gowns and had her hair done, dressed only in a skimpy chemise.

> ## 'SHE WAS AN EXTRAORDINARY COMBINATION OF PERFECT PHYSICAL BEAUTY AND THE STRANGEST MORAL LAXITY. IF SHE WAS THE LOVELIEST CREATURE ONE HAD EVER SEEN, SHE WAS ALSO THE MOST FRIVOLOUS.'
> Antoine-Vincent Arnault

Eight months after the death of her first husband, Pauline married Prince Camillo Borghese. Napoleon was appalled that she would remarry so soon, but Borghese was one of the richest men in Italy. He owned one of the world's finest diamond collections and the Villa Borghese in Rome. The marriage brought Pauline 70,000 francs a year, part ownership of the Villa Borghese, two carriages and numerous other baubles. However, from their wedding night onwards, the marriage was a disaster. There were rumours that Borghese was either gay or a transvestite. A more plausible explanation was that the prince was just not sufficiently well endowed for the new princess. As one biographer put it, Prince Borghese 'somewhat disappointingly had a very small penis. Pauline, whose nymphomania was periodic but intense, scorned all but very large ones.' As Pauline herself put it in a letter to her uncle: 'I would rather have been Leclerc's widow on just 20,000 francs a year than be married to a eunuch.'

PRODIGIOUS PROMISCUITY

Unhappy in Rome, Pauline headed back to France. On the way she stopped in Florence, where she commissioned the most famous sculptor in Italy at the time, Antonio Canova, to make two statues of her. Canova had already fulfilled several commissions for Napoleon, so it was only natural that he should sculpt the emperor's favourite sister. However, Pauline wanted to be sculpted as Venus and decided to pose nude. This shocked the sculptor, who had formerly worked for the unusually pious Pope Clement XIV (1769–74). It is said that Canova's hands shook when he applied modelling clay to her body. When she was later asked how she could possibly pose nude, she replied: 'Why not? It was not cold, there was a fire in the studio.' The statue of Pauline as Venus Victrix so appalled her husband that he kept it in the attic where no one could see it.

Back in Paris, Pauline exhausted a number of lovers. Then she took up with society painter Philippe Auguste de Forbin who was endowed with, it was said, 'usable gigantism'. She could not get enough of him, but his huge size caused her vaginal distress. France's leading gynaecologist was called in, who said that Pauline's uterus was swollen by constant excitement and her vagina showed signs of damage due to friction. Forbin was persuaded to join the army and was posted out of harm's way.

In Nice, Pauline hired a young musician named Félix Blangini to 'conduct her orchestra'. She bedded the leading actor of the day, François Talma, and 25-year-old Colonel Armand Jules de Canouville, aide to Marshal Berthier, Napoleon's chief of staff. Again her brother stepped

Napoleon Bonaparte

1769–1821

Napoleon was supposed to have had a very small penis. An object purporting to be his member was bought at auction in 1977 by American urologist Dr John K. Lattimer. It was said to look like 'a maltreated strip of buckskin shoelace or shrivelled eel', when it went on display at the Museum of French Art in New York. The organ has also been described as 'a shrivelled sea horse', 'a small shrivelled finger', and 'one inch long and resembling a grape'. But then, it had been pickled for over 150 years.

On the other hand, it may explain his impulse to power. As a young man, he wrote that sexual love was 'harmful to society and to the individual happiness of men'. At school, his only friend was a pretty boy who was later drawn into overtly homosexual circles. He had a number of unsuccessful encounters with girls. Then, at the age of 18, he deliberately lost his virginity to a prostitute from the Palais Royal in Paris. It was '*une expérience philosophique*', he wrote in his notebook.

At 25, Napoleon fell in love but was, again, rejected. As a result, he wrote a love story that is little short of pornographic. While he rose through the ranks, Napoleon was unattractive with his lank hair and scruffy appearance. He proposed to a widow who refused him.

Napoleon became a hero during the French Revolution and took a fancy to Joséphine Tascher-Beauharnais, who danced naked with other mistresses before the head of the Directory, Paul Barras. When Barras tired of her, he gave Napoleon command of the army in Italy if he would take her off his hands. Napoleon, surprisingly, married her.

With Napoleon away in Italy, Joséphine took a string of lovers, while Napoleon wrote her love letters, expressing his desire in the most graphic terms. But as his power grew, the boot was on the other foot. He would invite actresses over and have them wait naked in an adjoining room until he had finished the business of state. Sometimes a message came telling them to put their clothes on and go home, because he was too busy to see them.

Napoleon divorced Joséphine in 1810 and married Marie-Louise, daughter of the Austrian emperor Francis I. But he was still in love with Joséphine and met her whenever possible. It is thought that he became impotent at the age of 42 after his disastrous campaign in Russia. He had a son and heir with Marie-Louise, though there were rumours that artificial insemination was used. She did not accompany him into exile, taking, instead, another lover. Joséphine was not allowed to go with Napoleon It was thought that his penis was removed during his autopsy.

in, posting Canouville to Danzig. When he died in 1812 during the retreat from Moscow, a locket carrying her picture was found hanging around his neck. She was inconsolable for days.

Pauline accompanied her brother into exile on Elba, where she threw balls for the inhabitants and wore her most fabulous dresses in an attempt to cheer up her brother. She gave him the Borghese diamonds to finance his last campaign. They were found in his carriage after the battle of Waterloo. Not allowed to accompany him in his final exile to St Helena, she returned to Rome where she enjoyed the protection of Pope Pius VII. She lived in the Villa Paulina, decorated to commemorate her brother's campaign in Egypt. When he died in 1821, she was overcome with grief.

With the help of the pope, three months before her death, she was reconciled with her husband, who had been living with his mistress in Florence. Legend has it that, on her deathbed, she asked a servant for a mirror. After gazing into it, she sank back, smiled and said: 'I'm not afraid to die. I am still beautiful.' Pauline was just 44. She asked for the coffin to be closed at her funeral. Canova's nude statue of her was to be brought out of storage and displayed in the church so that the mourners could appreciate her beauty. The statue is now on show in the Villa Borghese.

VICTOR HUGO

NEVER *MISÉRABLE*

1802–1885

The poet, dramatist and novelist Victor Hugo was the most important writer of the French Romantic movement. He was a man of immense energy, both in his literary career and in his love life. Not only did he have a prodigious output of books and plays, he also had sex with a great many women – at the height of his powers at a rate of four a day. He also indulged in various sexual perversions including voyeurism and, possibly, incest.

Victor Hugo was a virgin when he married at the age of 20, but he quickly made up for lost time. On his wedding night, he coupled with his innocent young wife, childhood friend Adèle Foucher, nine times. He wore her out. After five difficult pregnancies in eight years, she called a halt to their sex life. Instead, she took up with the rather less demanding literary critic, and friend to Hugo, Charles-Augustin Sainte-Beuve. This nearly caused a duel between the two men and certainly led to their estrangement.

Hugo turned to Juliette Drouet, an actress and courtesan who had been the mistress of a number of famous men. She remained his faithful mistress for the rest of her life. Hugo, however, was anything but faithful. Juliette taught him the whole gamut of sexual delight and, armed with this sentimental education, Hugo was soon able to declare: 'Women find me irresistible.'

Hugo loved women who were passionate, witty and challenging, but he was not unduly discriminating in his choice of sexual partners. He had sex with married women, provided they were not living with their husbands. He would have a young prostitute visit him directly after breakfast. Then he would bathe and dress before having lunch with an actress, making love to her before and after the meal. In the afternoon he would visit a courtesan, and then have sex with Juliette Drouet in the evening. Juliette estimated that between 1848 and 1850 he had sex with over 200 other women.

In 1844, he took up with Léonie d'Aunet, a young noblewoman who had run away with a painter. Her jealous husband had her followed by the police, who caught her in the act with Hugo. At the time adultery was a criminal offence in France. Léonie was thrown in jail, but Hugo escaped imprisonment by invoking his privilege as a peer (he had been nominated to the Chamber of Peers in 1845). When Léonie was freed, he divided his time between her and Juliette who, he said, was his 'true wife'. Though he saw her every day, he wrote her over 17,000 love letters, many of which were very explicit about sexual matters.

> 'A WOMAN WHO HAS ONE LOVER IS AN ANGEL, A WOMAN WHO HAS TWO LOVERS IS A MONSTER AND A WOMAN WHO HAS THREE LOVERS IS A WOMAN.'
> Juliette Drouet

At the age of 70, Hugo seduced the 22-year-old daughter of fellow writer Théophile Gautier, priding himself on teaching her new tricks. He was carrying on an affair with the actress Sarah Bernhardt at the same time. At the age of 80 Hugo's young grandson caught him making love to a housemaid. 'Look little Georges,' said Hugo, 'that's what is called genius.'

Juliette was 77 when she died in Hugo's arms. He lived on for another two years. It was said that his spirit was broken by her death, but according to his diary his sex drive was unaffected.

Satyriasis

An abnormally high sex drive in a male is called satyriasis. It takes its name from the satyrs in Greek mythology, who were the half-man, half-goat companions of Pan and Dionysus. In classical art, they are often depicted with an erection. Satyriasis has sometimes been considered a mental disorder. Men who suffer from bipolar disorder often go through periods of hypersexuality. It can manifest itself as sexual addiction or priapism, where the penis remains permanently erect.

In the four months leading up to his death at the age of 83, amazingly he recorded eight bouts of lovemaking.

WATCHING

As well as having sex, Hugo loved to watch it being performed. He was a life-long voyeur. As a youth, he would hide in a wardrobe in his mother's house so he could watch the maid as she got out of bed. He spent hours studying the nude statues in the Luxembourg Gardens. He was particularly drawn to Juliette because she had been a famous model and erotic sculptures of her body were sold to private collectors.

He was a fan of the *tableaux vivants* that Emma Hamilton had pioneered and that were then taken to Paris by English actresses. Seeing nipples in public particularly excited him. But when he became a leading literary and political figure he had to avoid scandal, so he hired prostitutes who specialized in stripping to perform for him in private. He considered these private shows as live pornography. His diaries also reveal that his interests included not just nudity but a particular penchant for women's feet.

When Napoleon III came to power in France, Hugo, an ardent republican, went into exile on the Channel Islands. His house on Guernsey had a secret staircase leading to concealed rooms where he could entertain his mistresses. He also had peepholes through which he could watch his guests making love.

AGONIES OF JEALOUSY

Hugo was very attached to his daughter Léopoldine and went through agonies of jealousy, especially when she reached the same age as the actresses and prostitutes with whom he was having sex. There have even been suggestions that he committed incest with her.

In *Les Misérables*, published in 1862, he wrote: 'The reader may at a pinch be introduced to a nuptial bedchamber, but never into the bedroom of a virgin. Such at the time would hardly be dared in verse; in prose it must not be attempted.

'It is the inside of a flower which has yet to open ... A budding woman is sacred ... the bosom which veils itself before a mirror as if the mirror were an eye, that chemise hastily pulled up to hide a shoulder when the furniture creaks or a carriage passes in the street ... the successive phases of clothing, none of that must be described ... A man's eye must show even more reverence at the rising of a young girl than at the rising of a star. The possibility of touching must convert itself into increased respect. The down on a peach, the dust on a plum ... the feathery powder of the butterfly's wing are coarse matters compared with the chastity which does not know that it is chaste ... The indiscreet touch of the eye is a ravishment of that vague penumbra.' Hugo was not above making free with Léopoldine's young friends, recording in his diary that he deflowered a ten-year-old friend of Léopoldine after her first communion.

The Second Empire

Because of his republican views, Victor Hugo went into exile during the Second Empire, which meant he missed all the fun. One of Napoleon III's ministers described the period as 'not so much an empire, more of a party'. It was the golden age of the *grandes cocottes* – also known as *les grandes horizontales* – the pampered courtesans who were Paris's most glamorous celebrities. Through their skills in the bedroom, these women were able to amass huge fortunes and managed to maintain luxurious residences with retinues of liveried servants.

One of the most famous was Cora Pearl, who was from Plymouth and who was once paid £10,000 for a single night with emperor Napoleon III. When the Prince of Wales asked to see Cora, she had herself served up at his dinner table on a silver salver. When the cover was removed, she was completely naked except for a string of pearls and a sprig of parsley. She had told dinner guests that she was going to serve them meat that they dare not cut.

Throughout her life Cora had trouble keeping her clothes on. Invited to a fancy dress party at the Restaurant des Trois Frères Provençaux, she dispensed with a costume and went as Eve. A visiting English journalist said: 'Her form and figure were not concealed by any more garments than were worn by the original apple-eater.'

She also appeared naked on stage, playing Cupid in the comic opera *Orphée aux Enfers* at the Théâtre de Bouffes-Parisiens. The whole of high society, including all the members of Paris's exclusive Jockey Club, turned out to see her. However, her career came to an end when a wealthy young man shot himself after her refusal to drop her other lovers. Homeless and penniless, she was taken in by the writer Julian Arnold. He was once sitting in his library after dinner when she walked in and dropped her dressing gown, so that he could see why, once, she had been so sought after.

Another courtesan who enjoyed being *au naturel* was Giulia Beneni, an Italian better known as *La Barucci*, who claimed to be the 'greatest whore in the world'. The Duc de Gramont-Caderousse took the Prince of Wales – the future Edward VII – to meet her. She turned up three-quarters of an hour late in a gown of transparent gauze. She dropped it and then, in defiance of protocol, turned her back on the prince so he could admire her perfect ivory buttocks. When the duc remonstrated with her, she said candidly: 'Well, you told me to show him my best side.'

Before he became king, Edward spent so much time in Paris enjoying himself that he had a special 'sex chair' that offered myriad sexual possibilities in Le *Chabanais*, a famous brothel. But even the Prince of Wales occasionally got his come-uppance. In 1867, he was having an affair with the Princesse de Sagan, the lovely and lascivious daughter of a banker at the court of empress Eugénie at Fontainebleau. Her husband was a hugely rich, stylish man, famous as both a wit and raconteur, who bore her infidelity with the self-control demanded of his class.

However, her eldest son did not. Returning early one day to find a gentleman's clothes strewn around her boudoir, he picked them up and threw them into the fountain. Edward emerged from the bedroom to find his clothes gone and had to traipse back to his hotel in a pair of borrowed trousers that were much too tight. The offending youth was banished from the family home, although his outrage may have been well founded. The Prince of Wales was rumoured to be the father of de Sagan's youngest child.

In 1873, Hugo returned to the topic of virginity in a poem where he described himself seducing a maiden, kissing her on her white shoulders until she 'ceased to be a virgin and turned into an angel'.

Like many great artists, he considered himself to be above normal morality. When one young woman touched his penis, he told her: 'It's a lyre.' Then he told her: 'And only poets know how to play them.'

WILLIAM GLADSTONE

'SAVING' FALLEN WOMEN

1809–1898

William Ewart Gladstone was one of the greatest British parliamentarians of the 19th century. Like his successor Lloyd George, he diced with scandal all his life. On several occasions his addiction to prostitutes almost brought him down, but somehow he managed to emerge unscathed, possibly because he did not feel morally compromised by his association with women of easy virtue. His diaries reveal that he atoned for his sins with a dose of self-flagellation.

Throughout his life Gladstone was torn between moral rectitude and a powerful sex drive. At puberty he discovered an overwhelming urge to masturbate, which, as he confided to his diary, came over him 'again and again, like a flood'. At Oxford, he befriended Richard Monckton Milnes, later a Tory MP and a suitor of Florence Nightingale. He had one of the biggest collections of pornography in Victorian England, and Gladstone became an enthusiastic user.

He began visiting prostitutes when he was a young man at Oxford in the 1820s. Tormented by guilt, he would scourge himself afterwards. But this did not seem to stem his appetite as he writes of returning to sin 'again and again'. He continued visiting prostitutes when he moved to London, only abandoning the practice, temporarily, when he married at the age of 29. Although marriage gave him an outlet for his sexual desire, his wife was frequently pregnant – they had four sons and four daughters. It was the practice in Victorian times for a gentleman to refrain from sexual intercourse with his wife when she was with child. It was not uncommon, of course, for the man to find another channel to relieve his frustration.

In the 19th century, the streets of London were awash with prostitutes. Despite the stifling strictures of Victorian values, gentlemen regularly sought the company of ladies of the night. Although he was married, Gladstone made no secret of his vice. He would even bring young prostitutes picked up on the streets back to 10 Downing Street, despite the fact that members of the cabinet begged him not to do so.

The 1865 Election

Disraeli and the Conservatives were kept out of office in Britain by a scandal in the run-up to the General Election in 1865. At the age of 79, the Liberal leader Lord Palmerston was cited in the divorce case of the attractive 30-year-old Mrs O'Kane. With the unofficial party slogan 'she was Kane and he was able', the Liberals won by a landslide.

UPLIFTING PASSAGES

Apologists point out that Gladstone was a fierce moralist and a lay preacher. Some contend that all he did with his 'erring sisters' was read them an uplifting passage from the Bible. Indeed, he did manage to guide some of the young women he brought home into honest employment. However, Gladstone admitted in his own diaries that his motives were, partly at least, 'carnal'. Passages are marked with a sign representing a whip, showing that he had atoned.

When Gladstone joined Robert Peel's government as president of the Board of Trade in 1843, he wrote in his diary that he was 'fearful [of] the guilt of sin returning again and again in forms ever new but alike hideous'. Conscious of his position, he tried to avoid prostitutes, returning to pornography instead. But by 1851, his diary shows that he was visiting a beautiful young prostitute named Elizabeth Collins regularly – sometimes every other day. One entry in his diary reads: 'Received (unexpectedly) remained two hours: a strange humbling scene'. After his visits, he noted, he always scourged himself. This continued when he became chancellor in 1852.

A man named William Wilson saw Gladstone picking up a prostitute near Leicester Square and tried to blackmail him. Gladstone handed over the blackmail demand to the police and Wilson was sent down for 12 months with hard labour.

There had been another brush with scandal involving a courtesan named Laura Thistlethwayte. They exchanged passionate letters and he visited her regularly both at her London town house and at her cottage in Hampstead. But Gladstone grew extremely wary when Laura began showering him with gifts to the point that he feared her extravagance would ruin her husband, Colonel Thistlethwayte.

As prime minister, Gladstone had a close friendship with the Prince of Wales's mistress, the actress Lillie Langtry. And in the 1870s there were rumours that he was having an affair with Madame Olga Novikov, who advised him on Russian affairs. However, he could not give up prostitutes. In 1880, when he was 70, he was still visiting brothels on what he called 'rescue work'. The situation became more difficult in 1882, when the threat of assassination over the Irish Home Rule Bill meant that he had to have a 24-hour police guard. Lord Rosebery, then a junior minister in the Home Office, warned him of the danger of some poorly paid policeman taking advantage of the situation and selling the story to the press. It did no good. Three months later the Tory MP Colonel Tottenham saw Gladstone talking to a lady of the night and decided to make some political hay in the House with it. Gladstone answered Colonel Tottenham's allegations with studied dignity. 'It may be true that the gentleman saw me in such conversation,' he said. 'But the object was not what he assumed or, as I am afraid, hoped.'

> ## 'HAS IT BEEN SUFFICIENTLY CONSIDERED HOW FAR PAIN MAY BECOME A GROUND OF ENJOYMENT?'
> William Ewart Gladstone

He survived, but even this close call did not stop him. In July 1886, his private secretary, Edward Hamilton, warned him that another blackmailer was at work. Gladstone promised Hamilton that he would stop, but his diaries record that he was still seeing prostitutes in 1892, though they may have accosted him rather than the other way around.

INFIDELITY TO THE MARRIAGE BED

In 1896, two years before his death, Gladstone sought to set the record straight. He wrote a statement and sent it to one of his sons, Stephen, who had become a clergyman. It read: 'With reference to rumours which I believe were at one time afloat, though I know not with what degree of currency: and also with reference to the times when I shall not be here to answer for myself, I desire to record my solemn declaration and assurance, as in the sight of God and before His Judgment Seat, that at no period of my life have I been guilty of the act which is known as that of infidelity to the marriage bed.'

However, his biographer H.C.G. Matthews noted that his diary entries concerning his visits to prostitutes 'certainly suggest... that he was guilty of other [sexual] acts'. It may be that he just liked to put himself in the way of temptation. Some of the girls called him 'Glad-eyes'. Others

Benjamin Disraeli

1804–1881

Gladstone's great political rival was Benjamin Disraeli, who is reputed to have said to Gladstone: 'When you are out saving fallen women, save one for me.'

As a young man eager to make his way, Disraeli borrowed heavily to buy into gold and silver mines in South America and to start up a newspaper with his friend John Murray. However, a stock market crash in 1825, when Disraeli was just 21, wiped him out. Left with massive debts, Disraeli wrote a novel about the collapse called *Vivian Grey*. It was so thinly fictionalized that it drew threats of a duel from Murray. The duel never took place, but it brought such notoriety to the book that Disraeli could pay off enough of his debts to keep going.

Disraeli then had a nervous breakdown and, to escape his remaining creditors, went off on a tour of the Middle East. He returned a changed man. Always a dandy, he was now positively effeminate, dressing in green velvet trousers and ruffles. He spoke openly at dinner parties of his passion for the East and, according to the painter Benjamin Haydon, 'seemed tinged with a disposition to palliate its infamous vice ... sodomy'. Disraeli's biographer, Jane Ridley, concurred. 'Bisexuality came as naturally to Disraeli as did Tory Radicalism,' she said.

Disraeli had a series of affairs with older women, some of whom were married. His affair with Henrietta Sykes became a public scandal. She was much older than him and had been married for 11 years to the ailing Sir Francis Sykes, the father of her four children. Her letters to Disraeli were signed 'your mother'.

Her husband turned a blind eye because he was having an affair with Clara Bolton at the time. Clara was another of Disraeli's former lovers. She was jealous and encouraged Sir Francis to break up Disraeli's affair with Henrietta. But soon after, he found his wife in bed with Disraeli's successor. In a fit of pique, he kicked her out of the house and placed a notice in the newspapers advertising her adultery and causing a scandal that tainted Disraeli along with everyone else involved.

It is hard to say just how much the scandal harmed him politically, since he seemed unelectable in any event. Voters did not appreciate his dandified dress, and his Jewishness counted against him. On the hustings he was greeted with cries of 'Shylock' and was pelted with chunks of rotten pork and ham.

When he was elected for Maidstone on his fifth attempt, there were accusations of offers of bribes to the electorate. This was a common enough practice, but Disraeli outraged the voters of Maidstone by promising a bribe and failing to pay up. In the resulting lawsuit, his court costs were paid by the latest woman in his life, Mary Anne Wyndham Lewis, the widow of his late rival for the Maidstone seat. It was a master stroke. This fresh scandal eclipsed the bribery allegations.

Mrs Wyndham Lewis was 12 years older than Disraeli, and she was rich. They married, but even his wife's fortune was not enough to discharge his debts. He left Maidstone and stood for Shrewsbury in 1841. It had a smaller electorate and, consequently, fewer voters to bribe.

Realizing his plight, his rivals for the seat plastered Shrewsbury with posters detailing his debts. They amounted to £21,000. Handbills pointed out that Disraeli needed to stay in Parliament or face debtors' prison. But the voters of Shrewsbury paid no heed and soon found their member making his way up the greasy pole.

called him 'Daddy-do-nothing'. When one young prostitute came home with him for a second time, Gladstone wrote that he had 'certainly been wrong in some things and trod the path of danger'. It could be that he craved the aura of sin so that he could indulge in masochistic sessions with the whip.

Gladstone was 82 when he gave up visiting whores, but his reputation lived on. 'Gladstone founded the great tradition,' ran one obituary, 'in public to speak the language of the highest and strictest principle, and in private to pursue and possess every sort of woman.'

FYODOR DOSTOYEVSKY

PUNISHMENT WITHOUT CRIME

1821-1881

The master of the brooding Russian novel, Fyodor Dostoyevsky was dubbed the 'Russian Marquis de Sade' by his contemporary Ivan Sergeyevich Turgenev. Both were imprisoned and both used whipping and other forms of violence in their lovemaking. However, towards the end of his life, Dostoyevsky found sexual satisfaction within the bounds of a happy marriage to a woman who endlessly indulged him.

Dostoyevsky's mother died of tuberculosis when he was 13. His father – a drunken, lecherous miser – was murdered by his servants in retribution for mistreatment. It was said that they were so enraged by his drunken outbursts that they poured vodka down his throat until he drowned.

Dostoyevsky himself was frail and awkward. In social situations his face and lips twitched, and in his twenties this nervousness developed into full-blown epilepsy. One attack was so severe it left him permanently disfigured with a bulging right eye. His condition caused further problems. When he grew passionate, his excruciating shyness turned into frenzy. He would gesture wildly and, some said, foam at the mouth. This cannot have made him very attractive to women and his only sexual outlet in his twenties was with prostitutes.

After his father died, he abandoned his career as a military engineer to become a writer in St Petersburg. His first novel, *Poor Folk*, published in 1846, was well received. Spotting the emergence of a rival, Turgenev wrote a satirical poem about the new writer. Dostoyevsky responded by parodying Turgenev in *The Possessed*.

SIBERIA

Dostoyevsky got involved with a circle of socialists in 1847. He was arrested, charged with revolutionary conspiracy and put in front of a firing squad. At the last moment a reprieve came, the sentence was commuted and Dostoyevsky was sent to Siberia. After four years in a labour camp, he was conscripted as a soldier. This allowed him a little freedom to meet people of the opposite sex finally. He had a few affairs with young women before taking up with Maria Dmitrievna Isayeva, the wife of a friend. She became a model for the female figures in his novels. A consumptive married to an alcoholic, she was regarded by Dostoyevsky as a paragon of female virtue. They married after her husband's death in 1857. On their honeymoon, he suffered an epileptic fit that was to set the tone of their marriage. Neither derived much sexual satisfaction from it and both were extremely unhappy. This may have influenced his work, which has a distinctly masochistic streak. Before Maria died after some seven years of miserable wedlock, he had already started an affair with Apollinariya 'Polina' Suslova, another female types who features in his work. She was sexually cold, with a sadomasochistic streak, and teased and tortured Dostoyevsky. He took out his frustration in gambling and, while becoming increasingly successful as an author, became plagued with debts. He took an almost

> 'I GO DOWN ON MY KNEES BEFORE YOU AND I KISS YOUR DEAR FEET A COUNTLESS NUMBER OF TIMES. I IMAGINE THIS EVERY MINUTE AND I ENJOY IT.'
> Fyodor Dostoyevsky

masochistic pleasure in losing at the tables. It is said that the publisher's advance on *Crime and Punishment* had to be paid by the day, since he would lose all the money at the casino each night. When travelling with Polina, he would pawn their belongings so he could continue gambling, and begged cash from his relatives.

FOOT FETISH

After Polina left him, Dostoyevsky decided that he should take up with someone who might bring some sort of domestic stability to his life. At the age of 45, he married his 20-year-old stenographer, Anna Snitkina. She worshipped him, saying she was 'prepared to spend the rest of my life on my knees to him'. However, it turned out to be the other way around. His letters to her are full of references to him kneeling before her and kissing her feet. 'I bear witness that I long to kiss every toe on your foot and you will see I shall achieve my purpose,' he wrote.

This was an interest he shared with other writers – for example, Thomas Hardy, F. Scott Fitzgerald, Victor Hugo and Aleksandr Pushkin, who devoted a passage of his verse novel *Eugene Onegin* to his obsession. Johann Wolfgang von Goethe wrote to his long-term lover Christiane von Vulpius, asking for a pair of 'danced-out shoes' to 'press to his heart'. She shared his obsession, calling his penis *Herr Schönfuss* – 'Mr Nicefoot'. This was after they had known each other for 15 years. Goethe eventually married Christiane after she saved him from being shot by two soldiers when Napoleon invaded Germany. However, marriage did not stop him chasing other women. After Christiane died, the 74-year-old Goethe asked his 19-year-old 'daughterling', Ulrike von Levetzow, to marry him. She refused.

No one is quite sure why some people are turned on by feet. It seems to be largely a male thing. Surveys show that between a quarter and three-quarters of 1 per cent of the adult population are sexually aroused by feet – and 70 per cent of them are men. Anna Snitkina had to put up with other things from Dostoyevsky. His letters are full of references to corporal punishment. In 1876, Dostoyevsky became obsessed with the Kroneberg case, writing about it extensively in *A Writer's Diary*. Thirty-one-year-old nobleman Stanislav Leopol'dovich Kroneberg was charged with torturing – by beating – his seven-year-old illegitimate daughter Maria. The defence was that Kroneberg was only punishing his daughter for what Dostoyevsky repeatedly calls her 'secret vice' – onanism. The court case dragged on for six days, with Kroneberg's mistress, Adelina Gesing, describing the bruises and welts on the young girl's body. Other witnesses talked of her being stripped

Foot Fetishism

The University of Bologna examined 381 Internet fetish discussion groups, in which at least 5,000 people had been participating, and discovered that 47 per cent of those interested in specific body parts or characteristics preferred feet and toes. Three per cent went for navels, ethnicity and breasts, while 2 per cent focused on legs, buttocks, mouths, lips and teeth. Among those people who preferred objects related to body parts, 64 per cent were interested in footwear, particularly shoes and boots. Some 12 per cent were turned on by underwear, 9 per cent by coats, body fluids and body size, 7 per cent by hair, 5 per cent by muscles, and 4 per cent by genital and body modifications such as piercing and tattooing. The lowest scores went to stethoscopes, wristwatches, bracelets, nappies and catheters. Body hair, nails, noses, ears, necks and body odour all scored less than 1 per cent.

Leo Tolstoy

1828–1910

Another Russian literary giant, Tolstoy spent his lifetime trying to give up sex. He lost his virginity at 16 to a prostitute. 'The first time my brothers dragged me to a brothel and I performed the act, I sat down afterwards at the foot of the woman's bed and cried,' he said.

Otherwise he had little time for women. 'Regard the company of women as a necessary social evil and avoid them as much as possible,' he wrote in his diary. But he did not take his own advice, admitting in later life to Anton Chekhov that he was insatiable. At 21, he seduced a dark-eyed servant named Gasha on the family estate. She was a virgin. 'Is what has happened to me wonderful or horrible?' he asked himself. 'Bah! It's the way of the world; everyone does it.' Soon after, he had another servant named Dunyasha. In later life, he looked back on her 'beauty and youth ... her strong womanly body. Where is it now? Nothing but bones.'

He desired his aunt, Alexandra Tolstoy, and dreamed of marrying his 'unique' and 'delicious' relative incestuously. Meanwhile he was carrying on with a peasant woman named Axinya, who bore him a son. However, Tolstoy simply abandoned his mistress and child when he decided to marry.

In 1862, Tolstoy married Sonya Andreyevna Bers, who was eager to be the wife of a famous writer. But first he made her read his diary, which detailed his sexual exploits. He wanted her to know everything about him, he said, but it led her to believe that he was only interested in physical love.

Their wedding night was not a success – from her point of view at least. She wrote of love, that the 'physical manifestations are so repugnant'. But her innocence and apprehension only fuelled his lust. Although she bore him 13 children, she never enjoyed sex.

However, Sonya remained devoted to Tolstoy, encouraging him in his work and copying his manuscripts. But further humiliation lay in store. In 1889, he published *The Kreutzer Sonata* which urged people to give up marriage and avoid sex. Sonya was pregnant at the time. 'That is the real postscript to *The Kreutzer Sonata*,' she wrote bitterly.

Try as he might, Tolstoy did not give up sex until the age of 82, when he admitted to a friend that he was no longer consumed by lust. Meanwhile, he blamed Sonya for luring him into sin. Sonya's desire was not encouraged by the fact that Tolstoy was going through an ascetic phase in which he no longer washed. He smelt like a goat and his feet were covered in dirt and sores.

Sonya turned her attentions to the pianist and composer Sergey Tanayev, sending Tolstoy into paroxysms of jealousy – though he did not stop demanding sex from her. On the other hand, when Tolstoy was writing his will with Vladimir Chertkov, leaving his works to the public, Sonya accused her 81-year-old husband of having a homosexual affair with Chertkov.

naked. Dostoyevsky used the courtroom scenes from the trial in *The Brothers Karamazov*, while in his work as a journalist he drew on the case to begin a debate on masturbation. During lovemaking he would often go into a frenzy, which could sometimes provoke an epileptic fit. Afterwards he would lie rigid, as if dead. Nevertheless the marriage was sexually satisfying on both sides. After 12 years of marriage, he was able to declare with confidence that 'ecstasy and rapture are inexhaustible'. This, too, may have been the result of his epilepsy, which sometimes affects the 'pleasure centres' in the brain.

There may have been a darker side to Fyodor Dostoyevsky's sexual life – his obsession with young girls. The idea of an older man corrupting a young girl is a regular theme in his books. There was a rumour that he had put this idea into practice when a governess brought a young girl – presumably a child prostitute – for him to bathe.

SIR RICHARD BURTON

A THOUSAND AND ONE ARABIAN NIGHTS

1821-1890

Sir Richard Burton was one of the great explorers of the Victorian era. He was one of the first non-Muslims to visit Mecca and led the search to find the source of the Nile. He wrote numerous books about his travels and translated some of the classics of Eastern erotic literature – the *Kama Sutra*, *The Perfumed Garden* and *The Arabian Nights* – which were, at the time, condemned as pornography. It is clear that he enjoyed first-hand experience of the sexual variations set out in these books.

Born the son of a British army officer, Richard Burton travelled extensively in France and Italy with his family as a child, which gave him a facility for languages. By the time he went to Oxford, he was fluent in French, Italian and its Béarnais and Neapolitan dialects, as well as Latin and Greek. He was even said to have had an affair with a Gypsy girl and learnt the rudiments of the Roma language. The Continent also provided a thorough sexual education, with the young Burton enjoying orgies with the prostitutes in Naples.

After two years, he was sent down from Oxford for a breach of college discipline and went out to Bombay with the army. Within a year, he was fluent in both Hindustani and Gujarati. He learnt at least seven other Indian languages and, over his lifetime, mastered more than 40 languages and dialects. He even set up house in India with 40 monkeys in an attempt to learn their language. Burton called the prettiest monkey his wife, wreathing her in pearls and seating her beside him at mealtimes.

He continued his sexual education among the women of Bombay and took a Hindu *bubu*, or mistress, who was expert at prolonging the act of love. 'She cannot be satisfied with anything less than twenty minutes,' he wrote. Later he met a beautiful Persian girl in a caravan near Karachi and pined after her for the rest of his life.

HOMOSEXUAL BROTHELS

As a result of Burton's facility with languages, he was used as an intelligence officer by Sir Charles Napier, who was trying to stamp out infanticide, wife-killing and pederasty in Sind. Napier sent Burton to investigate the homosexual brothels in Karachi, in which young boys were entertaining British soldiers. Burton came back with a report so graphic in its detail that it was plain that he had

The Vulva

The *Kama Sutra* says: 'The vulva contains a tube shaped to the penis, which is the swing in which the Love-God rides. Opened with two fingers, it causes the love juices to flow. This tube and the sunshade of the Love God [the clitoris] are the two organs characteristic of women. The sunshade of the Love God is a nose-shaped organ placed just above the entrance of the God's dwelling, and full of the veins which secrete the juice of love. Not far from it, within the vulva, is the duct of the full moon, which is filled with this juice. There is also another vascular area. When these three zones are rubbed with the finger, the woman is brought into condition.'

The Perfumed Garden says: 'God has given this object a mouth, a tongue, two lips and a shape like the footprint of a gazelle on the sands of the desert. When a desirable woman walks, her natural parts should stand out under her clothing; when she is in heat, they should become turgid and moist – and grip, and suck firmly upon, the male organ.'

participated, particularly in some of the more unusual sadomasochistic practices on offer. Like many people of that era, he seemed to enjoy flagellation. Napier shut down the brothels but, after he left India, the report was circulated, despite the fact that it was meant to have been kept secret. Disgraced, Burton returned to England.

Burton obtained leave from the army to make the hajj pilgrimage to Mecca for the Royal Geographic Society; he disguised himself as a dervish, since any Christian found entering the holy city would be killed. Preperations for the pilgrimage entailed hanging out in Cairo to brush up his Arabic. When it was published, his account of the trip brought him fame.

Next he headed for another forbidden city – Harar in Somalia. It was the centre of slavery in East Africa and no Christian had ever been there. In 1855, he joined an expedition to find the source of the Nile. When that failed, he returned to London, then went off to the Crimean War, where he trained Turkish irregular horsemen. He set out on another expedition to find the source of the Nile in 1857 and discovered Lake Tanganyika with John Hanning Speke. When Speke returned to London, he claimed that he had discovered the source of the Nile – Lake Victoria. Burton disputed this and the two fell out.

> ## 'DO WHAT THY MANHOOD BIDS THEE DO, FROM NONE BUT SELF EXPECT APPLAUSE.'
> Sir Richard Burton

PRACTICE OF POLYGAMY

In 1860, Burton travelled across the United States by stagecoach to visit the Mormon capital, Salt Lake City. While others were condemning the Mormon practice of polygamy, Burton maintained that it was the natural state of mankind.

On his return, he married Isabel Arundel, a Catholic whom he had met in Boulogne 12 years earlier following his disgraced expulsion from India. He was sent as consul to Fernando Po, which gave him the chance to explore West Africa and study the sexual practices there. He was then posted to Brazil, later returning to Damascus as consul. He was delighted to be back in the Middle East, but he found himself surrounded by enemies and was recalled. After a summer in Iceland, he settled in Trieste, where he remained for the rest of his life.

PRIVATE PUBLICATION

In Trieste, Burton spent his time writing and translating. Believing that the wisdom of the East in sexual matters should be available in the West, he risked prosecution and imprisonment to translate and publish the *Kama Sutra of Vatsyana*, the *Ananga Ranga* and *The Perfumed Garden of Cheikh Nefzaoui*. These were printed secretly. He published openly an unexpurgated 16-volume edition of *The Arabian Nights*, also known as *One Thousand and One Nights*. He also translated Latin erotic classics.

Burton's version of *The Arabian Nights* netted him 10,000 guineas, the first serious cash he had earned from writing. 'Now that I know the tastes of England, we need never be without money,' he said.

Of *The Perfumed Garden*, he told a friend: 'It is a marvellous repertory of Eastern wisdom; how eunuchs are made, and are married; what they do in marriage; female circumcision, the Fellahs copulating with crocodiles, etc.'

The Kama Shastra Society

The Kama Shastra Society was founded in 1882 by Sir Richard Burton and Forster Fitzgerald Arbuthnot, a fellow orientalist who had been born in Bombay. After being educated on the Continent, he returned to India where he worked as a government official. He was initiated into oriental literature by Edward Rehatsek, a learned but eccentric Hungarian who led the life of a fakir in Bombay. Arbuthnot met Burton and his wife there in 1876.

The goal of the Kama Shastra Society was to 'remove the scales from the eyes of Englishmen who are interested in Oriental literature'. It published the *Kama Sutra* and other erotic masterpieces. Necessarily, these books were published secretly and circulated privately to avoid prosecution by the Society for the Suppression of Vice under the UK's Obscene Publications Act of 1857. Known as Lord Campbell's Act, it had already led to the jailing of other writers and publishers.

According to Lord Campbell, the Lord Chief Justice, the trade of pornographic material was 'a sale of poison more deadly than prussic acid, strychnine or arsenic'.

Burton and Arbuthnot deliberately defied British law when they published the *Kama Sutra*. Meeting in secret, they arranged with a publisher named Payne to print the first 250 copies of the English-language edition. On the title page it said that the text was 'translated from the Sanskrit and annotated by A. F. F. and B. F. R.' – simply reversing their initials. Their justification was that millions of Orientals had access to the texts in one form or another, so what harm could be done by English gentlemen reading the work? With their own identities disguised, Burton and Arbuthnot restricted the circulation of the book to the membership of the society. They went to such great pains to protect their identity and the secrecy of the society that little is known about it even today.

Publicly his translations were condemned as the 'garbage of the brothel', but he maintained that nothing could be judged obscene since taboos and tastes vary from culture to culture. To illustrate this, he liked to tell the tale of a group of Englishmen visiting a Muslim sultan in the desert. In full view of the Englishmen, the sultan's wife fell off her camel. Her dress was hitched up and her private parts were on display to all. 'Was the sultan embarrassed?' Burton would ask. 'Quite the opposite. He was pleased, because his wife had managed to keep her face covered throughout the incident.'

SEXUAL MUTILATION

Burton saw nothing wrong in pornography. When in England he studied in the library of Richard Monckton Milnes, taking a particular interest in material on flagellation and sexual mutilation. Burton's travel books also detail the sexual mores of the places he visited, often hinting that he took part.

But no one can be sure quite where his own tastes lay. He had a Byronic love of shocking people, once telling a priest: 'Sir, I'm proud to say I have committed every sin in the Decalogue.'

When he died in 1890, his wife burnt the new edition of *The Perfumed Garden* that he had been preparing. She then wrote a biography of her husband in an attempt to make him appear a good Catholic. After it was finished, she burnt the diaries and journals that covered the last 40 years of his life.

LEOPOLD VON SACHER-MASOCH

ENSLAVEMENT TO A WOMAN

1836–1895

Leopold von Sacher-Masoch was an Austrian writer and journalist. He was a socialist and humanist who wrote about the integration of Jews and the emancipation of women. Seen in his time as a rival to Turgenev and a potential successor to Goethe, he is now known only for his novel *Venus in Furs* – about a man who wants to enslave himself to a woman – and for the perversion of 'masochism' to which he lent his name.

Leopold von Sacher-Masoch was born in what is today Lviv in the Ukraine but was then Lemberg, the German-speaking capital of the Polish kingdom of Galicia and Lodomeria, a province of the Austrian Empire. A Roman Catholic, he was the son of the Austrian police director, but did not begin learning German until the age of 12. After graduating from Graz University, he returned to Lemberg where he became a professor.

He began writing about Austrian history, then developed an interest in the folklore of his native Galicia, publishing a series of volumes between 1860 and 1880. These were translated into Russian, French and Ukrainian. He later moved to Paris.

THE LEGACY OF CAIN

In 1869, he published *Venus in Furs* as part of a longer series known as the *Legacy of Cain*, which was never completed. The novel drew heavily on Sacher-Masoch's own life. It tells the story of a man who dreams that he is talking about love to Venus while she is swathed in furs – an idea he took from the painting *Venus with a Mirror* by Titian. He tells the dream to a friend named Severin, who offers him the manuscript of a book called *Memoirs of a Suprasensitive Man* as an antidote to his obsession with cruel women. In the manuscript, the protagonist Severin as a ten-year-old is bound hand and foot and whipped by his cruel aunt wearing a fur jacket. 'Under the lash of a beautiful woman my senses first realized the meaning of woman,' he says. 'In her fur jacket she seemed to me like a wrathful queen, and from then on my aunt became the most desirable woman on God's earth.'

As a child Severin read the legends of martyrs and the torments they suffered. 'To suffer and endure cruel torture from then on seemed to me exquisite delight, especially when it was inflicted by a beautiful woman,' he says. 'I felt there was something sacred in sex; in fact, it was the only sacred thing. In woman and her beauty I saw something divine, because the most important function of existence – the continuation of the species – is her vocation. To me, woman represented a personification of nature, Isis, and man was her priest, her slave. In contrast to him she was cruel like nature herself, who tosses aside whatever has served her purposes as soon as she no longer has need for it. To him her cruelties, even death itself, still were sensual raptures.'

> 'MAN IS THE ONE WHO DESIRES, WOMAN THE ONE WHO IS DESIRED. THIS IS WOMAN'S ENTIRE BUT DECISIVE ADVANTAGE. THROUGH MAN'S PASSIONS, NATURE HAS GIVEN MAN INTO WOMAN'S HANDS.'
>
> Leopold von Sacher-Masoch

Masochism

The German neuropsychiatrist Richard von Krafft-Ebing coined the term 'masochism' in his book *Psychopathia Sexualis*, first published in 1886 – while Sacher-Masoch was still alive. Krafft-Ebing wrote: 'I feel justified in calling this sexual anomaly "masochism", because the author Sacher-Masoch frequently made this perversion, which up to his time was quite unknown to the scientific world as such, the substratum of his writings ... During recent years facts have been advanced which prove that Sacher-Masoch was not only the poet of Masochism, but that he himself was afflicted with this anomaly. Although these proofs were communicated to me without restriction, I refrain from giving them to the public. I refute the accusation that I have coupled the name of a revered author with a perversion of the sexual instinct, which has been made against me by some admirers of the author and by some critics of my book.'

Severin is obsessed with finding a beautiful woman who will wear furs and whip him. He becomes infatuated with Wanda von Dunajew. Severin asks to become Wanda's slave and encourages her to treat him in ever more degrading ways. At first Wanda demurs, but slowly she begins to take advantage of him, while at the same time deriding him. She wears fur and whips him. Severin's feelings of exquisite humiliation are described as 'suprasensitivity'. He travels to Florence with Wanda, pretending to be her servant 'Gregor'. There she recruits three African women to beat and humiliate him. Wanda then finds herself a new lover, a young Greek cavalry officer named Alexis Papadopolis. The idea is to torment Severin with pangs of jealousy, but this only makes him more ardent. 'Nothing can intensify my passion more than tyranny, cruelty, and especially the faithlessness of a beautiful woman,' he says.

Upping the stakes, Wanda submits to Alexis, then allows Alexis to whip Severin until, finally, the spell is broken and he is cured of his love for Wanda. The book ends on a feminist note – a woman can only be a master or a slave to a man until there is equality between the sexes in education and work. Only then can there be companionship.

LIFE FOLLOWS ART

Only 1,225 copies of the book were printed for private circulation. The type was then broken up. It was intended to be part of a series of novels under the six strands Love, Property, Money, the State, War and Death. Sacher-Masoch only completed the first two, Love and Property. *Venus in Furs* is the fifth novel in the Love strand.

The model for Wanda von Dunajew was the writer Fanny Pistor, who approached Sacher-Masoch under the fictitious name of Baroness Bogdanoff, asking for his advice on her literary efforts. Sacher-Masoch agreed to become her slave for six months, on 8 December 1869 signing himself into bondage. His one stipulation was that she must wear furs as often as possible, especially when she was in a cruel mood. They travelled to Venice, rather than Florence. But, as in the book, she travelled first class, while he travelled in third class as her servant and using the name 'Gregor'. In the novel, Wanda has their portrait painted, she reclining in furs with a whip and Severin at her feet. In life they were photographed in much the same pose, with Fanny holding the whip casually in her hand. Fanny then took a lover, an Italian actor named Salvini, but the affair between her and Sacher-Masoch petered out, rather than reaching the dramatic climax it does in the book.

Ludwig II of Bavaria

1845–1886

Ludwig II of Bavaria is known as 'Mad King Ludwig', perhaps unjustly. He was deposed on the grounds of mental illness without a medical examination being made and died a day later in mysterious circumstances. But he was, shall we say, eccentric.

On his accession in 1864, the pretty 19-year-old king summoned the composer Richard Wagner to Munich. The king instructed him to complete his *Ring* cycle and put all worries about money from his mind. Wagner bowed low in gratitude. King Ludwig sank to his knees, clutched the composer and swore an oath of eternal fidelity.

Naturally, Wagner hid from the king the nature of his relationship with his lover, Cosima Liszt. Ostensibly she was his secretary. As such, she handled their correspondence, which was so passionate that she grew jealous.

In Munich, Wagner's interminable private audiences with Ludwig set tongues wagging, not least because Wagner was a Protestant and a noted revolutionary. Wagner's high camp mode of dressing in silk and furs, and his addiction to perfume, were a gift to satirists. The king preferred thigh boots, tight breeches and army uniforms.

Ambitious courtiers circled. One faction tempted Wagner with a young woman called Agnes Street to use his influence with the king on their behalf. Meanwhile, with all Wagner's talk of Siegfried, Brünhilde and the joys of Valhalla, the chronically unstable king began to lose his grip on reality.

When King Ludwig discovered the true nature of Wagner's relationship with Cosima, he accused the composer of 'adultery' and 'betrayal'. Wagner grew so unpopular that he was forced to leave Bavaria. The king consoled himself by building magnificent castles. The first was the theatrically neo-Gothic Neuschwanstein, decorated with scenes from Wagner's operas. In 1869, he built the even more extravagant Linderhof, which featured a huge artificial grotto illuminated with coloured electric lights that would be the envy of any modern theme park. He finally went over the top with Schloss Herrenchiemsee, which he intended as an elaborate copy of Versailles.

A proud Bavarian, Ludwig looked down on his mother's Prussian background. Once king, he refused to see her and referred to her only as 'my predecessor's wife'. He never got around to having a wife himself, though he was engaged to Duchess Sophie of Bavaria. The engagement was broken off and it is generally assumed that Ludwig was gay. For the last 17 years of his life, he was closely attached to the master of his stables.

After 22 years on the throne, Ludwig's extravagant building plans had left Bavaria practically bankrupt. In 1886, he was declared insane, though the historian Ghislain de Diesbach said that he was merely 'an eccentric and misanthrope who despised the human condition while still remaining desperately attached to it'. Forced to abdicate, he was found drowned in Lake Starnberg.

In 1873, Sacher-Masoch married Aurora von Rümelin, who wrote a number of novels under the name Wanda von Dunajew. The marriage was unhappy and they split up after ten years. In 1906, after Sacher-Masoch's death, Aurora published the sensational memoirs *The Confessions of Wanda von Sacher-Masoch*, writing that when she was 15 her father left the family destitute. She said that she did not want to play his 'Venus in Furs' but he forced her, through fear of returning to destitution, to play the role. Throughout his life, he continued writing books with dominant, even sadistic characters in a central role. Meanwhile he tried to force her to take other lovers so that he could experience the pain and humiliation of being a cuckold.

During their marriage, Aurora says that they paid court to King Ludwig II of Bavaria. After they split up, Wanda returned to penury while Sacher-Masoch went on to have more mistresses, at least one more wife and other children, all the time following his fantasy of playing slave to 'Venus in Furs'.

ALGERNON SWINBURNE

'A BRAGGART IN MATTERS OF VICE'

1837-1909

The poet and critic Algernon Swinburne had a life-long obsession with flogging. He boasted of his heterosexual prowess, though he was probably homosexual. He also posed as a bestialist, a word even attributed to him in the *Oxford English Dictionary*. The work he published under his own name was widely condemned as perverted filth. The work he published anonymously was worse. Then there was the work he did not publish at all, but merely circulated privately among a small coterie of Victorian fans of erotica.

Born to an aristocratic family, Swinburne had a puny figure and a huge head covered in flowing locks of carrot-coloured hair. His manner was extremely effeminate and he had a high-pitched voice that turned falsetto when he got excited.

At Eton, he found his métier at the infamous flogging block. On one occasion he bathed his face in cologne before a beating, believing that it would heighten his senses. Another old boy recalled a birching with fear rather than pleasure: 'You had to take your trousers and underpants off and kneel on a block, held down by two college servants. You were birched on your bare bum. I was trembling all over, as white as a sheet, absolutely terrified. I got six strokes, which actually drew blood, and when I got back into my class everyone was shouting 'Where's the blood? Where's the blood?' I had to take my shirt-tail out and show the blood spots.' Nevertheless, Swinburne maintained a life-long nostalgia for the flogging block at Eton.

After he left school, he wrote to his friend the homosexual poet George Powell, who was still at the school: 'I should like to see two things there again, the river – and the block.' He also asked for the details of the latest floggings. 'The topic is always most tenderly interesting,' wrote Swinburne, 'with an interest, I may say, based upon a common bottom of sympathy.' Aptly chosen words. Powell indulged Swinburne by sending him a used birch. Swinburne was beside himself and longed to be back at the site of his former delights. 'To assist unseen at the holy ceremony,' he wrote, 'I would give any of my poems.' Powell then sent him a photograph of the old flogging block, which is now kept in the Eton College Museum. Swinburne was excited, but wanted more. 'I would give anything for a good photograph taken at the right minute,' he said, knowing exactly when that would be – 'say the tenth cut or so.'

> 'ONE OF THE GREAT CHARMS OF BIRCHING LIES IN THE SENTIMENT THAT THE FLOGGEE IS THE POWERLESS VICTIM OF THE FURIOUS RAGE OF A BEAUTIFUL WOMAN.'
>
> Algernon Swinburne

Swinburne became a regular client at a flagellation brothel in St John's Wood, known as 'Grove of the Evangelist'. Customers were whipped by rouged blond girls, while an older woman took their money.

In 1861, he met the great collector of pornography Richard Monckton Milnes, who encouraged Swinburne to write. Swinburne addressed their mutual interest in sadomasochism in his poetry. This brought a torrent of criticism. The historian and essayist Thomas Carlyle said that Swinburne was 'standing up to his neck in a cesspool, and adding to its contents'. Another critic accused Swinburne of 'grovelling down among the shameless abominations which inspire him with frenzied delight'. *Punch* magazine dismissed him as 'Swine Born'.

He contributed anonymously to the famous erotic monthly *The Pearl*, which flourished from July 1879 to January 1881. He also wrote S&M classics including *The Flogging Block*, *Charlie Collingwood's Flogging* and *The Whippenham Papers*, which ended up in the private case of the British Library, along with the rest of Monckton Milnes' collection. However, in 1863 he fell out with Monckton Milnes because the latter had taken to beating a boy of the lower classes, while Swinburne believed that flogging should be an exclusively upper-class pastime.

Swinburne's *Ballads and Poems I*, published in 1866, caused a sensation, especially the poems written in homage to Sappho of Lesbos. It is generally assumed that Swinburne's own interests were homosexual, or uranist, to use the term then current. He was close friends with the homosexual painter Simeon Solomon and was an associate of the Pre-Raphaelites; he once chased Solomon around Dante Gabriel Rossetti's house – both were naked. At an Arts Club dinner, Swinburne got drunk and spoke of his horror of sodomy, though he talked about it incessantly.

NOT UP TO SCRATCH

As far as one can tell, Swinburne seems to have been impotent with women. On one occasion Rossetti paid the American actress and dancer Adah Isaacs Menken £10 to sleep with Swinburne. She tried on several occasions, but said she was 'unable to get him up to scratch' and returned the money. She complained that she could not 'make him understand that biting's no use'. On the other hand, Swinburne – perhaps to refute rumours of uranism, which was then illegal – claimed that he had enjoyed a 'riotous concubinage' with Adah. And when Turgenev asked him what the most original and unrealized thing he wanted to do was, he replied: 'To ravish St Geneviève during her most ardent ecstasy of prayer – but in addition, with her secret consent.'

In 1868, the 18-year-old Guy de Maupassant visited Swinburne at George Powell's cottage in Normandy, to be confronted, after lunch, with a gigantic portfolio of pornographic photographs of men taken in Germany. 'I remember one of an English soldier masturbating on a pane of glass,' said Maupassant. Powell kept sucking on the fingers of a flayed hand, which was used as a

An Eton Flogging

An eyewitness to a flogging at Eton wrote: 'A cry rose behind me. "Hullo, there's going to be a swishing!" and a general rush was made towards the upper end of the schoolroom. The victim doomed to execution was a very white-skinned, curly-headed lad called Neville and several dozens of fellows clambered upon forms and desks to see him corrected. I got a front place, my heart thumping. Two fellows deputed to act as holders-down stood behind the block and one of them held a birch of quite alarming size which he handed to the Lower Master as he stepped down from his desk. I had pictured a rod as nothing more than a handful of twigs but this thing was nearly five feet long, having three feet of handle and nearly two feet of bush. As the master grasped it and poised it in the air, addressing a few words of rebuke to young Neville, it seemed a horrible instrument for whipping so small a boy with. Neville knelt on the block and the Master inflicted upon his naked posterior six cuts that sounded like the splashings of so many buckets of water. I turned almost faint.'

Sappho

c.630–612 BC

The poet Sappho was born around 612 BC on Lesbos, an island just off the coast of Turkey. Although she gave both her name and the name of her island to female homosexual love, she was not in fact a lesbian. She was married to a wealthy merchant called Cercolas – his name derives from *kerkos*, Greek for penis. Then she took two male poets as her lovers and later leapt to her death from the White Rock of Leucas for love of the handsome ferryman Phaon. This is the same rock that Aphrodite, the goddess of love, was supposed to have leapt from on account of her love for Adonis.

However, Sappho also ran a school for girls where they were taught poetry, music, singing and dance. Already in Sparta they had developed an all-girl version of pederasty, where a woman teacher took on a young girl as her pupil in exchange for sexual favours. The Greek writer Plutarch mentions that 'in Sparta, even honest married women fell in love with young girls' – possibly because their men were always off fighting and Spartan fighting men were expected to sleep with one another in order to build their *esprit de corps*.

Sappho became famous for her poetry, much of which concerns her relationship with girls – though her brother Charaxus was also the subject of some poems. At the time, women formed informal associations from which men were excluded, and there would be a lot of drinking and a certain amount of nudity and intimacy. Sappho's work dealt with the passions and jealousies that flourished in this heated atmosphere and women would come from all over Greece to attend her readings.

Other poets' work makes reference to lesbian practices on Lesbos, particularly tribadism, and Lesbos was famed for its nude beauty contests. However, Lesbos was known for all types of sexual freedoms. Indeed, in Classical Greek the verb 'to lesbianize' means to perform fellatio.

paperweight. The couple also kept a large pet monkey which Swinburne 'titillated'. It slept each night with Powell and defecated in the bed. At night, the house was full of strange noises, which Maupassant thought an indication that sadistic practices were being indulged in. But he decided that Swinburne and Powell were not having a homosexual relationship, but rather were having sex with the monkey and the 14-year-old servant boys Powell had sent out from England. The monkey was eventually hanged by one of the servant boys in a fit of jealousy.

MONKEY MEAT

When Maupassant visited again, he was served meat that he strongly suspected was monkey. According to local gossip, Powell 'ate only monkey – boiled, roasted, sautéed, or in a confit'. On this occasion, Maupassant said the monkey was spit-roasted. He was also given a drink so strong that it nearly knocked him out and he fled. On a final visit, his attention was drawn to an inscription above their door. It read: '*Chaumière de Dolmancé*' – 'Dolmancé's Cottage'. Maupassant asked the Englishmen if they knew who Dolmancé was (the hero and homosexual corrupter of Sade's *La Philosophie dans le Boudoir*). Indeed they did, they replied, 'with terrifying expressions on their faces'. Again Maupassant fled, avoiding Swinburne and Powell thereafter.

Swinburne had another monkey which he dressed in women's clothing. It was seen by a young man who paid a visit when he was living in a tent on the Isle of Wight. When Swinburne was making advances to the boy while extolling the virtues of 'unisexual love', the monkey attacked him in a fit of jealousy. Again, on a subsequent visit, he was served grilled monkey. But this may all have been a front. Oscar Wilde thought so.

ADELINA PATTI

THE SOPRANO WHO REACHED FOR THE LOW NOTES

1843-1919

Abel canto coloratura soprano, Adelina Patti was queen of world opera for more than 50 years. Earning huge fees at the height of her career, she became the richest prima donna of the late 19th century. She was married three times and details of her love life made her notorious. But it was a bizarre affair with a midget that made her the talk of show business.

Born to a musical family in Madrid, Adelina Patti moved with her family to New York where her father helped manage the Astor Place Opera House. She made her stage debut there at the age of eight. At 16, she appeared in the title role of Donizetti's *Lucia di Lammermoor* at the New York Academy of Music, and at 18 she took to the stage at London's Covent Garden where she became an overnight sensation.

Using London as a base, she conquered the Continent. She could learn a role after two rehearsals and at the height of her career had a repertoire of 42 operas. The crowned heads of Europe showered her with jewellery. In 1862, she sang Howard Payne's *Home, Sweet Home* at the White House for Abraham and Mary Lincoln, after their son Willie had died of typhoid. She also sang the song for Queen Victoria, who was moved to tears.

The composer Giuseppe Verdi said that she was the greatest vocalist he had ever heard. When she performed an aria from Gioacchino Rossini's *The Barber of Seville* in front of the composer, adding her own embellishments, he applauded vigorously and said: 'That was wonderful – who wrote it?'

Adelina was also transcendently beautiful. A critic wrote that she had a 'delicately chiselled head, fine mobile features and the guileless eyes of a doe – white marble turned into flesh, surrounded by a dark frame of hair'. She was such a noted beauty that Pear's Soap used her in their advertising, picturing her emerging from her bath.

In Paris, the celebrated illustrator Gustave Doré threatened to kill himself in her boudoir if she would not make love to him. A young man from Milan who turned her head was rejected because he did not have enough money, and a young Puerto Rican named José Rios, whom she met in 1858, followed her back to New York and trailed around the Continent behind her.

BEHIND KINDLY SCREENS

At the age of 25 Adelina attracted the attention of Napoleon III. He sent his equerry, Henri, Marquis de Caux, backstage to convey his compliments. The middle-aged marquis was immediately smitten but, cash-strapped, he could not propose. In his youth he had inherited a fortune, but had frittered it away. By the time he met Adelina, he had spent more than his entire yearly allowance in one Parisian restaurant alone, the Maison-Dorée, until he was refused further credit. But he did provide some form of compensation. Another Frenchman said that the marquis was 'never more appreciated by the ladies than

> 'PEOPLE WENT TO HER PERFORMANCES NOT TO HEAR A GREAT ARTIST BUT TO SEE A GREAT WANTON – A BEAUTIFUL SENSUALIST THE FAME OF WHOSE ADULTERIES HAD OVERSPREAD THE GLOBE.'
>
> *The Wasp*, California, March 1885

during those intervals when conversations were held behind scented fans, and grave indiscretions committed behind kindly screens'.

Despite the marquis's age and relative poverty, Adelina liked the idea of having a title. She proposed and married in virginal white. At the wedding breakfast, the 58-year-old Italian tenor Giovanni Mario, who often played opposite Adelina, leaned over to the British music critic Sutherland Edwards to whisper: 'The marquis, much as he might be attached to his fascinated bride, has never made love to her as much as I, her constant lover, have done.' This rather put a damper on the marriage and both began having affairs.

After seven years, Adelina fell for her new leading man, Italian tenor Ernesto Nicolini, who left his wife and five children. The marquis was furious at their very public affair and forbade his wife to appear on stage with Nicolini again. She ignored him and starred opposite Nicolini in *La Traviata* in St Petersburg. In her dressing room, the marquis complained that she had soiled the title he had brought her. She said that he could have the title back. The couple separated in 1877.

In 1881, she toured the US in a luxuriously appointed private railway carriage. By then she was charging $5,000 a night, which had to be paid in gold before the performance – and she had a parrot trained to shriek: 'Cash! Cash!'

It took her eight years to obtain a divorce from the Marquis de Caux, and it cost her half her fortune. In 1886, she married Nicolini and they moved to Craig-y-Nos Castle in Wales. They remained happily married until his death in 1898. Less than a year later, the 56-year-old Adelina married Baron Rolf Cederström from Stockholm who was 30 years her junior. They stayed together until her death 19 years later.

GENERAL MITE

As we have seen, Adelina Patti enjoyed variety in her sex life. However, in 1882, while she was still married to the Marquis de Caux and in a full-time relationship with Ernesto Nicolini, she spotted a picture of a midget called Dudley Foster in the window of Bundell's Curiosity Dime Museum in New York. Foster was from Nova Scotia and performed under the stage name General Mite. Twenty years old, he was 56 centimetres (22 ins) tall and weighed less than 4.5 kilograms (10 lbs).

Charles Baudelaire (1821–1867)

French poet and critic Charles Baudelaire was famous for his 1857 collection *Fleurs du Mal* ('The Flowers of Evil'). As a student in Paris, he caught venereal disease from a prostitute called Sarah la Louchette ('Squint-eyed Sarah'), whom he immortalized in early poems. The disease later killed him. After he came into his inheritance, he squandered it on clothes, good food and wine, books, paintings, opium and hashish. He took a mulatto woman named Jeanne Duval as his mistress, and wrote erotic masterpieces , such as *La Chevelure* – 'The Head of Hair'.

Richard von Krafft-Ebing said: 'Baudelaire came of an insane and eccentric family. From his youth he was psychically abnormal. His *vita sexualis* was decidedly abnormal. He had love-affairs with ugly, repulsive women, negresses, dwarfs, giantesses. About a very beautiful woman he expressed the wish to see her hung up by her hands and to kiss her feet. This enthusiasm for the naked foot also appears in one of his fiercely feverish poems as the equivalent of sexual indulgence. He said women were animals who had to be shut up, beaten and fed well. The man displaying these masochistic and sadistic inclinations died of paretic dementia.'

La Belle Otero

1868–1965

Like Adelina Patti, Augustina Otero Iglesias could have any man she fancied. Ostensibly a dancer, singer and actress in the music hall, she made a career out of being the mistress of famous men, making and losing over $25 million during her lifetime. She had affairs with the Prince of Wales, later Edward VII, kings of Spain and Serbia, Russian archdukes, the Khedive of Cairo, the duke of Westminster, the writer Gabriele d'Annunzio and railroad heir William K. Vanderbilt.

King Leopold II of Belgium, she said, 'was not very generous to start with, but I taught him how to give. He was an apt student.' They were lovers for three or four years and he gave her several opulent residences. Prince Albert I of Monaco 'was not very virile and I don't think he got his money's worth ... But as long as he didn't care, neither did I, and he seemed to enjoy taking me where we could be seen together publicly.' Then there was Prince Nicholas of Montenegro, who became the country's one and only king. He presented her with 'a simply gorgeous diamond bracelet and at least five ... beautiful watches' before persuading her to visit his palace. 'I saw practically nothing the whole trip,' she complained. 'All the Prince wanted to do was to make love to me, so I obliged.'

However, her great love was Aristide Briand, then a junior minister in the French government. According to La Belle Otero: 'He was ... hideously ugly. He was fat. He dressed like a slob – often there'd be the remains of an omelette on his vest – his nails were black, but there was a fascination to him I never found in any other man.' The downside was that he could only afford 'an occasional cheap jewel and flowers'. But there were compensations. 'Once ... he made love to me eight times before morning, and he was 50 years old at the time,' she recalled.

Another less-than-fastidious lover was Czar Nicholas II of Russia. He had a bad complexion and rarely bathed. Nevertheless, she 'grew quite fond of him' though 'he had the strangest views about sex'. He was also terrified of being assassinated. 'There were always half-a-dozen huge, black-bearded armed guards at our bedroom door, some more at every window, and, if there was a rear exit, he'd have half a regiment posted there,' she recalled. 'It almost felt like I was undressing in an army barracks or a bull-fighting arena. If I moved a chair suddenly or dropped a perfume bottle, Nick would jump out of bed and scream with fright.'

But then La Belle Otero liked having sex in unusual places. She made love to Baron Lepic in a hot-air balloon floating 60 metres (200 ft) above the river Aude in France in 1902. The New York *World* reported that 'the gondola remained high above the earth for more than an hour'. La Belle Otero said: 'It was an experience every woman should enjoy.'

It was said that her nymphomania stemmed from her having been raped at the age of 11. A broken pelvis left her unable to have children and she sought to avenge herself on men for the rest of her life. It is also said that the twin cupolas of the Carlton Hotel in Cannes are modelled on her breasts.

Adelina made a deal with the proprietor of the museum and was allowed to whisk the tiny man off to her bedroom. The affair caused a sensation. General Mite was himself not unencumbered. He had met the future Mrs Mite in Liverpool in 1880, and they arranged to travel together and married in Manchester in 1884.

Given Adelina's eclectic tastes, it should come as no surprise that New York society turned its back on her. The Vanderbilts no longer invited her to their balls. Elsewhere, she would be entertained only by men, as upstanding ladies thought it improper to fraternize with her. Tolstoy recorded the scene when the matrons of St Petersburg walked out on her performance. She took British citizenship in 1898.

According to the German sexologist Richard von Krafft-Ebing, the only one of Adelina's contemporaries to share a fetish about dwarfs or midgets was the controversial, decadent French poet and critic Charles Baudelaire.

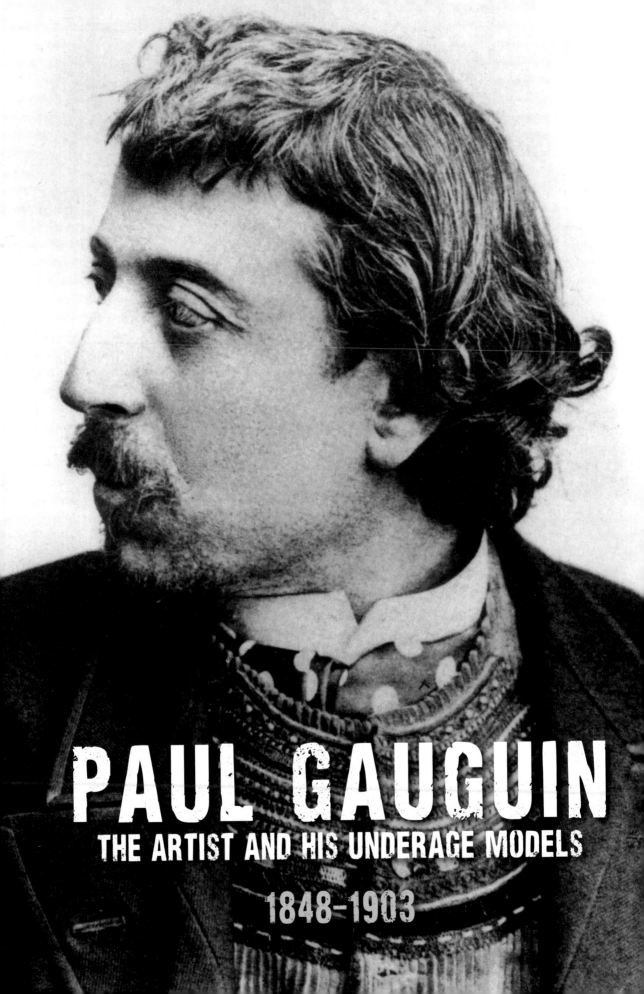

PAUL GAUGUIN
THE ARTIST AND HIS UNDERAGE MODELS

1848-1903

Paul Gauguin was one of the greatest painters of the late 19th century. After spending two years at sea, he became a stockbroker but gave it up for art. The result was poverty and separation from his wife and family. He spent much of the rest of his life in the South Seas, where he could enjoy sexual freedom, particularly with underage girls. Like that other great painter of the day, Amedeo Modigliani, Gauguin felt he had to have sex with a model before he could paint her.

Gauguin's father, a liberal journalist, was forced into exile by the accession of Napoleon III and Gauguin spent much of his childhood in Peru, where nudity was a common sight. At 17 he decided to travel the world as a sailor and lost his virginity in Le Havre before setting sail. He was entranced by tales told by other sailors of the sexual freedoms of Polynesia. Indulging in a little of this freedom himself, he had sex with an opera singer in Rio and a Prussian passenger on board his ship, catching syphilis along the way.

When he returned to France at the age of 23, his guardian got him a job at the stock market and introduced him to Danish governess Mette Sophie Gad – 'a beauty with a heart of stone'. They were married, but he took to visiting prostitutes behind her back. His growing interest in art led him to go and see the erotic sensation of the age, Edouard Manet's *Olympia*, which shows a naked young courtesan staring directly out of the canvas. Gauguin was much taken by the girl's black maidservant, an Afro-Caribbean model named Laure, who reminded him of the girls he had known in Peru.

THE FEMALE NUDE

Gauguin began painting, showing particular interest in the female nude. With the stock-market crash of 1882 he quit to become a full-time painter. But the financial crisis had hit the art market too. Reduced to penury, he separated from his wife, who returned to Denmark with their children.

Gauguin spent much of his time in the artist colony at Port Aven in Brittany, where getting the local Bretons to pose nude was a good deal cheaper than paying the professional models in Paris. To earn some money, he went to work on the construction of the Panama Canal. On his way back to France, he stopped at Martinique. He wrote to his wife: 'I can tell you that here a white person has great difficulty in keeping his virtue intact, for the wives of Potiphar are everywhere ...' Potiphar was the Egyptian captain in the book of Genesis whose wife tried to seduce Joseph. In desperation, she tore his clothes off and later claimed that he raped her, offering his clothes as proof. As a result, Joseph was imprisoned.

'EVERY NIGHT FRENZIED YOUNG GIRLS INVADE MY BED. LAST NIGHT I HAD THREE OF THEM TO KEEP ME COMPANY.'
Paul Gauguin

'The day before yesterday, a young negress of sixteen – and my word she was pretty – offered me a guava, which had been split and squeezed at one end,' Gauguin wrote. 'I was about to eat it when a yellow-skinned notary grabbed the fruit from me and threw it to the ground.' The mulatto was an educated man, who knew the ways of the local women. 'You are a European and

Teha'amana

In Tahiti the middle-aged Gauguin gave his love of young girls full rein. One day, while taking a break from work, Gauguin made a trip down to the western end of the island. He stopped to share a meal with a local family, and the mother of the clan, a handsome woman of about 40, asked him the purpose of his journey.

'I am looking for a wife,' he said.

'Look no further', she said. She had a daughter. Gauguin asked her three questions: 'Is she young? Is she pretty? Is she healthy?' The answer to all three was yes.

'Okay,' said Gauguin. 'Go and get her for me.'

The woman disappeared, while Gauguin ate a meal of wild bananas and crayfish. Half an hour later, the woman returned. She brought with her a young girl of about 13, wearing a transparent dress of pink muslin. Through it, Gauguin said, he could see her golden skin and her nipples standing out hard from her breasts. The beautiful young girl sat down beside him and he asked three more questions.

'Aren't you afraid of me?'

'No,' she said softly.

'Have you ever been ill?'

'No.'

'Would you like to come and live in my hut?'

'Yes.'

It was as easy as that. Her name was Teha'amana, which means 'the Giver of Strength'. They lived together openly. She became his model and the mother of his child.

you don't know the ways of the country,' he said. 'You must never eat fruit without knowing where it comes from. This fruit possesses a charm; the black girl has rubbed it on her sexual parts, and after you have eaten it you will be hers to command.'

Gauguin promised his wife he would be on his guard. 'I shall not succumb,' he said. 'You can rest assured about my virtue.' However, in his wood carving entitled simply *Martinique*, he depicts a naked Martiniquan Eve picking the forbidden fruit. In the place of the serpent he portrays a goat and a monkey, two potent symbols of sexual licentiousness, urging Eve on. Judging from the size and firmness of her breasts, the girl was young, perhaps the 16-year-old he mentioned in his letter.

Back in Paris, he met a beautiful mulatta who became his mistress and the model for the nude sculpture *La Femme Noire*. After visiting Vincent van Gogh in Arles and impregnating 20-year-old seamstress Juliette Huet, who had modelled for him, Gauguin set off for Tahiti. On the way, he grew his hair so that the Polynesian women jeered at him, calling him *taata vahine* or 'man-woman'. Nevertheless, he found young Tahitian girls creeping into his hut for sex at night.

SEXUAL DEMONSTRATIONS

Gauguin attended the rites of a local religious sect, the Areois, who preached free love and proselytized wherever they went. Members were forbidden to marry. They practised infanticide to deter permanent relationships and, with missionary zeal, put on displays of erotic dancing and sexual demonstrations.

Captain Cook witnessed one of these shows: 'A young man, nearly six feet tall, performed the rites of Venus with a little girl about eleven or twelve years of age, before several of our people and a great number of natives, without the least sense of its being indecent or improper, but, as it appeared, in perfect conformity to the custom of the place. 'Among the spectators were several women of superior rank, who may properly be said to have assisted in the ceremony; for they gave instructions to the girl how to perform her part, which, young as she was, she did not seem much to stand in need of.'

Vincent Van Gogh

1853–1890

Compared to Gauguin's colourful sex life, that of van Gogh was positively grey. The two young women to whom he proposed as a youth rejected him with horror. He turned to prostitutes, preferring older, faded women whom he could cosset. Clasina Maria Hoornick, already pregnant and with a five-year-old daughter, moved in with him. He called her *Sien* – 'My Own'. With almost masochistic glee, van Gogh tidied up after her, fed her and looked after her daughter. He used her as his model and tried to reform her. He failed in this, but he did succeed in getting her to attend the public baths in order to wash.

She bore him a son and gave him a dose of gonorrhoea that put him in hospital for three weeks. He bore his condition stoically, saying it did not compare to the pains of childbirth she was suffering. Through his art, he said, he was trying to elevate Sien and all prostitutes. But his drawings of her show her scrawny and misshapen with a scraggy neck and drooping breasts. She is sad, pathetic and old before her time. He left her after she went back on the streets, and she drowned herself in 1904.

In Paris, van Gogh surrounded himself with old prostitutes, before moving on to Arles. When Gauguin visited van Gogh there, the latter was enamoured with a girl named Rachel who worked at *Maison de Tolérance* No.1, run by Madame Virginie. Van Gogh would visit each evening to talk to Rachel. Gauguin was more of a man of action and took her straight to bed. Van Gogh ran home to get a razor with which he threatened Gauguin, then ran off. Later, van Gogh cut the lobe of his ear off and gave it to Rachel, who screamed and fainted.

There is a strong homosexual element in Tahitian culture. In island mythology both gods and men make love to each other. The hula-hula was originally a homoerotic dance, with the dancers bumping and grinding against one another. Gauguin joined in the hula-hula – though, according to his own account, he preferred doing it with a nubile young girl. However, he was nearly overwhelmed by his homosexual feelings for a boy named Jotefa, with whom he walked naked in the forest. The contours of the young man's body appeared to him so graceful that he could almost have been an hermaphrodite. His beauty and fragrance set Gauguin's temples throbbing, and he had to cool off by jumping in a mountain stream.

Promiscuity was interfering with his work, so Gauguin took a wife or *vahine* – a girl called Teha'amana, who was barely in her teens. He painted her naked with another nude Tahitian woman, writing on the painting: 'What, are you jealous?'

Returning to Paris to exhibit his paintings, he boasted of this 13-year-old child-bride, who was now pregnant. He then seduced Judith, the 13-year-old daughter of the Swedish sculptress Ida Ericson-Mollard, later taking 13-year-old 'Annah the Javanese' also as his mistress and model.

Gauguin returned to Tahiti, where he was briefly reunited with Teha'amana, who had married. But there was no shortage of other young girls to share his bed. The delightful young Pau'ura moved in. He claimed she was 13 but, according to her birth certificate, she was fourteen-and-a-half. They had a son named Emile.

Plagued with syphilis, Gauguin left Pau'ura and moved to the Marquesas, where he lived in the *Maison du Jouir* – House of Orgasm. He continued painting and sleeping with his underage models. 'I was aware that my skill as a painter depended on the physical and moral possession of the model,' he said. He had another child by 14-year-old Vaeoho and spent his time trying to corrupt the pupils of a nearby girls' school.

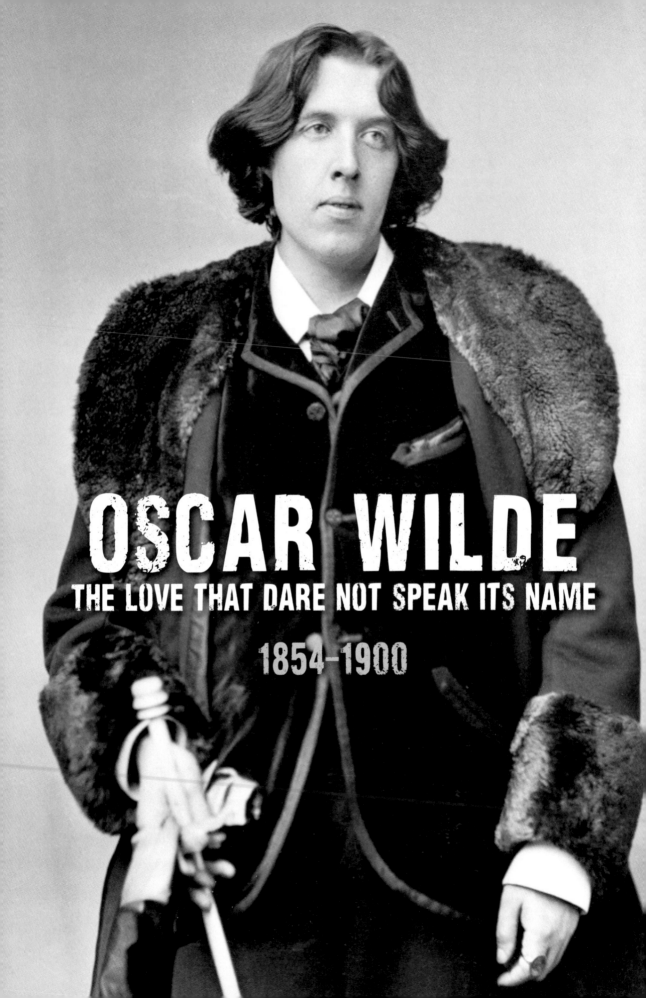

OSCAR WILDE

THE LOVE THAT DARE NOT SPEAK ITS NAME

1854–1900

The witty and erudite writer Oscar Wilde is seen as a gay martyr – a man destroyed by society's prejudice against homosexuality. However, he was not, by and large, having sex with other men, but rather underage boys. These days he would have received a much longer jail term than the two years to which he was sentenced in 1895, and he would have spent the rest of his life on the sexual offenders' register.

Oscar Wilde's father, Sir William Wilde, was a womanizer whose lack of personal hygiene repelled his fastidious son. Lady Jane Wilde dressed her son in girl's clothes until he went to school. At boarding school, there were no sexual adventures. 'I was nearly sixteen when the wonder and beauty of the old Greek life began to dawn upon me,' said Wilde. However, the day he left school another boy came up and kissed him. Tears ran down his face.

At the time John Pentland Mahaffy, a noted classical scholar at Trinity College Dublin, was writing a book entitled *Social Life in Greece*, and he encouraged Wilde to lend a hand. This was the first book to contain a frank discussion of 'Greek love' – that is, the romantic affections between an older man and a beautiful young boy. Wilde called Mahaffy 'my first and best teacher... the scholar who showed me how to love Greek things'. In 1877, they sampled the pleasures of Greece together, taking a holiday there that summer.

GREEK LOVE

At Oxford, Wilde wrote poetry celebrating male lovers in Greek history. Because of his openness about his proclivities, Wilde was considered a dangerous friend at Oxford. However, with the coining of the word 'homosexual' on the Continent in 1886, the sexual love between two men began to be thought of, in intellectual circles at least, as a psychological problem that required the attention of a doctor, rather than a crime that belonged in the courts. Wilde picked up on this. He said that fellow Magdalen undergraduate Augustus 'Gussy' Cresswell 'is charming though not educated well: however he is "psychological" and we have long chats and walks'. Wilde used the word 'spooning' to describe another undergraduate's activities with a choirboy. According to the *Oxford English Dictionary*, by that time spooning already meant 'to lie close together, to fit into each other, in the manner of spoons'. Wilde also wrote a poem called 'Choir Boy', detailing what he wanted to do in the stalls.

Wilde mixed with other uranists, who believed, like the Greeks, that men gave up same-sex love when they reached marriageable age. He began to show an interest in girls. There were a number of flirtations before he fell in love with Florence Balcombe. However, he delayed his proposal because he had been diagnosed with syphilis, and Florence married Bram Stoker, the author of *Dracula*.

> 'WILDE TREATED ME AS AN OLDER BOY TREATS A YOUNGER ONE AT SCHOOL ... WHAT WAS NEW TO ME AND WAS NOT (AS FAR AS I KNOW) KNOWN OR PRACTISED AMONG MY CONTEMPORARIES: HE "SUCKED" ME.'
> Lord Alfred Douglas

Green Carnation

Oscar Wilde has long been associated with green carnations. The fashion had started in Paris in 1891, where homosexual men had formerly worn green cravats. Green was the colour favoured by effeminate men in classical Rome and committed uranists began to sport green carnations in their buttonholes, as a badge of honour. Minutes before the curtain rose at the St James's Theatre for the premiere of *Lady Windermere's Fan* in February 1892, a dozen young men, some wearing make-up, took their seats in the stalls wearing green carnations.

However, scandal was never far away. In September 1894, Bosie's friend Robert Hichens published, anonymously, the novel *The Green Carnation*. This was clearly based on the love affair between Oscar and Bosie and, by the end of the year, it had gone through four editions. The book confirmed everyone's worst suspicions. It even portrays Bosie as lusting after a nine-year-old boy – indeed, Bosie had expressed a desire for Oscar's nine-year-old son Cyril. The book further infuriated the Marquess of Queensberry. Not only did it make it clear what was going on between his younger son and Oscar, it also painted a vicious portrait of him, and people were soon asking what he proposed to do about it.

Coming down from Oxford, Wilde lived with like-minded young men in Salisbury Street off the Strand. He was smitten by Lillie Langtry when she came for tea, and threw himself at a number of actresses. However, since he grew his hair long, dressed in a flowing velvet jacket and knee breeches, and could be seen holding a single lily as he walked down Piccadilly, he was considered rather fey. On his tour of the US, he was widely mocked and scorned, while male followers painted their faces and rouged their cheeks.

After the rejection of two more marriage proposals, Wilde settled on 23-year-old Constance Mary Lloyd, the sister of another friend at Oxford. He immediately set about trying to 'cure' his homosexuality by having sex with a number of prostitutes. When he proposed to Constance, she immediately accepted, though she had already condemned some of his work for its lack of 'morality'. Wilde was attracted to her slim, boyish figure, but he still desired the real thing. And once he was married, he felt quite safe going off with other men.

REPELLED

After Constance gave birth to their two sons, she lost her boyish figure and became round and womanly. This repelled Wilde. 'When I married, my wife was a beautiful girl, white and slim as a lily, with dancing eyes and rippling laughter like music,' he told Frank Harris. 'Within a year or so the flower-like grace had all vanished; she became heavy, shapeless, deformed. She dragged herself about the house in uncouth misery with drawn blotched face and hideous body, sick at heart because of our love. It was dreadful. I tried to be kind to her, forced myself to touch and kiss her; but she was sick always and – oh! I cannot recall it, it is all loathsome. I used to wash my mouth and open the window to cleanse my lips in the pure air.'

Pregnancy he considered a deformity; menstruation was unbearable. 'There is no comparison between a boy and a girl,' he told Harris. 'Think of the enormous, fat hips which every sculptor has to tone down, and make lighter, and the great udder breasts which the artist has to make small and round and firm.' When it came to sex: 'A woman's passion is degrading. She is continually tempting you. She wants your desire as a satisfaction for her vanity more than

The 1885 Act

Following the publication of 'The Maiden Tribute of Modern Babylon' in the *Pall Mall Gazette*, which uncovered the trade in underage girls, the Tory government passed 'An Act to make further provisions for the Protection of Women and Girls, the suppression of brothels, and other purposes'. However, maverick Liberal MP Henry Labouchère introduced an amendment that read: 'Any male person who, in public or private, commits, or is party to the commission of, or procures or attempts to procure the commission by any male person of, any act of gross indecency with another male person, shall be guilty of a misdemeanour, and being convicted thereof shall be liable at the discretion of the court to be imprisoned for any term not exceeding two years, with or without hard labour.'

Wilde failed to appreciate the danger even in 1889, when the Criminal Law Ammendment Act was used to prosecute those involved in the Cleveland Street scandal.

The police had raided a homosexual brothel at 19 Cleveland Street. When the owners were arrested, they gave the names of their aristocratic clients. These included Lord Arthur Somerset, the earl of Euston and Prince Eddy, the oldest son of Bertie, Prince of Wales, and grandson of Queen Victoria. The names of these high-born gentlemen were kept out of the subsequent trial, which earned the low-born brothel keepers nine months' hard labour. However, Ernest Parke, the crusading editor of the *North London Press*, published the names of Somerset and Euston.

Somerset fled to France where he stayed until his death in 1926, but Euston sued Parke for libel. He claimed that he had been given a flier advertising *poses plastiques* at 19 Cleveland Street. Naturally, he said, when he went there and discovered what was really going on, he was appalled and fled.

However, a young boy named Saul who worked at the brothel said that Lord Euston had picked him up on the street and that he had taken Euston back to Cleveland Street for sex. But Euston was 'not an actual sodomite', Saul said. 'He likes to play with you and then "spend" on your belly.' Nevertheless, Parke was sent down for a year with hard labour, while Lord Euston was fully rehabilitated. He was appointed aide-de-camp to Edward VII at his coronation in 1901.

anything else, and her vanity is insatiable if her desire is weak, and so she continually tempts you to excess, and then blames you for the physical satiety and disgust which she herself created.' Sodomy had long been against the law, but in 1885 the Criminal Law Amendment Act also outlawed other acts of 'gross indecency' between men. This did not stop Wilde picking up young men in public lavatories. He even brought some of his young conquests home. Wilde also had procurers supplying underage sexual partners, and was sleeping with Fred Atkins, a female impersonator, male prostitute and professional blackmailer. In 1891, he met Lord Alfred Douglas, nicknamed 'Bosie', who was still a student at Oxford. They had a brief affair. Sharing an interest in 'Greek love', they took to swapping young partners. The Savoy Hotel eventually threw Wilde and Douglas out. They had been staying in adjoining rooms, sharing young rent boys. The chambermaids complained of the Vaseline, semen and human excrement on the sheets.

The whole thing was brought crashing down when Douglas's father, the Marquess of Queensberry, accused Wilde of being a 'somdomite [sic]'. Wilde sued, but when it became clear that Queensberry was going to produce some of Wilde's rent boys in court, he withdrew the suit. However, he was now open to prosecution under the 1885 act.

In court, the chambermaids from the Savoy and the rent boys were called to testify. Wilde made an eloquent speech in his own defence. When asked about 'the love that dare not speak its name' – a line from one of Douglas's poems – he talked of the love between an older, intellectual man and a joyful youth as a beautiful and noble thing.

HAVELOCK ELLIS

THOSE WHO CAN, DO

1859-1939

Proclaimed the 'Darwin of sex', Havelock Ellis was the author of *Studies in the Psychology of Sex*, which came out in seven volumes between 1897 and 1928. He also conducted free sex clinics for men and women for 40 years. Although he was seen as a pioneer, he had little experience of the issue he discussed. He did not manage to get an erection until he was 60 and was only turned on by the sight of a woman urinating.

At the age of 12, Havelock Ellis was taken to London Zoo by his mother. Caught short, she crouched down and urinated on a gravel path while Ellis looked on. His favourite sister said, 'She is flirting with you.' It was an incident that would affect him for the rest of his life.

After being sent to Australia for his health when he was 16, Ellis returned to London to study medicine. He practised for a while in the slums of London, then gave up medicine for writing, publishing his first book, *The New Spirit*, at the age of 30. Subsequently, he began collecting material on sex for his life's work. But although he was interested in sex, he already knew he was no good at it.

He was completely inexperienced at the age of 25 when he wrote a fan letter to Ralph Iron, the author of *The Story of an African Farm*. The author turned out to be a woman, 29-year-old Olive Schreiner, who was a veteran of a number of affairs. They corresponded, then met. Although a feminist, Olive longed to be dominated by a strong man; in Ellis, she found a weedy intellectual. Nevertheless, when she read his journals, she discovered that he was a virgin and decided to deflower him. She did not find him unwilling.

LIMP AND FLACCID

Olive whipped Ellis off to a country cottage she had rented in Derbyshire. During a brisk walk across the dales, she grabbed his crotch to feel his penis. It did not respond. Back in the cottage, she lay naked on the sofa while he caressed and kissed her vulva. Unfortunately that did no good either. While she became wild and inflamed, he remained limp and flaccid. Then came the final ignominy – premature ejaculation.

Olive persisted, but this sad scene was repeated again and again. 'She possessed a powerfully and physically passionate temperament,' Ellis wrote, but he could not match it. She gave up her ambition to marry him and returned to South Africa.

Six years later, Ellis received a fan letter of his own. It was from 28-year-old school governess Edith Lees. She was pretty, petite and curly haired, though he preferred the fact that she was

Urophilia

The 19th-century German sexologist Georg Merzbach noted that few women found erotic pleasure in urine. However, he reported the case of a woman in the late 19th century who masturbated while holding a bottle of men's urine under her nose. She also waited outside men's lavatories in order to smell the urine and masturbated openly as she watched men leave. It is thought that she was aroused by the hormone androsterone, made in the liver by the metabolism of the male sex hormone testosterone and secreted in the urine. It has also been noted that male guinea pigs arouse uncooperative mates by urinating on them.

forthright and intelligent. When she proposed marriage, he pleaded poverty and expressed concerns about his privacy. She promised to share their living expenses, and give him space to work. They shared the cost of a wedding ring and married in December 1891. He did not tell her about his impotence until they were on their honeymoon in Paris. She was somewhat put out as she wanted a baby, but agreed to a marriage of companionship, thinking him 'beautiful' and her spiritual lover. He did not even attempt to make love to her, though occasionally he fondled her in bed.

> ‘A WOMAN IS A SHIP WITH TWO HOLES IN HER BOTTOM.’
> Olive Schreiner

Edith held out for three months, then explained that, although she had had affairs with men, she preferred women. By then she was having an affair with a woman called Claire. This gave Ellis the opportunity to interview her for the first volume of his *Studies in the Psychology of Sex*, which was on *Sexual Inversion*. His co-author was John Addington Symonds, who covered male homosexuality. The book was banned in Britain as an 'obscene libel'. When the ban was challenged in the High Court, on the grounds that the book was of 'scientific value', the judge ruled against the plaintiffs, saying: 'That is a pretence adopted for the purpose of selling a filthy publication.' The other volumes were published in Britain and the USA, but until 1935 they were only available to doctors.

LESBIAN ACTIVITIES

After the death of her next lover, a fragile painter named Lily, Edith returned to her husband. She wrote books and plays, and gave lectures as Mrs Havelock Ellis – her favourite was on Oscar Wilde. When she resumed her lesbian activities, he responded with his own sexless affairs. Nevertheless, they sparked jealousy in his increasingly neurotic wife. She was outraged when the 57-year-old Ellis fell for the 24-year-old Mneme Smith, the daughter of a friend. When Mneme married, Ellis became enamoured of the American birth-control advocate Margaret Sanger. This brought Edith back from a US lecture tour to have a nervous breakdown. Her doctor told Ellis that she was on the verge of insanity. It was a great relief to all when she went into a diabetic coma and died in September 1916.

AT LAST, A MIRACLE

Two years later, a 30-year-old Frenchwoman named Françoise Cyon visited Ellis to collect a fee for having translated one of Edith's books into French. Later, she returned for marital advice. She had had one child by a lover and another by a Russian journalist, who had recently left her. During her treatment by Ellis, she wrote to him telling him that she loved him. While he could be open about sex in an academic setting, he could not find the words to warn her of his impotence. She found out for herself when they went to bed.

Then a miracle happened. Ellis was lying down fully clothed caressing Françoise when she found that she had to go to the bathroom. He followed and, at the sight of her urinating, found he had an erection for the first time in his life. Finally he was able to practise what he preached. While the uninhibited Françoise walked about the house naked and they spent hours kissing, fondling and involved in mutual masturbation, if she really wanted to arouse him, all she had to do was take him out for a walk in the rain and urinate in the garden.

Marie Stopes

1880–1958

A contemporary of American birth-control campaigner and activist Margaret Sanger, Marie Stopes set up the first birth-control clinic in Britain. She wrote extensively about women's sexual pleasure though, again, she had not experienced what she was talking about – at least, not for the first 36 years of her life.

After studying botany, she was researching the production of coal at the University of Munich when she had her first kiss from a Japanese man, Kenujiro Fujii, who was not culturally versed in kissing and had to be shown how. He was married and their relationship continued chastely until he was divorced. Then she dumped him.

Though her writings make it clear that she was opposed to lesbianism, she had long relationships with two older women – Clothilde van Wyssk, one of her teachers at North London Collegiate, and doctor and author Helen McMurchy, a Canadian who took a passionate interest in Marie. It seems unlikely that these relationships were consummated as Marie only found out about masturbation at the age of 29.

At 31, she married Dr Reginald Gates, but she did not realize that anything was missing from her marriage until Alymer Maude, a translator of Tolstoy, came to live with them and informed her of the basic mechanics of sex. From then on, she read avidly. In 1916, she sued for the annulment of her marriage on the grounds of non-consummation. A doctor was called in and testified to her virginity.

'With regards to your husband's part, did it ever get rigid at all?' she was asked in court.

'On the hundreds of occasions when we had what I thought to be relations, I only remember three occasions when it was partially rigid, and then it was never effectively rigid,' she replied.

'And he never succeeded in penetrating your private parts ...'

'No, he did not.'

Notwithstanding, in 1918 she published *Married Love or Love in Marriage* and *Wise Parenthood*, which advocated birth control. The books were banned in America and derided in Britain but became bestsellers, with translations into more than 30 languages.

That same year, she married fellow birth-control advocate Humphrey Roe and finally lost her virginity. Although she gave birth to a son at the age of 44, her second marriage was not much more successful than her first. After 20 years of frustration, she asked her husband for a letter granting her the right to carry on extramarital affairs. Roe provided it, whereupon she began to entertain the young men who queued up for the 58-year-old whom they imagined was an expert at sex.

However, trouble was coming. Ellis asked her to befriend one of his admirers, the novelist and fellow advocate of free love Hugh de Selincourt. Behind Ellis's back, their friendship developed into something else.

De Selincourt proved to be a master at lovemaking, prolonging the action endlessly without coming himself. Françoise made light of the physical aspects of the affair, but Ellis protested. 'Do you imagine that coitus is unimportant?' he said. 'Olive said to me once that when a man puts his penis into a woman's vagina it is as if he put his finger into her brain and stirred it round and round.'

Françoise insisted that her affair had not affected her feelings for him. She gave up de Selincourt, but could not move in with Ellis because he could not support her. However, Margaret Sanger stepped in, paying Françoise a salary as Ellis's secretary, and she continued to water his garden for the rest of his life.

HENRI DE TOULOUSE-LAUTREC

'LITTLE COFFEE POT WITH THE LARGE SPOUT'

1864-1900

Henri de Toulouse-Lautrec is remembered for his restricted height and his vivid depiction of the decadent nightlife of *fin-de-siècle* Paris. He spent most of his short life living in brothels, surrounded by naked and semi-naked women, and watched them at work. He also frequented lesbian bars and had fetishes about parts of the body not normally considered erogenous – hands, backs and nostrils.

In his early teens, Toulouse-Lautrec suffered a series of accidents that broke both his legs. They did not heal properly and grew no further, while his torso grew to an adult size. However, for a man just under five feet tall, he had disproportionately large genitals. He described himself as the 'little coffee pot with the large spout', while lovers referred to him as the 'prick on paws' and the 'prick on wheels' – and also, majestically, as 'the tower'.

With his malformation, he could not share his aristocratic father's love of field sports, nor expect to marry a girl of his own class. Showing some talent for art as a child, Toulouse-Lautrec left the family estates in the Midi at the age of 19 and headed for Paris. Some time later he lost his virginity with a young model named Marie Charlet, provided by fellow students at the atelier of Ferdinand Cormon. She was just 16 but had a broad range of sexual experience behind her. Sexually abused by her drunken father, she had left home, supporting herself by nude modelling and casual prostitution. She was uninhibited, with an insatiable sexual curiosity. Toulouse-Lautrec's dwarfism intrigued her, which was very satisfactory from his point of view. Marie introduced him to the world of sex and to the type of women who would give him pleasure. She also left him with few illusions about the relationship between men and women. He told a friend that he would like to 'find a woman who had a lover uglier than me'.

As it was, he took a series of beautiful lovers. He moved to Montmartre where he stayed with his friend René Grenier and his wife Lily. Among his surviving erotic drawings there is one of a nude Lily performing oral sex on Toulouse-Lautrec. He then became the lover of model-turned-artist Suzanne Valadon, mother of Maurice Utrillo. She was wildly promiscuous. In a letter to him in 1890, she invited him to 'come and sleep over when you want only not before half past midnight' and signed off the letter: 'I give you a kiss on your (little bedroom slipper etc).' They stayed together for over ten years.

Another beauty who gave herself to him was Jane Avril, a dancer at the Moulin Rouge. She worked under the name *La Mélinite* – 'The Explosive'. She was famed for her 'Botticelli-like' beauty and, though she feigned prudery, her *décolleté* reached nearly to the waist. She was also reputedly a lesbian.

THE DEAD RAT

Toulouse-Lautrec would sometimes try to use his pencil as a tool of seduction. In Le Rat Mort – the restaurant where he ate – when he spotted a pretty woman, he would not hesitate to go over to her and

> 'HE WOULD PURR WITH DELIGHT AS HE PLUNGED HIS FACE INTO A WOMAN'S BOSOM, WRAPPING HER TWO ENORMOUS BREASTS AROUND HIM LIKE A COMFORTER MADE OF HUMAN FLESH.'
> Thadée Natanson

sketch her as a way of introducing himself. 'Le Rat Mort' means 'the dead rat'; it also means 'bored stiff' in French colloquial jargon. But many of the great artists of this period, Degas particularly, called their models rats. As well as being a hangout for artists, Le Rat Mort appears in works by Degas, Manet and Forain. It had a large gay and lesbian clientele. The poet Arthur Rimbaud cut the wrist of his homosexual lover Paul Verlaine there for a dare.

Maison close

Under Napoleon, brothels in France were legalized and regulated. They had to be registered and the prostitutes had to submit themselves to regular health checks. During the First Empire, *maisons de tolérance* or *maisons closes* sprang up all over Paris. There were also *maisons d'abattage*, which were cheaper and less salubrious. Brothels had to be run by a woman, usually an ex-prostitute. Among the most exquisite houses to flourish throughout the 19th century were Le Chabanais, Le One Two Two, Le Sphinx, La Fleur Blanche, L'Etoile de Kléber and Le Palais Oriental in Reims, which matched in splendour its Parisian counterparts. Hotel Marigny, a homosexual brothel near the Opera, was opened in 1917. Marcel Proust visited it regularly under an assumed name.

During the Second World War, the German occupation forces reserved the top 20 brothels for the use of German officers and French collaborators. This made the brothels extremely unpopular with the French public. In 1946, they were outlawed and approximately 1,400 registered brothels were closed down.

In 1891, Toulouse-Lautrec began the first of his famous posters for the Moulin Rouge. Following his break-up with another lover, Berthe la Sourde, he began to frequent brothels. By 1894, he had moved into a high-class bordello on the Rue des Moulins where he could not only indulge his sexual appetites, but also paint unposed nude and semi-nude women. 'The professional model is always like a stuffed owl,' he said. 'These girls are alive.'

He would eat, drink and sleep with the girls there, only venturing out to ogle the scantily clad dancers at the Folies Bergère. The madams would make sure he was well fed and served him their finest wines. He also entertained there. 'What do you expect?' he said, when someone was shocked by an invitation to meet him in a *maison close*. 'I just feel more at home there than anywhere else.'

At least five brothels rented him a room where he stayed as if it was a hotel. And in 1899, when he travelled to Bordeaux, he wrote ahead to a brothel there, reserving a room.

Toulouse-Lautrec loved nude female flesh so much that he could not sketch it without being overwhelmed with the desire to caress it, and press himself against it. 'The body of a beautiful woman is not made for love,' he once said. 'It is too exquisite.'

He would spend hours caressing a woman's hand, pressing it against his cheeks, ears and nose, smelling its dampness without ever quite letting his lips touch it. For more than 20 nights he reserved the same seat in the orchestra stalls of a Paris theatre so that he could watch Marcelle Lender dance the bolero. 'I simply come to see Lender's back,' he said. 'Take a good look at it. You've never seen anything so magnificent.'

When a woman took off her stockings, Toulouse-Lautrec would grab them, roll them into a ball and inhale the scent with his eyes closed. He would smell women's hair and the pits of their elbows and knees, but most of all he loved to smell their armpits, which he called 'tobacco shops'. Being short, he could plunge his head into the cleavage of any big-breasted woman he

Arthur Rimbaud

1854–1891

Arthur Rimbaud was a French Symbolist poet, adventurer and general ne'er-do-well. Born in rural France, Rimbaud was obsessed with masturbation from an early age. He developed a passionate interest in the lyric poet François Villon, condemned to death by Louis XI, probably for sodomy. In 1870, he began writing seductive letters to the Parnassians – a group of Parisian poets led by Paul Verlaine – claiming to be older than he was. Their journal *La Charge* published his poem 'Three Kisses', but they were unable to publish 'Nina's Replies', which compares heterosexual love to a stable full of warm dung, or 'Vénus anadyomène', which portrays Aphrodite as a fat old lady rising from a bathtub, 'her wide crotch hideously embellished with an anal ulcer'.

In 'The Sly Women' and 'At the Cabaret Vert', he described waitresses with huge breasts who invite him to suckle. His poems are full of ugly women and reek of misogyny. They are also peppered with naked buttocks and *renifleur* – 'sniffers' – who loitered around urinals in the hope of sex.

He alienated the poet Charles Clos by using his poems as lavatory paper and is said to have urinated or masturbated into the milk drunk by pianist and composer Ernest Cabaner, who hosted artistic soirées in his rooms on the Rue Racine. It was alleged that at poetry readings he would shout 'Shit!' at the end of every line, and stab anyone in the audience who objected.

Verlaine and Rimbaud set off on a trip around northern Europe, celebrating the sexual nature of their affair in the grossest of terms. In a letter to Rimbaud, Verlaine says: 'I am your old cunt, ever open or opened.' In the poem 'The Good Disciple' he invites the reader to 'Climb on my backside and throb'. According to Edmond Goncourt, Rimbaud frequently boasted of being the recipient of anal sex. 'Rimbaud, Verlaine's lover, that glorious one of abomination and disgust,' Goncourt wrote in his journal, 'arrived at a café and, laying his head on the marble of the table, began to describe his latest doings in a loud voice: "I am killed, I am dead. Jean fucked my arse all night long, and now I can't keep my shit in."'

They lived in the most degrading circumstances. According to Goncourt, Rimbaud did not mind 'a little shit and cheese' on the body of an unwashed partner because he loved so much to 'gamahuche' – a Victorian word that means both to fellate and to perform cunnilingus, though here it probably refers to rimming. And in his letters to Verlaine, Rimbaud begs him to 'shit on me'.

There was an S&M aspect to their relationship. One day in Le Rat Mort, Rimbaud told Verlaine to put his hand on the table, then he pulled a knife from his pocket and slashed Verlaine's wrist. An eyewitness said that Verlaine then 'went out with his sinister companion and received another two knife wounds in the thigh'. There were frequent knife fights in bars and 'if a little blood flowed, they soon ran to make it up over pints of bitter ale or brandy'.

By this time Verlaine's wife was seeking a divorce on the grounds of adultery. In a letter to an old friend, Verlaine boasted that he and Rimbaud were willing to undergo an anal examination to 'prove' that they were not lovers. 'If necessary we are ready, Rimbaud and me, to show our cunts (virgin) to the whole group,' he wrote. Given their lamentable lack of attention to personal hygiene, this would not have been pleasant.

Eventually Verlaine shot Rimbaud and was sent to jail for two years. At 20, Rimbaud gave up writing and became a slave trader in Africa. But he had not given up his other ways. He lived with an Abyssinian woman but when a young infibulate Ethiopian girl entered his house, he cut her open to use her. He also kept a boy. Like Toulouse-Lautrec, he died aged 37.

came across. He also had a fetish about finely chiselled nostrils, as he usually had to look up at a woman's face, and a penchant for redheads.

Toulouse-Lautrec's work also portrayed the brutal side of brothel life – the girls lining up, naked from the waist down, for their weekly medical inspection or lying back exhausted with their legs apart, ready to be used again. He kept an album of his lovers in the throes of orgasm. As if in revenge for the trick played upon him by nature, he would often depict lovers with horribly deformed bodies.

ANDRÉ GIDE

ATTRACTED BY DEFORMITY

1869–1951

Nobel Prize-winning author André Gide wrestled with homosexuality in his life and in his work. He made an effort to marry and even had a child by a mistress. But from an early age he knew he was a pederast. He was repelled by almost everything about homosexual practices, enjoying only mutual masturbation with young boys. Towards the end of his life, he took his perversion to more extreme limits.

André Gide was born into wealth and position. An only child – and sickly – he was overprotected by his puritanical mother. His father died when Gide was 11 and he was expelled from school for masturbation. Horrified, his mother took him to a doctor, who threatened castration as a cure.

Although Gide was considered a dunce at school, and left to his own devices while growing up in isolation in Normandy, he became a prolific writer. At the age of 13, he fell in love with his 15-year-old cousin, Madeleine Rondeaux. He called her his 'mystic lodestone' and worshipped her for the rest of his life.

He published his first book, *The Notebooks of André Walter*, at the age of 22. The following year he met Oscar Wilde in Paris. Gide kept a journal for over 60 years, but he tore out and destroyed the pages that cover the three weeks he and Wilde spent together. At the time, according to Lord Alfred Douglas, Wilde was reading *Psychopathia Sexualis* in preparation for the aborted production of *Salomé*. The book had just been translated into English. In it, author Richard von Krafft-Ebing coined the word 'homosexual', considering same-sex love a psychological rather than a criminal condition.

Gide's first recorded sexual experience occurred with a 14-year-old Arab boy named Ali, who hung around his hotel in Tunisia. The boy offered himself in the nearby sand dunes. Gide feigned reluctance but soon gave in. Horrified at what he had done, he tried to swim back to the shores of heterosexuality by going with a 16-year-old female prostitute named Meriem who, he said, looked like a child. However, when he was with her, the only way he could perform was to imagine that she was her little brother, a young lad who, he wrote, was 'black and

Magnus Hirschfeld (1868–1935)

Known as the 'Einstein of sex', Magnus Hirschfeld opened the Institute for Sex Research in Berlin in 1919, which took advantage of the liberal atmosphere of the newly founded Weimar Republic. The institute housed an immense library on sex and a museum of sex, and provided medical consultations and educational services.

In 1896, after working as a general practitioner, Hirschfeld had written a pamphlet on homosexuality called *Sappho and Socrates*. The following year he helped form the Scientific Humanitarian Committee to promote homosexual rights and repeal Paragraph 175, the section of the German penal code that criminalized homosexuality. Hirschfeld himself identified 64 possible types of intermediary sexual identities between masculine heterosexual male and feminine homosexual male, and coined the term 'transvestite'.

When the Nazis came to power, they tightened Paragraph 175 further. They attacked the institute. It is thought that stock newsreel footage of book-burning shows the destruction of the institute's library. Hirschfeld, a Jew, had already left Germany and did not return. He died in Nice in 1935.

slim as a demon'. But he had to give up the 'treatments' Meriem was providing when his mother came to nurse him through a bout of tuberculosis.

The following year in Algiers Gide met Wilde and Douglas, who were on holiday, indulging themselves with hashish and 13-year-old Arab boys who 'fluted on our reeds for us'. Wilde procured a young musician named Mohammed for Gide, who provided the highlight of Gide's sexual life. Wilde then returned to London, leaving Gide and Douglas to enjoy ever-younger Arab boys. Douglas was heartbroken when one of his lovers, Ali, went with a female prostitute. He lamented to Gide: 'Boys, yes boys, as much as he likes. But I will not stand for him going with women.' Gide fell for a 15-year-old servant boy named Athman, whom he called his 'black pearl'. He wanted to take Athman back to Paris with him, telling his mother that he could 'help around the house'. His mother forbade it, saying that her servant would leave if a 'Negro' came to live with them. Gide and Douglas then travelled to Florence where they met up with Wilde again, shortly before the storm broke and Wilde ended up in jail.

IN THE ARMS OF BOYS

Despite fresh attempts at heterosexual love, Gide failed to establish a sexual relationship with a mature woman, while encounters with young boys were consistently satisfying. He consulted a doctor about what he considered to be a hopeless perversion, explaining that he only felt sexually 'normal' in the arms of a boy. The doctor advised him to marry. 'Get married without fear,' he said, 'and you'll quickly realize that all the rest exists only in your imagination.'

So, when Gide's mother died, he married his beloved Madeleine Rondeaux. It was a *marriage blanc* – a sexless marriage. Gide, it has been said, suffered from 'angelism', the inability to make love to an idealized partner. Thanks to his mother, he believed that 'good' women had no sexual feelings, while bad women – prostitutes – were to be feared as much as 'throwers of vitriol'.

> 'AFTER MOHAMMED HAD LEFT ME, I SPENT A LONG TIME IN A STATE OF QUIVERING JUBILATION AND, ALTHOUGH I HAD ALREADY ACHIEVED PLEASURE FIVE TIMES WITH HIM, I REVIVED MY ECSTASY OVER AND OVER AGAIN.'
>
> André Gide

It has to be said that he was not much better when it came to homosexual relations. He compared having sex with another man to 'a huge vampire feeding upon a corpse'. But with pederasty things were different. He merely swapped masturbating himself when he was a boy for masturbating another boy – and being masturbated by another boy.

Madeleine did not complain about the lack of physical love in their marriage. She considered their relationship to be spiritual. She did not even mind when Gide went back to Algeria and returned with the servant boy Athman. However, she became upset in 1916, when he fell deeply in love with Marc Allégret, the 16-year-old son of Elio Allégret, who had been best man at their wedding. The two eloped to London and Gide adopted Marc. In a fit of pique, Madeleine burnt all his correspondence – 'the best part of myself' he complained later. However, Gide understood her feelings when Marc returned home one night after visiting the artist, writer and film director Jean Cocteau.

Psychopathia Sexualis

In 1886, Richard von Krafft-Ebing – professor of psychiatry at Strasbourg, Graz and Vienna – published the first edition of *Psychopathia Sexualis*, a groundbreaking study of sexual aberrations. It coined the terms sadism, masochism and homosexuality. The book was given an academic title to discourage lay readers. This ploy failed, though some of the more provocative passages in the book were written in Latin for the same reason. One of the most influential books on sex, it was the first to study female sexual pleasure and the importance of clitoral orgasm. However, Krafft-Ebing continued to see women as sexually passive and recorded no female sadists or fetishists among his case studies.

He believed that the purpose of sex was procreation and that any form of desire that did not lead to that ultimate goal was a perversion. However, he did not believe that this applied to homosexuality. After interviewing a large number of homosexuals – even though homosexual practices were against the law in Germany and the Austro-Hungarian empire at the time – he concluded that homosexuality was a sexual inversion that occurred in the foetus.

One of his case studies was that of Count Sandor, a female-to-male transsexual. He noted that her masculine appearance might support the idea of a genetic cause for transsexuality and proposed that transgenderism might be treated by surgery, rather than by psychology or psychiatry.

His work was condemned for immorality and for justifying perversion. Krafft-Ebing also incurred some enmity from the Austrian Catholic Church by associating the desire for sanctity and martyrdom with hysteria and masochism, and by denying the perversity of homosexuality. *Psychopathia Sexualis* first appeared in English in 1892. Since then, it has become overshadowed by the work of Sigmund Freud.

As if to cause Madeleine great hurt, Gide had a heterosexual affair with Elizabeth van Rysselberghe, the young daughter of his friend the Belgian neo-impressionist painter Théo van Rysselberghe. He had known Elizabeth throughout her childhood. This time his lover was anything but spiritual and she gave birth to a daughter named Catherine.

SEX SCANDAL

In 1924, Gide caused a scandal with the publication of *Corydon*, a collection of essays advocating homosexuality. It was widely condemned. However, he found a fan in the American lesbian poet Natalie Barney. She invited him to tea at her Temple of Friendship in the Rue Jacob in Paris, where they were surrounded by cavorting nudes – girls, unfortunately, from Gide's perspective. He also travelled to Berlin and met Christopher Isherwood at Dr Magnus Hirschfeld's Institute for Sex Research, the first such institute in the world. Gide had gone there to view one particular curio – a boy who had a perfect pair of female breasts.

After a long estrangement, Gide was reconciled with his long-suffering wife during her final illness. In 1938, Madeleine died. He used his sexless marriage as background material in his novel *Et Nunc Manet in Te*. Eventually, Elizabeth van Rysselberghe left her husband and moved to Paris to be near Gide and look after him.

In his autobiography, *Unless the Seed Dies*, Gide recalled that, as a child, he was sexually aroused 'by a profusion of colours or unusually shrill sweet sounds'. He was also aroused when he broke his favourite toys or heard stories about crockery being smashed to pieces. Later in life, he was attracted to deformed, crippled or in other ways hideous children – recognizing in them, perhaps, a reflection of himself.

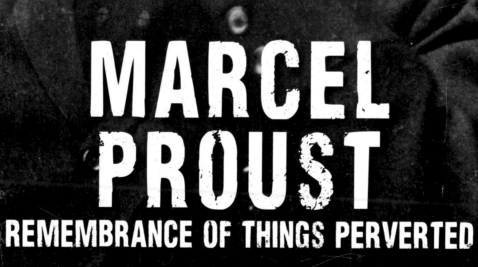

MARCEL PROUST

REMEMBRANCE OF THINGS PERVERTED

1871-1922

In his seven-volume novel *À la recherche du temps perdu*, Marcel Proust chronicled the social life of *la belle époque* – life in metropolitan France before the old order was swept away by the First World War. It is semi-autobiographical and many of the female characters in it were, in fact, male in real life. Proust made little attempt to hide his homosexuality during his lifetime, even owning a homosexual brothel. But his interest in rats was one perverted secret that he wanted only a few trusted intimates to share.

As a child, Marcel Proust found girls as attractive as boys. One day while playing in the garden, he saw Marie de Benardaky, an 'elegant, tall and beautiful' blonde. He fell in love with her and spent every free minute pursuing her. However, his parents discouraged the match.

In fictional accounts of Marcel's youthful romps, Marie becomes Gilberte and they tickle and fight. 'I held her gripped between my legs like a young tree which I was trying to climb,' he wrote. 'In the middle of my gymnastics, when I was already out of breath with the muscular exercise and the heat of the game, I felt, like a few drops of sweat wrung from me by the effort, my pleasure express itself in a form which I could not even pause for a moment to analyze. Whereupon Gilberte said good-naturedly: "You know, if you like, we might go on wrestling a little bit longer."'

INVITATION TO THE BROTHEL

Despite these heterosexual feelings, he refused older classmates' invitations to accompany them to the brothel. He had a lifelong distaste for prostitutes, at least female ones, but he went along with the most handsome boy in the class in an attempt to seduce a girl working in a cheese shop. She threw Proust out on his ear, along with the flowers he had brought her. Meanwhile, he was writing love letters to younger boys and, to the horror of his parents, masturbating incessantly. His father was so worried that he gave Marcel ten francs to visit a brothel. It was a disaster. He lost the money, but not his virginity.

He complained to his grandfather that he had broken a chamber pot and was too agitated to perform. But already, he confided to his friend, he was involved in mutual-masturbation sessions with pederasts. Then, 'in a moment of madness', he consented to anal sex. Proust even told his father about this. His father was not very angry, though he considered Marcel's 'error a surprise'. But maybe it was not such an error. By the autumn of 1888, he had written a sonnet entitled 'Pederasty', celebrating the joy of the love of young boys. Like other burgeoning homosexuals, he justified himself with reference to Socrates and classical Greece, and claimed that 'sensual and intellectual friendships are better for a young man with a keen sense of beauty ... than affairs with stupid, corrupt women'.

> 'THE NEIGHBOURS IN THE ADJOINING ROOM MAKE LOVE ... EVERY DAY WITH A FRENZY THAT MAKES ME JEALOUS.'
> Marcel Proust

To everyone's surprise, Proust's youthful beauty came to the attention of the famous courtesan Laure Hayman. He doted on her, thereby confusing his school friends. While away on

Zoophilia

Having sex with animals is illegal –
and there was a time when the beast
concerned was prosecuted too. In
1750, a man named Jacques Ferron
was hanged for having intercourse
with a she-ass in France. According
to an account of the trial: 'Several
respectable citizens (including
the abbot of the local monastery)
appeared as witnesses and declared
that they had known the donkey for
many years and that it had always
behaved itself virtuously and as a
good donkey should. The court then
acquitted the donkey, declaring that
it obviously must have been raped.'

military service, he kept falling in love with the wives and girlfriends of the other men. He found he could love a woman from a safe distance and spend hours mooning over photographs of sweethearts that comrades had brought with them, but he could not deal with women on an intimate basis.

When his mother urged him to marry, he said that he felt love only for young girls. But young girls did not stay young once they were married. 'One can have a young girl only once,' he said. 'I do so understand Bluebeard: he was a man with a weakness for young girls.' From time to time he made some genuine effort to marry. The writer Anatole France offered his 18-year-old daughter. Proust was tempted, but he hesitated and found himself relieved when she married someone else.

Thanks to Laure Hayman's salon, he had an entrée into literary and artistic circles where he moved at ease. The salon was also full of homosexual men. He learnt 'moschant', the secret language of French homosexuals. Soon he was deeply involved in the gay scene. But he also showed an interest in the beautiful young actress Louisa de Mornand. He gave her a copy of his French translation of John Ruskin's Gothic guidebook the *Bible of Amiens*, with a dedication on the cover which read: 'He who Louisa cannot win / Must be content with Onan's sin.' Proust had already proved himself adept at this.

THE 'GERMAN VICE'

Even when Louisa invited him to her apartment, the relationship remained chaste. He merely watched her read in bed before she fell asleep. By then he was partial to the 'German vice', as homosexuality became known after a sex scandal at the highest levels of Kaiser Wilhelm's court. But he continued to feign interest in women for the sake of his mother.

Proust hired a handsome amanuensis with no qualifications for the position and a young chauffeur. Meanwhile, he wrote openly about homosexuality and was surprised when he could not find a publisher. There were still concerns about the homosexual undertones in *À la recherche du temps perdu* – translated into English as *Remembrance of Things Past* or, more recently, *In Search of Lost Time*. But Proust was adamant. If he could write about pederasty without ever mentioning it, 'I should then have all the pederasts on my side, because I should be offering them what they like to hear. Precisely because I dissect their vice (I use the word vice without any suggestion of blame), I demonstrate their sickness, I say precisely what they most abhor, namely that this dream of masculine beauty is the result of a neurotic defect.'

Research for *À la recherche du temps perdu* took Proust to Turkish baths and male brothels run by Albert Le Cuziat but funded by Proust himself. A male prostitute at the house on the Rue de l'Arcade gave a unique insight into Proust's sexual needs. The house had a window into a room where the male prostitutes played cards. Clients looked through it and made their selection.

Bodil Joensen

1944–1985

Danish actress Bodil Joensen was an animal lover who ran a small farm, but her notoriety came from the numerous pornographic films she appeared in where she had sex with animals. Brought up by a strict Christian mother who beat her, she was sexually assaulted when she was 12. Her mother blamed her for this and whipped her. Turning to animals for affection, her dog, Lassie, became her best friend, companion and lover. She wore a picture of him in a locket around her neck all her life.

Excited by the sight of animals mating, Bodil set up a breeding farm, which she called 'Insemination Central'. Rumours spread that she had a unique method of handling aggressive animals such as boars. These rumours were spread by farmers' wives who did not want their husbands working with an attractive, single farm girl.

Bodil began her career in pornography at the age of 17. By 25, she had established herself in the subgenre of bestiality, making more than 40 movies between 1969 and 1970. She came to international fame with the film *Boar Girl*, in which she has sex with male pigs. In the 1971 pseudo-documentary *Animal Lovers*, she informs the interviewer that she has had sex with boars, dogs and horses. She said she had only had sex once with a human male and was not impressed. A scene follows with Bodil and Lassie on a bed. Lassie is encouraged to perform oral sex on her before she masturbates him, sucks him and inserts his penis into her vagina. Then she has sex with a boar.

The pinnacle of her career was *Animal Farm*, made in the late 1970s. In it she is shown performing acts of intercourse and fellatio with pigs, horses and chickens. There is also a scene in which a woman inserts live eels into her vagina.

By 1980, Bodil had become hooked on tranquillizers, drank heavily and had put on weight, bringing her career in pornography to an end. She became incapable of taking care of her farm and was jailed for 30 days for neglecting the animals, which had to be put down. Bodil went on the streets as a prostitute. In her final interview, she said: 'In my position it is hard to turn down anything, no matter how disgusting ... for me, staying alive in the hooking business is hell.'

Bodil died in 1985 of cirrhosis of the liver.

CAGED RATS

'He picked his partner and went upstairs,' said a young man frequently selected by Proust. 'A quarter of an hour later, I knocked on the door, went in and found Marcel already in bed with the sheet pulled up to his chin. He smiled at me. My instructions were to strip off all my clothes and remain standing by the door while I satisfied myself under the anxious gaze of Marcel, who was doing the same. If he reached the desired conclusion, I smiled at him and left without seeing any more than his face or touching him. If he didn't reach the desired conclusion, he would gesture for me to go and Albert would bring two cages.'

Each cage contained a famished rat. Albert would set the cages together and open the doors. The two starving animals would then attack each other, making piercing screams as they tore each other to bits. This brought Proust to orgasm.

Proust confessed all to Gide. 'During a memorable night of conversation (of which there were so few that I remember each of them well) Proust explained his preoccupation with combining the most diverse sensations and emotions in order to achieve orgasm,' Gide wrote. 'That was the justification for his interest in rats, among other things ... In any case Proust wanted me to see it as such. Above all I saw it as an admission of some type of psychological inadequacy.'

GRIGORY
RASPUTIN
THE MAD MONK
c.1872–c.1916

Grigory Yefimovich Novykh was one of Russia's greatest lovers. Not only was he happy to make love to any woman who came along, but he also popularized self-flagellation among women in tsarist Russia, teaching his followers that they must sin first before they could be redeemed. And he was happy to flash his 13-inch penis at anyone who wanted to see it. His byname – Rasputin – means 'the debauched one'.

Rasputin was born some time between 1863 and 1873 in the village of Pokrovskoye in Siberia. The children of the village would bathe naked in the local pond, and the young girls quickly picked him out for special attention because of his inordinately large penis. A further initiation into the world of sex came at the hands of Irina Danilov Kubasova, the pretty wife of a Russian general. She lured him into her bedroom where she and six of her maids were on hand to seduce him.

According to his daughter, Rasputin had some sort of religious revelation after cavorting with three Siberian girls he chanced upon swimming in a lake. He then joined a sect of flagellants named the Khlysty. Rasputin preached that one was nearest to God when feeling 'holy passionlessness' induced through the sexual exhaustion that came after prolonged periods of debauchery. One of the sect's practices was known as 'rejoicing', a ritual that sought to overcome human sexual urges by engaging in group sexual activities so that, through consciously sinning together, the sin's power over the human could be nullified.

At 20, Rasputin married Praskovia Feodorovna, who gave him four children. However, he was soon expelled from his village by a respectable priest and took to the road with his wife and Dunia Bekyeshova, one of Irina Danilov Kubasova's maids, who became his lifelong mistress. Together they wandered around Russia, with Rasputin initiating hordes of other women into the rites of the Khlysty in unrestrained orgies 'in any convenient place, the woods, a barn, or the cottage of one of his converts'. Praskovia was not fazed by his countless mistresses. 'He has enough to go around,' she said.

REDEMPTION THROUGH SEXUAL RELEASE

Rasputin's doctrine of redemption through sexual release attracted numerous respectable guilt-ridden women, many of whom found they could enjoy sex for the first time. His unkempt appearance and peasant manners added to his attraction as a 'holy satyr'. For his female followers, as his biographer Robert Massie pointed out, 'making love to the unwashed peasant with his dirty beard and filthy hands was a new and thrilling sensation.' Many of his lovers dowsed themselves in perfume beforehand, since his own body odour was so powerful.

By the time he reached St Petersburg, Rasputin had a powerful reputation as a mystic, a healer and a clairvoyant. In 1905, he was introduced at court. Tsar Nicholas's son Alexis was a

'RASPUTIN'S ASSASSIN AND ALLEGED HOMOSEXUAL LOVER, FELIX YUSOPOV, CLAIMED THAT HIS PROWESS WAS EXPLAINED BY A LARGE WART STRATEGICALLY SITUATED ON HIS PENIS, WHICH WAS OF EXCEPTIONAL SIZE.'
Orlando Figes

haemophiliac and Rasputin was called on to tend him. He was able to successfully ease the child's condition, perhaps through hypnosis. The boy was sometimes close to death. 'God has seen your tears and heard your prayers,' Rasputin told the tsarina. 'Fear not, the child will not die.'

He gave practical advice, halting the use of leeches, whose saliva contained an anticoagulant. He stopped the administration of aspirin, then thought to be a wonder drug but which prevents blood clotting. He kept the boy away from doctors and recommended rest. By relaxing the child, he allowed the natural healing processes to work.

While Rasputin remained a paragon of chastity and humility in court, outside he continued in his scandalous ways. Women gathered in his apartment eager for an invitation to visit his bedroom or the 'holy of holies' as he called it. Usually he would be found in the dining room surrounded by female disciples who took turns to sit on his lap while he instructed them on the mysteries of the resurrection. On one occasion, he gave a graphic description of the sex life of horses, then grabbed one of his distinguished guests by the hair and pulled her towards his bedroom, saying: 'Come, my lovely mare.'

A GLIMPSE OF PARADISE

On other occasions, Rasputin would sing and his followers would dance wildly before collapsing in a rapturous swoon or being taken into the holy of holies for a personal glimpse of paradise. Eventually attendance at his gatherings became so fashionable that husbands would boast that they had been cuckolded by Rasputin.

In 1911, the prime minister drew up a long bill of Rasputin's offences and the tsar expelled him from court. However, he was soon recalled by the tsarina, who feared for her son's life. When tsar Nicholas was called to the front during the First World War to take personal command of his troops, the tsarina was left in charge and Rasputin began to meddle in government affairs. They were so close that there were rumours that they were lovers. Meanwhile she became increasingly unpopular because she was German by birth.

An attempt had been made on Rasputin's life on 29 June 1914 when Khionia Guseva, a former prostitute who had been one of his followers, stabbed him in the belly when he was visiting his wife and children in Pokrovskoye. 'I have killed the antichrist,' she cried. Although she ruptured the stomach wall and part of his intestine protruded, after surgery Rasputin recovered, though he continued to take opium for pain relief.

On 30 December 1916, a gang of conservative noblemen fed him poisoned cake and wine. When he fell into a coma, Prince Felix Yussupov, a homosexual

Religious Masochism

Extreme masochism was common among religious fanatics in the Middle Ages who scourged themselves to mortify the flesh. Although, at the time, these puritanical zealots were thought to be demonstrating their devotion to Christ, it appears to modern eyes that they were actually 'getting off' on sado-masochism. In his book *The Pursuit of the Millennium*, published in 1962, the author Norman Cohn mentions a 14th-century monk who 'shut himself up in his cell and stripped himself naked ... took his scourge with the sharp spikes, and beat himself ... till blood poured off him ... One of the spikes on the scourge was bent like a hook and whatever flesh it caught it tore off ... He stood there bleeding and gazed at himself. It was such a wretched sight that he was reminded of the appearance of the beloved Christ.'

Catherine the Great

1729–1796

Catherine the Great was one of the world's greatest nymphomaniacs From an early age the German-born Catherine was a very sensual woman. She would lie in bed at night and masturbate with her pillow between her legs. At 16 she was married to her 17-year-old cousin Peter, the German-born grandson of Peter the Great and heir to the throne of Russia. However, the marriage bed did not hold all the delights Catherine longed for. Peter was an alcoholic, impotent and feeble-minded. For him, bed was where you played with your toys.

For six years, Catherine contented herself with horse riding and voracious reading. But the empress Elizabeth, Peter's aunt and Russia's reigning monarch, wanted her to have children in order to continue the Romanov line. On an out-of-the-way island in the Baltic, Elizabeth arranged for Catherine, still a virgin, to be left alone with Sergei Saltykov, a Russian nobleman and accomplished womanizer.

After one night with Saltykov, Catherine could not get enough sex. Two miscarriages occurred in rapid succession. Then she went to term with Paul, who was whisked away by Elizabeth and presented to the Russian people as heir to the throne.

Soon after, Catherine's husband Peter underwent an operation to correct a malformation of his penis and make him potent. He began taking a string of mistresses. However, he does not seem to have had sex with his wife, who by this time had had a second child by a young Polish nobleman named Count Stanislas Poniatowski. 'I do not know how it is my wife becomes pregnant,' Peter said. When he found out, Poniatowski returned to Poland in disgrace.

Catherine replaced him with a dashing officer in the Horse Guards, Count Grigori Orlov, who soon impregnated her. She managed to conceal her swelling belly under the hooped dresses that were then in fashion. When she felt the child coming, one of her servants helpfully set his own house on fire in order to distract Peter.

Catherine's infidelity maddened Peter and, when he came to the throne in 1761, he was determined to divorce her. But Peter was deeply unpopular. Dressed in a lieutenant's uniform, Catherine rode to St Petersburg where Orlov was stationed. With the army behind her, she proclaimed herself empress. Peter was arrested. He abdicated, but was murdered eight days later.

Once on the throne, Catherine refused to marry Orlov. He got his own back by seducing every attractive woman who came to court. When he seduced Catherine's 13-year-old cousin, Catherine kicked him out. She replaced Orlov with a cavalry officer, Prince Grigori Potemkin, who refused to attend court until Catherine had sent away all her other favourites. The 35-year-old Potemkin loved to frolic in the royal sauna with the 43-year-old Catherine. However, he put on weight, which repelled the empress. She continued to refer to him as 'husband', but he only retained his position at court by hand-picking handsome young cavalry officers for her pleasure. Candidates were checked for syphilis before their virility was tested by one of Catherine's ladies-in-waiting.

Catherine continued in this way into her sixties. The myth has come down that she died when trying to have sex with a horse because no man could satisfy her. The horse, it was said, was lowered on to her by a crane that broke, crushing her to death. There is, however, no evidence to support this scandalous tale. Catherine died at the age of 67 two days after suffering a massive stroke, and no equine involvement was evident.

rebuffed several times by Rasputin, took the opportunity to abuse him sexually before shooting him four times. A second assassin pulled out a knife and castrated Rasputin, throwing his severed penis across the room. Rasputin was then tied up and thrown in the icy Neva river, where he drowned finally. His severed penis was recovered later by a servant, who gave it to a maid. During the Revolution she fled to Paris, where she kept the member in a polished wooden box. Last seen in 1968, it was said to look like 'a blackened, overripe banana, about a foot long', thus comparing well with Napoleon's severed organ.

MATA HARI
THE COURTESAN SPY
1876–1917

Executed in France as a German spy in 1917, Mata Hari found fame as an exotic dancer, often appearing nude – particularly at parties held for her lesbian circle by the American poet Natalie Barney. What led to her downfall was her fetish for uniforms. Among her lovers were high-ranking officers on both sides during the First World War, but she would also sleep with ordinary soldiers for free.

Mata Hari was born Gertrude Margareta Zelle in the Netherlands in 1876. When she left her convent school at the age of 18, she answered a newspaper ad placed by an officer of Scottish descent who was serving in the Dutch colonial army. Thirty-nine-year-old Captain Campbell MacLeod was advertising for a wife. They married, and for two years they lived in Holland, where she gave birth to a son.

In 1897, her husband was posted to the Dutch East Indies. Over the next five years they lived in Java and Sumatra. She gave birth to a daughter, but her son died, possibly of complications relating to the treatment of syphilis contracted from his parents. However, another story is told – that the boy was poisoned by a native soldier incensed by the fact that his girlfriend, the boy's nanny, had been seduced by MacLeod.

MacLeod openly kept a native wife and a concubine. He was a violent alcoholic who beat Gertrude when she flirted with other officers. In 1902, they returned to Europe and separated. She moved to Paris. 'I thought that all women who left their husbands went to Paris,' she said.

Gertrude earned a living as an artists' model and performed as a circus bareback rider under the name Lady MacLeod. Fellow model Suzanne Valadon appeared in nude horse-riding spectaculars in front of an invited audience. It is not known whether Gertrude took part in these, but she was certainly seen naked on horseback at one of Natalie Barney's garden parties.

In 1905, she found fame as an exotic dancer. She took the stage name 'Mata Hari', a Malay expression for the sun – literally 'eye of the day'. In the Dutch East Indies, she had studied Javanese dancing and put out the story that she was the daughter of a 14-year-old temple dancer who had died giving birth to her. She had then been raised by priests, who taught her dances sacred to the Hindu god Shiva, and first danced naked for them in front of a Hindu altar at the age of 13.

Salome

The dance of the seven veils does not appear in the Bible. Indeed the name Salome does not even appear in the New Testament. The Gospels according to Matthew and Mark say that the daughter of Herodias danced for King Herod, before asking for the head of John the Baptist. However, Flavius Josephus's *Jewish Antiquities* named her and detailed her family relations. The Bible certainly does not mention her taking her clothes off.

The dance of the seven veils is an invention by Oscar Wilde in his play *Salomé*, which could not be staged in Britain at the time it was written because the portrayal of biblical characters was banned. The play premiered in Paris in 1896. In 1905, Richard Strauss used the play as the basis for his one-act opera *Salomé*, and kept the dance of the seven veils in.

Making her debut at the Musée Guimet on 13 March 1905, she was an instant success, largely because she stripped off her clothes and flaunted her body. Her provocative movements garnered wild acclaim and her act also chimed with the orientalism that was fashionable at the time. The critics raved. One of them, Edouard Lepage, said: 'Her flexible body at times becomes one with the undulating flames, to stiffen suddenly in the middle of contortions ... with a brutal gesture, Mata Hari rips off her jewels ... throws away the ornaments that cover her breasts. And, naked, her body seems to lengthen way up into the shadows! ... She beats the air with her shattered arms, whips imperturbable night with her long heavy hair.'

> **'I NEVER COULD DANCE WELL. PEOPLE CAME TO SEE ME BECAUSE I WAS THE FIRST WHO DARED TO SHOW MYSELF NAKED TO THE PUBLIC.'**
> Mata Hari

SMALL BREASTS

Mata Hari usually appears in photographs wearing a bejewelled bra. She was self-conscious about her small breasts, and sometimes was obliged to wear a small piece of cloth to cover her crotch. These were certainly abandoned when she gave private performances before Natalie Barney and her exclusively female gatherings.

The writer and actress Colette, who also performed nude at Natalie Barney's parties, said that she was 'a dancer who did not dance much'. Describing Mata Hari's performance before a mixed audience, she said: 'The only pleasant certainties on which her drawing-room audience could count were a slender waist below breasts that she prudently kept hidden, a fine, supple moving back, muscular loins, long thighs and slim knees. It should be said that the finale of her dance, the moment when Mata Hari, freed of her last girdle, fell forward modestly upon her belly, carried the male – and a good proportion of the female – spectators to the extreme limit of decent attention.'

However, Colette preferred the nude Mata Hari to the clothed one. With her clothes on, Colette said, she could be rather pretentious. By 1910, numerous imitators had sprung up and the intellectual elite began to question the authenticity of her performance, seeing it as cheap exhibitionism rather than a genuine expression of Eastern culture. Nevertheless she continued to be booked to perform at important social events across Europe.

To supplement her income from performances, Mata Hari became a courtesan, taking numerous wealthy men as her lovers. These included a colonel in the Dutch Hussars, the French minister of foreign affairs, a French general, a Russian captain, a German crown prince and an officer in the German Hussars, who set her up in an apartment. She hired herself out at $7,500 a night, though she also extended her favours for free. When she was 40 she took on two boys, one aged 17, the other 18. Broadly speaking, she was susceptible to the attractions of a uniform.

EMPLOYED AS A SPY

During the First World War, Holland remained neutral. This meant that Mata Hari could travel freely across borders. The French employed her as a spy. However, she was arrested on 13 February 1917 in Paris and accused of spying for the Germans. In July she was given a two-day trial in front of a military court, convicted and sentenced to death by firing squad. On the morning of 15 October 1917, she was awoken by a nun, who reprimanded her for showing too much leg while putting on

Colette

1873–1954

Mata Hari's one-time rival Colette was a sexual omnivore. At the age of 20, she seduced and married 35-year-old Henry Gauthier-Villars, a friend of the family. Known simply as 'Willy', he produced pornographic postcards and maintained a stable of ghostwriters. Willy encouraged Colette to write about the amorous adventures of a young girl. Published under her husband's name, the Claudine novels were hugely successful. Colette also posed for his postcards.

Willy was constantly unfaithful with would-be Claudines, who often put on lesbian shows for him. On one occasion Colette caught him fornicating with Charlotte Kinceler, a foul-mouthed, hunchbacked dwarf. He also encouraged Colette, who described herself as 'sexually impartial', to have sexual liaisons with his mistresses. She also took male lovers of her own, going on to seduce their other mistresses. She had an affair with wealthy American lesbian poet Natalie Barney. 'My husband kisses your hand,' Colette told Barney. 'I kiss all the rest.' When Colette came back home, Willy got her to act out what she had done with Natalie with one of his mistresses.

Colette then took up with a lesbian transvestite, Sophie-Mathilde-Adèle-Denise de Morny, Marquise de Belboeuf – also known as Missy, Mitzi or Uncle Max. Missy had taken to wearing men's clothes early in life to discourage her husband's advances. She was also wealthy, so Colette left Willy and moved in with her. However, Missy was as unfaithful as Willy, maintaining a string of actresses, models, shop girls and young female factory workers.

Colette began performing naked before lesbian gatherings. Then she went on the professional stage, usually picking parts where at least partial nudity was required. With Missy, she starred in a nude lesbian romp that sparked a riot. Meanwhile, Colette was entertaining herself with a succession of young gigolos.

At the age of 40 Colette had a baby daughter and married the father, journalist Henry Bertrand Léon Robert, Baron de Jouvenel des Ursins. During their marriage she achieved her greatest fame, publishing *Chéri* in 1920 and *The Ripening Seed* in 1923. However, she was tormented by jealousy over her husband's affairs. De Jouvenel also complained of his wife's obsession with 'love, adultery and half-incestuous relationships' – Colette took the virginity of de Jouvenel's teenage son and carried on a five-year affair with him.

After divorcing de Jouvenel, Colette married again at the age of 52. Her new husband was 35-year-old Maurice Goudeket, who had expressed his ambition to marry her when he had first read her books as a youth. They went to live in Saint-Tropez. Colette continued her lesbian liaisons and, in 1944, she achieved literary success again with *Gigi*.

her stockings in front of the prison doctor. She was then taken by car from Saint-Lazare prison across Paris to the barracks of the old fort at Vincennes. Twelve Zouaves had already been drawn up as a firing squad.

Mata Hari refused a blindfold. One story has it that she threw open her coat to show her naked body in an attempt to put the firing squad off, declaring: 'A harlot, yes, but traitor, never.' However, a British journalist covering the execution said that she was wearing a silk kimono under her cloak. She was not bound and stood calmly in front of the firing squad until the officer dropped his sword. The sound of the volley rang out. Mata Hari slowly fell to her knees with her head still held high, staring at those who had killed her. Then she fell backwards. A non-commissioned officer drew his revolver. He bent over, placed the muzzle of the revolver against her left temple and pulled the trigger. She was just 41.

Mata Hari's body was not claimed by her family and was sent to a medical school for dissection. Later her mummified remains were given a home in the Museum of Anatomy in Paris. They have since been lost.

PERCY GRAINGER

NO ONE IS STRANGER THAN GRAINGER

1882–1961

Australian composer Percy Grainger was a very strange man. This was hardly surprising, given his family background. When his pregnant mother discovered that his father had had a baby with another woman, she banned him from her bedroom, giving birth to Percy while contemplating a Greek statue in the hope that it would imbue the child with its beauty. She would not touch her child, fearful of infecting him with syphilis, but beat him mercilessly if he missed a piano lesson.

Throughout his life, Percy Grainger was deeply into S&M. Adopting his mother's veneration for all things blond, blue-eyed and Nordic, he became a proto-Nazi, though when he had a chance to put his lust for pain to some good use during the First World War he ran away to America.

During his childhood he was deeply influenced by the Greek statues around the family home, but further anatomical study was curtailed when his mother caught him making copies of his father's collection of nude paintings and put a stop to it.

At the age of 13 Grainger was enrolled at the Conservatorium of Dr Hoch in Frankfurt. It was there that he met Mimi Kwast, the daughter of his piano teacher. She was in love with the composer Hans Pfitzner, the cuckolder of Mahler, and eventually ran off to marry him. It was then that he discovered his peculiar sexual desires. 'By sixteen or seventeen, I was sex crazed,' he wrote.

Stories of people being whipped excited him in particular and he had already begun auto-erotic experiments in sadomasochism. He was also an exhibitionist and would present himself totally naked, spread-eagled on the lid of a grand piano, at an open window, no matter how cold the weather. In winter, he would strip off out of doors and pose naked as a statue, or sketch himself nude. He was happy to pose nude for photographs and encouraged his girlfriends to do likewise.

OUTRAGED

At his mother's request, Grainger wore his peroxide blond hair long. Many people mistook him for a homosexual. He was outraged – homosexuality was far too run of the mill. Grainger raved about good-looking young men and he was particularly enthusiastic about Nordic blondes. But his own mother was the most perfect example of Nordic womanhood. They were often mistaken for brother and sister, and they slept together, making their relationship doubly incestuous. Grainger described his relationship with his mother as 'the only truly passionate love affair of my life'.

Grainger wanted children of his own, but for his own purposes. He wrote to a girlfriend: 'You know that I long to flog children. It must be wonderful to hurt this soft unspoilt skin ... and when my girls begin to awaken sexually I would gradually like to have carnal knowledge with them ... I would love to explain things to them and open to their eyes in this area the whole way of the world without shame or shyness or cowardice ... Why should a man not be sensual with his own children?'

> 'I HAVE ALWAYS DREAMED ABOUT HAVING CHILDREN AND WHIPPING THEM, AND TO HAVE A SENSUAL LIFE WITH MY OWN DAUGHTERS.'
> Percy Grainger

Pygmalionism

As a youth, Percy Grainger suffered from pygmalionism. The condition is named after Pygmalion, the mythological Greek sculptor who fell in love with Galatea, one of his female statues. At his request the goddess of love, Aphrodite, brought the statue to life. Pygmalionism refers to people who have a fetish about statues and mannequins.

Several cases have been documented. In ancient times, Clisyphus had sex with a statue of a goddess in the Temple of Samos by placing a piece of meat in the crotch. In *Psychopathia Sexualis* Krafft-Ebing reported that, in 1877, 'a gardener fell in love with a statue of the Venus de Milo and was discovered attempting coitus'.

Roman wedding ceremonies began in the Temple of Priapus where the bride sat on the erect phallus of a statue of the god. St Augustine of Hippo said that this robbed the woman of her dignity, not her virginity or her fertility. More recently Indian women have used a sacred phallus to rupture their hymens before marriage.

Fortunately, he did not get the opportunity to indulge these desires. In fact, he advised his girlfriends not to get pregnant. 'Do you know that a woman's breasts, after she has had children, always hang down and she can never get them nice and firm again,' he warned one girlfriend.

Grainger scrupulously recorded his kinky urges in his letters and photographed himself, meticulously noting the camera details, location, number of lashes and whip employed.

In 1900, Grainger visited Amsterdam where he saw every possible perversion played out before his eyes. He began to collect pornography about German whipping clubs. 'I live for my lusts and I don't care if they kill me or others,' he told a friend. 'No sadist can call life poor or disappointing who can realize his cruellest, wildest dreams. When we successfully follow and realize our lusts we are lords indeed. I would not exchange with the angels.'

In 1901, Grainger and his mother moved to London, where Grainger fell in love with Mrs Frank Lowry, a 40-year-old woman whose husband allowed her complete sexual freedom. When Grainger had his first orgasm with her, he thought he was going to die. However, he concluded that no matter how earth-shattering sex was, it was still not as good as a sound thrashing.

Grainger returned to Germany to study under composer Ferruccio Busoni, who lived in a house in Berlin filled with cripples and paupers, who acted as his willing slaves. Grainger lodged at a boarding house run by Mimi Kwast's mother, who tried to interest him in her second daughter, Evchen. Then Mrs Lowry turned up. Soon she was evicted from her hotel because the management objected to Grainger's nocturnal visits. She moved into the boarding house too, scuppering the romance with Evchen. Meanwhile Busoni's pretty wife took a fancy to Grainger, but he was more interested in their two boys, Raffaello and Benvenuto, who were 'fine featured, bright eyed, soft limbed ... as fair to see as children could be'.

On a tour of Denmark, he fell for his friend Herman Sanby's fiancée Alfhild de Luce, whom he said looked like his mother. They entered a curious *ménage à trois*. When Alfhild said Grainger's mother 'looked like the devil', he left and took up with another Nordic beauty named Karen Holten. Though the whip continued to play a part in their relations, Grainger also enjoyed sliding 'my thick strong phallus into your inner fjords'. When he went off on a concert tour, he wrote to her regularly with details of his self-flagellation. He stuck needles in his flesh and beat himself four or five times daily, boasting of giving himself up to a thousand lashes.

Gustav Mahler

1860–1911

Since Luchino Visconti's 1971 film *Death in Venice*, it has been commonly assumed that Gustav Mahler was a closet paedophile lusting after young boys. In fact Mahler was something of a womanizer. He did not die in Venice and it was regular heterosexual love that killed him.

Although outwardly a prude, as a student Mahler regularly went with prostitutes. At 19, he fell in love with a postman's daughter named Josephine Poisl who wanted nothing to do with him. Next came blue-eyed soprano Johanna Richter. Again she rejected him, perhaps because he was Jewish or perhaps because he was just plain ugly. 'In spite of his ugliness, he had a demoniacal charm,' wrote British composer and feminist Ethel Smyth. 'But intercourse with him was like handling a bomb cased in razor blades.'

In his twenties, Mahler went through several women. When he was 26, he had an affair with Marion von Weber – 'the most beautiful person in Leipzig'. She was four years older than him and married with three children. The humiliation of being a cuckold drove her husband out of his mind and she dropped Mahler out of guilt. Later, 21-year-old Alma Schindler – 'the most beautiful woman in Austria' – moved in on him. She was already having an affair with her music teacher and noted composer Alexander von Zemlinsky, and had a brief fling with the painter Gustav Klimt. Mahler was 41 when they married. She became suspicious of his relationships with other women at the opera house. In her diaries, she began to complain of Mahler being a poor lover, if not impotent. Mahler consulted Sigmund Freud, who concluded that Mahler wanted to marry his mother and was a homosexual. By this time, Alma had taken up with the architect Walter Gropius. Mahler was diagnosed with heart disease, exacerbated by his wife's infidelity, and died aged 50.

The German novelist Thomas Mann was writing *Death in Venice* when he heard of the death of Mahler, and he consciously gave his protagonist Aschenbach some of the characteristics of the composer. In the book Aschenbach was a writer, but in the film Visconti makes Aschenbach a German composer. He used Mahler's music as the soundtrack, reinforcing the idea that *Death in Venice* is about Mahler and his yearning for little boys. It is not. It is about Thomas Mann and his yearning for little boys.

He wrote from Port Said, telling her of his experiences in a brothel with four 'not unattractive' women. He was disappointed by the pictures of nude women that the Arabs tried to sell him, but he enjoyed watching a beautiful golden-brown girl do the can-can naked. He paid five shillings to watch an Arab boy have sex with a Greek girl and was impressed with how bored she looked. He also liked the Arab boys who dived naked for pennies. Reaching Australia, he went swimming with naked men. One chap particularly impressed him. 'His sexual parts were so astoundingly Grecian; graceful and round without being clumsy and floppy,' he wrote. 'It is to my mind the very rarest thing to see men or boys with prettily formed appetizing sexual parts.'

In Norway, he boasted of having sex with two sisters and begged Karen to send him a picture of herself nude, so he could compare their bodies to hers. 'Sometimes, when I call to mind how long I still must wait until your flesh and my flesh meet,' he wrote, 'and that it is quite impossible for us to be united in half-an-hour's time, a madness overflows over me ... Then I must pull, hit, cut, whip, tear and burn some pain in myself. Afterwards I feel much less unsatisfied.'

He wrote that he wanted to tie Karen up and whip her too, and then rape her. He even expressed the urge to attach fish-hooks to a woman's breasts and raise her on a pulley. He wanted to pluck her pudendum. He wanted his testicles eaten like two boiled eggs. Would she like to be licked by a dog – or by another woman?

JAMES JOYCE

DIRTY BOOKS AND SOILED SUGGESTIONS

1883-1941

When it was first published, James Joyce's most famous work, the novel *Ulysses*, was banned in both Britain and America for obscenity, though the author would never permit himself to make an obscene remark in front of a woman. However, this did not mean that he was blameless, merely that he confined his perversions to his long-suffering wife.

Educated by Jesuits, James Joyce briefly considered becoming a priest, but soon concluded that there was no way he could live up to a vow of celibacy. He had already lost his virginity at the age of 14 in Nighttown, Dublin's seedy red-light district. He was a regular user of the girls there until he met his life-long partner, the semi-educated chambermaid Nora Barnacle. However, during his visits there he contracted syphilis, which he treated himself by cauterizing the chancre. This got rid of the symptom but not the disease, and it is thought that the eye trouble that dogged his later life might have been caused by syphilis.

By the time he met Nora, Joyce had turned against religion. In 1903, he visited Paris, returning when his mother was diagnosed with cancer. Despite her pleadings, he would not go to confession or take communion. When she fell into a coma and died, he refused to kneel at the bedside.

'A PRIEST IN A NIGHTSHIRT'

Joyce famously had his first date with Nora on 16 June 1904, the day on which the events recounted in *Ulysses* are supposed to have taken place and now celebrated in Dublin as Bloomsday, after Leopold Bloom, one of the central characters of the novel. When Joyce met Nora, he knew he had found his soulmate and gave up prostitutes. But he refused to be married by 'a clerk with a pen behind his ear or a priest in a nightshirt', so they left Ireland for the Continent, travelling first to Zürich, then settling in Trieste, which was part of the Austro-Hungarian Empire until the end of the First World War.

Nora called Joyce 'simple-minded Jim' and thought he was a weakling. That is also how he saw himself, and he felt that he was in need of the firm hand of motherly discipline. 'I would be delighted to feel my flesh tingling under your hand,' he wrote. 'I wish you would smack me or flog me even. Not in play, dear, in earnest and on my naked flesh. I wish you were strong, *strong*, dear, and had a big full proud bosom and big fat thighs. I would love to be whipped by you, Nora love.'

It is not known how Nora reacted to this. She certainly disapproved of his published work. When told that *Ulysses* showed a unique insight into a woman's mind, Nora said that Joyce knew 'nothing at all about women'. However, he continued to let the scatology he used in his books intrude into his personal correspondence.

> 'LOVE BETWEEN MAN AND MAN IS IMPOSSIBLE BECAUSE THERE MUST NOT BE SEXUAL INTERCOURSE, AND FRIENDSHIP BETWEEN MAN AND WOMAN IS IMPOSSIBLE BECAUSE THERE MUST BE SEXUAL INTERCOURSE.'
> James Joyce

'The smallest things give me a great cockstand,' he wrote when they were separated in 1909, 'a whorist movement of your mouth, a little brown stain on the seat of your white drawers ... to feel your hot lecherous lips sucking away at me, to fuck between your two rosy-tipped bubbies.' When Nora did not answer this letter, he quickly backpedalled. 'Are you offended, dear, at what I said about your drawers?' he wrote. 'I know they are as spotless as your heart.'

As well as being interested in soiled linen – something that comes up in his work – Joyce was also intrigued by underwear *per se*. He even carried around a pair of doll's panties in his pocket. When he was drunk, he would slip them over his fingers and walk them across the table, to the bemusement of those who had come to talk to the great writer.

Joyce had been a heavy drinker from his early youth. He used alcohol as a form of contraception, drinking until he was incapable. He and Nora had just one child, Lucia, who persuaded them to marry in 1931. Lucia was psychoanalyzed by Carl Jung, who came up with a diagnosis of schizophrenia. After reading *Ulysses*, Jung concluded that her father was a schizophrenic too.

Toilet Training

Havelock Ellis wrote of a man in the 19th century who, as a young boy, was allowed to stay in the same room when maids were defecating in a portable toilet. As his interest in female buttocks grew, he began to eroticize the act of excretion. As an adult he was caught masturbating over a similar toilet containing the faeces of a woman to whom he was sexually attracted. His own faeces held no appeal. Neither did those of women he was not attracted to.

'SOMETHING TO WRITE ABOUT'

Nora was fiercely loyal to Joyce, even though he urged her to sleep with other men so he would 'have something to write about'. She did not take him up on the offer. However, in 1919, he stayed with a woman named Marthe Fleischmann in Zürich. He told a friend that he first saw Marthe when 'she was in a small room in the act of pulling the chain'. This turned him on and, later that night with Marthe, he explored 'the coldest and hottest parts of a woman's body'. This left Joyce with a hankering for dark Semitic women and, after he moved to Paris in 1920, he fell in love with Amalia Popper, one of his students. Her wealthy father, a Jewish businessman, put a stop to the relationship.

Joyce suffered from glaucoma, cataracts and iritis, an inflammation of the iris. He had more than a dozen operations on his eyes, leaving him nearly blind. The syphilis that he contracted in his early youth is also thought to have contributed to his death in Zürich in 1941, after he underwent surgery for a perforated duodenal ulcer.

CONCERNING MASTURBATION

By the time of his death, the ban on the publication of *Ulysses* had been lifted. Written over a seven-year period from 1914 to 1921, the novel was first serialized in the American journal *The Little Review* in 1918. However, in 1920, after a passage in the novel concerning masturbation was published, Anthony Comstock's New York Society for the Suppression of Vice saw red and took action. At a trial the following year, the magazine was declared obscene and the book banned.

Carl Jung

1875–1961

While Swiss psychoanalytic pioneer Carl Jung was happily diagnosing Joyce and his daughter Lucia as schizophrenics, he was no picture of mental health himself. An early admirer of Hitler, whom he declared was a 'spirit vessel', he changed his mind later when the Nazis made it clear that they were not really introducing 'the twilight of the gods'. Jung also called a patient who had a phobia about catching syphilis a 'filthy swine'.

Jung admitted to having a 'religious crush' on Freud after being sexually assaulted by a man he worshipped when he was a boy. Freud divined that there was a homosexual dimension to their relationship, though neither appears to have acted on it.

During his 52-year marriage, Jung seems to have confined himself to seducing his patients. This began in 1909, when he admitted that there were 'polygamous components' to his relationship with a patient who begged him to impregnate her.

In 1910, 22-year-old Toni Wolff came to him as a patient. This caused the 35-year-old Jung to 'confront his subconscious'. In other words, he wanted to have sex with her. After three years, he was plunged into a near breakdown that lasted several years. But they developed a 'creative relationship' and Toni helped him search out his anima, the female part of his psyche – though she also managed to find the male part of his anatomy. He decided that Toni was his 'femme inspiratrice', while his wife Emma was merely the mother of his five children. Love, he claimed, was a 'many faceted gem', while Emma was a 'simple cube'. For 40 years, he managed to maintain the two women in a triangle. 'The prerequisite for a good marriage,' he said, 'is the licence to be unfaithful.'

However, in strait-laced Zürich where they lived, Toni was not content to be a mistress. She wanted Jung to divorce his wife and marry her. Despite the many comforts of psychoanalytic theory, she turned to booze and cigarettes and died of a heart attack at the age of 64.

Meanwhile a disproportionately large number of Jung's patients and followers were women. They were powerfully attracted to him and gathered round him to form a sizeable coterie, known somewhat irreverently as the *Jungfrauen*. One of them was the feminist, spiritualist and theosophist Olga Fröbe-Kapteyn. She founded the Eranos group, which introduced Eastern practices to Western thought. At least once an Eranos meeting degenerated into an orgy. It is 'the nearest I ever came to wicked abandonment', said one participant.

Some of the women in the circle claimed to have been the bear-like Jung's mistresses. One claimed that he was not up to much as a lover, while another, Jolanda Jacobi, said that he was undersexed. Unfazed, Jung replied that she presumably had not been his mistress after all.

Sylvia Beach, proprietor of the famous bookshop Shakespeare and Company, published an edition of *Ulysses* in Paris on 2 February 1922, Joyce's 40th birthday. In 1933, Random House imported the French edition, only to have it seized by US customs at the dockside. However, in December 1933 – the same week Prohibition was repealed – US District Court Judge John M. Woolsey ruled that 'in *Ulysses*, in spite of its unusual frankness, I do not detect anywhere the leer of the sensualist. I hold, therefore, that it is not pornographic.' Consequently, the book could not be considered obscene or banned. This ruling was confirmed by an appeal court. Bodley Head published an edition in England in 1936.

Although H.G. Wells might have had a point when he complained of Joyce's 'cloacal obsession', *Ulysses* is generally considered one of the greatest books ever written. But then Wells was just a straightforward womanizer.

T.E. LAWRENCE

AGONIES OF LOVE

1888-1935

In his spotless white Arab robes, T.E. Lawrence – Lawrence of Arabia – was assumed by many to be a sexless innocent. However, from his first encounter with the Middle East, he began an affair with a young boy. Then, after being beaten and sodomized by a Turkish bey during the First World War, his tastes turned darker. He became a dedicated masochist who, back in Britain, would travel the length of the country for a flogging.

T.E. Lawrence achieved fame as Lawrence of Arabia for his ability to handle Arabs and endure the hardships of the desert. He was uniquely talented in both departments. He never expressed so much as a passing interest in women and admired the Arabs' easy ways with homosexuality. As for him, the hardships of the desert were not something to be endured, but enjoyed. He was a lifelong masochist. From an early age, his mother would beat him on the bare bottom for minor infractions. This held no fear for him and he took his punishment like a man.

At school he was caught in a masturbation session with another boy and nearly expelled. Instead, he got another caning from his mother, much to his relief. At Oxford, fellow student Vyvyan Richards fell for him, but Lawrence took no notice. 'He had neither flesh nor carnality of any kind,' said Richards. 'He received my affection, my total subservience as it were his due. He never gave the slightest sign that he understood my motives or fathomed my desire ... I realize now that he was sexless – at least that he was unaware of sex.' It is clear from the earlier incident at school that this was plainly untrue.

> ## 'SEVERAL, THIRSTING TO PUNISH APPETITES THEY COULD NOT WHOLLY PREVENT, TOOK A SAVAGE PRIDE IN DEGRADING THE BODY, AND OFFERED THEMSELVES FIERCELY TO ANY HABIT WHICH PROMISED PHYSICAL PAIN OR FILTH.'
> T.E. Lawrence

Lawrence read Classics and expressed an intellectual interest in Greek pederasty. Meanwhile he was mortifying the flesh with midnight dips in the frozen River Cherwell, fasting and feats of endurance – including canoeing around Oxford's sewer system.

At 20, he proposed to Janet Laurie, a friend of the family. She laughed. They had never touched, kissed or discussed their feelings, and in any case she fancied his brother. Hurt, Lawrence learnt Arabic and went on a walking tour of Syria. Outside Aleppo, he was attacked and, seemingly, sexually molested, though his own accounts of the incident are contradictory.

Returning to Syria to supervise a dig for the British Museum, he fell for a 14-year-old servant boy with big brown eyes named Selim Ahmed, who nursed him through a bout of dysentery. He dedicated *The Seven Pillars of Wisdom* 'To S.A.: I loved you ...' The dedication was followed by a homoerotic poem that had to be toned down by Robert Graves. The locals called Selim 'Dahoum' – 'the dark-skinned one'. He posed naked for Lawrence, who made a sculpture of him in sandstone that was prominently displayed on the roof of the house they shared in Carchemish. They also swapped clothes, so it was Dahoum who first got him into Arab costume.

In *The Seven Pillars of Wisdom* Lawrence makes very clear his warm acceptance of homosexual love and his disgust at its heterosexual counterpart. He writes: 'The public women of the rare settlements we encountered in our months of wandering would have been nothing to our numbers, even had their raddled meat been palatable to a man in healthy parts. In horror of such sordid commerce, our youths began indifferently to slake one another's needs in their own clean bodies – a cold convenience that, by comparison, seemed sexless and even pure.' Elsewhere he finds 'friends quivering together in the yielding sand with intimate hot limbs in supreme embrace'.

During the First World War, Lawrence joined the army and ordered men to be beaten rather than court-martialled – especially those indulging in homosexual activity – even though flogging had been outlawed in the British army 30 years before.

After his famous raid on Aqaba, Lawrence went on an undercover mission to Deraa. He was captured by the Turks and was stripped and beaten with a 'Circassian riding whip', which he lovingly described. In a letter to Charlotte Shaw, wife of playwright George Bernard Shaw, he confessed to giving away his 'bodily integrity' in order to 'earn five minutes respite from pain'. It is not clear, however, whether he gave himself to the bey and his servants or was anally raped by a number of Turkish soldiers who robbed him forever of 'the citadel of my integrity'.

Spanking

In the 16th century, poet, dramatist and spy Christopher Marlowe (1564–93) had his own take on spanking:

When Francis comes to solace with his whore,
He sends for rods and strips himself stark naked;
For his lust sleeps, and will not rise before
By whipping of the wench it be awaked.
I envy him not, but wish I had the power,
To make myself his wench but one half-hour.

CHELSEA PARTIES

After he returned to England, Lawrence told Robert Graves that he felt the urge to be whipped and liked being buggered. By 1922, he was attending flagellation parties in Chelsea, held by a German called Jack Bilbo, also known as Bluebeard. Fearing that he might spill the beans, Lawrence wrote to the Home Secretary, asking for Bilbo to be deported.

Meanwhile Lawrence employed a strapping Aberdonian youth named John Bruce to beat him. Lawrence told Bruce that he had a stern relative known as the 'Old Man' or 'Uncle R', who threatened to tell the world that Lawrence was illegitimate if he did not submit to punishment for his alleged misdeeds; 'I have my mother to consider,' he said. Lawrence would turn up with a list of his infractions and details of the punishments he must endure. On one occasion he travelled to Aberdeen from Plymouth for a flogging. That time he took the train, though he often travelled to and from his beatings on his motorbike to increase his suffering.

SEVENTY-FIVE STROKES

The chastisement began with a birch cane applied to the bare buttocks. Then a metal whip was used. Lawrence would get an erection with the first stroke and the punishment only stopped when he ejaculated – sometimes as many as 75 strokes later. 'Uncle R' also ordered

The English Vice

In the late 18th and early 19th centuries, flagellation was known as *le vice anglais*. The French put the English penchant for flagellation down to excessive drinking, while the Germans saw it as the perfectly natural expression of sexual sadism. It was quite unknown in Italy or Spain.

Brothels in London specializing in flagellation started in 1760 with Mrs Jenkins' establishment. By 1800, there were many of them. The 'queen of the rod' was Mrs Theresa Berkley of 28 Charlotte Street, Portland Place. 'Her instruments of torture were more numerous than those of any other governess,' said a devotee. 'Her supply of birch was extensive, and kept in water, so that it was always green and pliant: she had a dozen shafts with a dozen whip thongs on each of them; a dozen different sizes of cat-o'-nine tails, some with needle points worked into them; various kinds of thin bending canes; leather straps like coach traces; battledores' – bats or paddles – 'made of thick sole-leather with inch nails run through to docket, and currycomb round hides rendered callous by many years of flagellation.'

If none of that tickled your fancy, she also had 'holly brushes; furze [gorse] brushes; a prickly evergreen called butchers' bush; and during the summer, glass and china vases filled with a constant supply of green nettles, with which she often restored the dead to life.' You could also be hung up to be beaten. And if a man wanted to beat a woman, Mrs Berkley herself would oblige.

In the spring of 1828, Mrs Berkley introduced a special apparatus to which gentlemen could be strapped while being flogged, known as the 'Berkley horse'. An English roué named Chace Price, a friend of James Boswell, invented a machine that could beat up to 40 people at a time. It was seen in operation in a London brothel in 1830.

Women were not to be left out. In the 18th century, there were female flagellation clubs. One met every Thursday in Jermyn Street. *Bon Ton* magazine of December 1792 carried a detailed description of the goings-on there: 'These female members are mainly married women who, tired of marriage in its usual form and the cold indifference which is wont to accompany it, determined by a novel method to re-awaken the ecstasy which they knew at the beginning of their married life ... The honourable society or club to which we refer never has fewer than twelve members. They draw lots for the order of procedure; then either a written speech is read or an extempore one delivered on the effects of flagellation, as it has been practised from the earliest ages up to the present day, in monasteries and convents, brothels and private houses; after which the six patients take their places and the six flagellants begin the practical demonstration, first uncovering those parts which, though less visible and less within reach of mishandling, are yet more sensitive and lively than others.

'The president of the club hands to each a stout rod, and begins the chastisement herself, with any variation she likes while the others watch. Sometimes, by order of the president, the whipping starts on the calves and goes up to the posterior, until the whole region, as Shakespeare says, from milk-white "becomes one red". After the president, the other flagellants take their turn.'

him to undergo privations, hard diets, physical hardships, emotional abuse, electric shocks and, compassionately, 'Swedish massage'. On one occasion Bruce received a letter telling him to hire a cottage, three horses and a groom. Lawrence was then to spend a week there swimming and riding. The week ended with a beating so merciless that the groom, who witnessed it, was physically sick.

At the end of these sessions, Bruce had to detail the punishment inflicted in a letter to 'Uncle R', which Lawrence said he must deliver by hand. It turned out that there was no 'Uncle R'. Lawrence got further thrills from reading of his own punishment and humiliation.

To escape from his celebrity, Lawrence returned to the services – where he enjoyed serving in the lowest ranks. He also let other soldiers and airmen beat him and sodomize him.

CHARLIE CHAPLIN

LITTLE TRAMPS

1889-1935

Charlie Chaplin was the first international film star. With his bowler hat, cane and funny walk, he was loved as an innocent little tramp by millions all over the world. In his private life Chaplin was also a tramp. But he was anything but little; Hollywood showgirls said he was hung like a horse. And there was no way he was innocent, spending much of his career deflowering underage girls.

Born in Elephant and Castle, London, in 1889, Charlie Chaplin learnt most of what he knew about comedy from the British vaudevillian Fred Karno. He also learnt a lot about sex from the same source. Any girl who wanted to work for Karno first had to visit his casting couch. Then, if he took her on, he would shamelessly exercise *droit de seigneur*.

In 1908, Chaplin fell in love for the first time with a young dancer from a troupe called Bert Coutts' Yankee Doodle Girls, which featured ahead of the Karno Company on the bill at the Streatham Empire. They were soon separated when the company was booked by the Folies Bergère in Paris. There Chaplin fled from a courtesan when he discovered that she was out of his price range.

When Karno toured the USA, Chaplin found the prices more to his liking. In Butte, Montana, he found the side streets were filled with hundreds of cribs with a young girl of 16 or so installed on each. They cost just $1. Chaplin was in heaven.

In Hollywood, Chaplin, his brother Sydney and Stan Laurel were signed up by Mack Sennett for his Keystone Studios. Alongside the Keystone Kops, Sennett – a man after Karno's heart – also had his Bathing Beauties. Many of the great actresses of the era started their movie careers in swimsuits as Sennett Bathing Beauties, or rather out of them on the couch in Sennett's office.

When Chaplin started his own studio in 1915, he took on ingénue Edna Purviance, as both co-star and lover. She starred opposite him in 35 films. Returning from New York, where he had signed a new contract that made him a rich man, Chaplin made a two-day stopover at the famous All Nations whorehouse in Chicago. But when Edna then had a fling with Hollywood's latest heart-throb, Chaplin dropped her and, as graduate of the Karno and Sennett school of seduction, dusted off a casting couch of his own. Whenever he was stuck for an idea on the set, he would call for one of the young female extras to perform fellatio on him while he tried to contact the muse. Meanwhile his brother Sydney Chaplin toured the local high schools, picking up star-struck schoolgirls.

A workaholic, Charlie had no time for such frivolity. He would only take a girl for 'an hour when I am bored'. Between pictures, though, he would chase what he called 'the most beautiful form of human life – the very young girl just starting to bloom'.

In 1916, he met child actress Mildred Harris at a party. She was just 14, but she had been a movie actress from the age of ten and had appeared practically nude in the notorious Babylonian scene in D.W. Griffith's epic *Intolerance*. Chaplin was immediately infatuated.

> 'IF I HAD KNOWN OONA OR A GIRL LIKE HER LONG AGO, I WOULD NEVER HAVE HAD ANY PROBLEMS WITH WOMEN. ALL MY LIFE I HAVE BEEN WAITING FOR HER.'
>
> Charlie Chaplin

The affair was actively encouraged by Mildred's mother, who was a wardrobe mistress at the studio and aware of Chaplin's tastes.

Mildred was already pregnant by the age of 16. Fearing a scandal, Chaplin married her, only to find out that the pregnancy was a false alarm. In 1920, Mildred really did get pregnant, but gave birth to a hideously deformed child who died after three days. The marriage broke up amid charges of cruelty and infidelity. Mildred had belatedly noticed the herds of young starlets who were going through Charlie's dressing room. Chaplin was too much of a gentleman to draw attention to the fact that Mildred herself had quit the conjugal bed for that of the notorious lesbian Alla Nazimova. They divorced.

Chaplin took off with ex-Ziegfeld Follies girl Peggy Hopkins Joyce to Catalina Island, where they were seen by locals cavorting naked. He then went through a roll-call of Hollywood stars, including the German beauty Pola Negri, whom he seduced on a bed of rose petals. His name was also linked with Thelma Moran Converse, who later became Lady Furness, and Winston Churchill's cousin Clare Sheridan, later a mistress of Mussolini. But these women were far too old for a man of Chaplin's tastes.

He met Lillita McMurray when she was six years old. She was, he said, 'the sweetest little thing you ever saw'. He took her under his wing and for nine long years he groomed her for a starring role. In 1923, she was leading lady in *The Gold Rush*. The studio announced that she was 19; in fact, she was just 15.

'FRIGHT GAVE WAY TO REVULSION'

At first, little Lillita had difficulty getting to grips with the part she was required to play. In Chaplin's hotel room, 'he kissed my mouth and neck and his fingers darted all over my alarmed body', she wrote. 'His body writhed furiously against mine, and suddenly some of my fright gave way to revulsion.'

Eventually, after a naked romp around his house, Charlie took her virginity on the tiled floor of the steam bath. Lillita was both surprised and flattered. He could have had any one of a hundred girls, she said. 'No, a thousand,' he said, correcting her. 'But I wanted to be naughty with you, not them.'

Chaplin was 35 and hated using condoms. Soon Lillita was pregnant. Chaplin suggested an abortion, but she refused. Then he offered her $20,000 to marry someone else. But it was her Charlie she wanted. There was talk of a paternity suit, which would bring with it, under California law, a charge of statutory rape that carried a penalty of up to 30 years in jail.

Sydney Chaplin
(1885–1965)

Chaplin's brother Sydney bragged to Darryl Zanuck that he could lay any woman in Hollywood. So Zanuck drove Sydney to Hollywood High School and picked out a teenage girl at random. Sydney went over to her. Within minutes he was showing her into the back of Zanuck's open tourer. Next time, Sydney told Zanuck, he should try and come up with something harder.

On one occasion Zanuck and Sydney checked into the Coronada Hotel, popular among honeymooners. There Zanuck pointed out a fresh-faced bride who was checking in with her brand-new husband. 'That's impossible,' said Zanuck.

After lunch, Zanuck heard himself being paged. The front desk told him to go to Sydney's room immediately. When he opened the door, he saw Sydney with the young bride naked on her knees giving him a blow job. Only years later did Zanuck discover that the whole thing had been set up. The 'bride' was an extra named Elizabeth McNeill and her 'husband' was from Central Casting.

John Barrymore

1882–1942

It is not quite clear what Chaplin intended to learn from Barrymore by training a telescope on his window. Barrymore was a notorious carouser who lost his first wife because he was often too drunk to make love to her. Famously Barrymore was so drunk he slept through the 1906 San Francisco earthquake, emerging from the rubble of his hotel wearing an immaculate flowered dressing gown to be pressed into helping clear up the debris by soldiers.

He lost his virginity at 15 to his stepmother, who seduced him. Later he slept with 16-year-old chorus girl Evelyn Nesbit, girlfriend of New York society architect Stanford White. When her family found out about the affair, they married her off to psychotic millionaire Harry K. Thaw. Then out of jealousy, Thaw shot White dead. Barrymore went into hiding until the scandal blew over.

After working his way through various showgirls, the 27-year-old Barrymore met 17-year-old heiress Katherine Harris. They married in 1910, but she could not cope with his drinking and his turbulent lifestyle. Hearing that his friend the illustrator James Flagg, who used Katherine as a model, was also sleeping with her, he confronted the artist.

'You've been living with my wife,' said Barrymore.

'No, you've been living with her,' Flagg replied. 'I've been sleeping with her.'

They divorced in 1917.

On the rebound, Barrymore then married Blanche Thomas, a suffragette who published poetry under the name Michael Strange. When they divorced in 1928, Barrymore headed for Hollywood. There he seduced, among many others, the 17-year-old Mary Astor. The next wife was 19-year-old Dolores Costello who played opposite him in *The Sea Beast*. She tried to wean him off the booze, taking him on a trip on his yacht after first throwing all the liquor over the side. He resorted to drinking her perfume, then grew paranoid. Jumping ship in San Francisco, he took a train across country, then a ship to London, where he signed a contract with producer Alexander Korda to make a film of *Hamlet*, his great stage role. On the first day of filming, he could not remember a single word, so he headed to India for spiritual healing and enlightenment.

Arriving in Calcutta, the first person he met on the dockside was a pimp who took him to a brothel, which looked more like a temple with marble pillars and hanging silks. He gave the madam $1,200 to close the doors for a month, so that he could continue his search for enlightenment undisturbed.

'I remained on the pillows for four busy weeks,' he said. 'I met only dancing girls and singing girls, all of them devout students of the *Kama Sutra*, which teaches that there are thirty-nine different positions for the worship of Dingledangle – the God of Love ... and I returned to America, fully restored.'

Chaplin quickly agreed that marriage to his beloved Lillita was the better option. On the way to Mexico to marry, he suggested she throw herself under the train.

They divorced after two years, during which time they had two children. Lillita secured a $1-million settlement, doubling her money by publishing her Bill of Divorcement detailing his shortcomings at 25 cents a copy. She said that during their 25-month marriage, Chaplin had maintained at least five long-term mistresses. He had often suggested that they liven up the marriage bed by introducing another young girl. He said that he wanted to film them having sex, or to do it in front of an audience. He also suggested that she indulge in an 'abnormal, against nature, perverted, degenerate and indecent act' – which turned out to be fellatio. However, oral sex was illegal under California law.

Chaplin was also a voyeur who kept a telescope trained on John Barrymore's bedroom window. In 1943, he married Oona O'Neill, daughter of playwright Eugene O'Neill. He was 54, she had just turned 18. Chaplin and Oona eventually went to live in Switzerland where they had eight children, the last fathered when he was in his seventies.

MAE WEST

'GOODNESS HAD NOTHING TO DO WITH IT'

1892-1980

ae West is remembered from her movie appearances as a stout, matronly figure, albeit with a lascivious turn of phrase. However, she had once been young and happy to show off her naked body on stage. Her first Broadway play, uncompromisingly called *Sex*, earned her a jail sentence. Her novel *The Constant Sinner* caused a scandal and she ran rings around Hollywood's Hays Office, which accused her of trying to corrupt public morals and obscenity.

Mae West said that she first found out about sex at the age of nine – from a medical book. 'It'd have been better had I not seen that book until I was twelve or thirteen,' she said. She claimed that, as a child, she had had a dream during which she had sex with a bear and enjoyed her first orgasm.

She also claimed to have seduced a handsome young teacher at school when she was 12. The consummation took place, she said, on the classroom floor after school was out. On another occasion, Mae said she first had sex at the age of 13, before she had her first period, with a 21-year-old actor. He had walked her home after an amateur show and made love to her on the stairs in the lobby of her apartment block with her fur coat wrapped around her.

Mae was also stage struck from an early age. At the amateur shows, she began singing 'novelty' – that is, saucy – songs with lashings of innuendo, in the way only a girl with some experience could. 'Even as a little girl, Mae's character songs were risqué,' said her older sister Beverly. She now rammed home the point by wiggling her hips suggestively. Her mother encouraged her.

Mae liked to hang out with boys and was proud that she could make them fight over her. She also liked being the only female at all-male parties where games included catch-as-catch-can kissing and more. 'I'd play with their – umm, you know,' she said.

Her first steady boyfriend was pianist Joe Schenek, though she claimed to have slept with the trumpet player and drummer in his band as well. She was no great fan of condoms, which were made from thick, unyielding rubber in those days. Instead, she preferred to rely on a sponge soaked in warm water inserted in the vagina.

FAN DANCER

Mae found herself an agent and became a fan dancer in burlesque. She was supposed to dance wearing a small G-string, while covering her body with two large feathered fans. But Mae could not be

The Hays Office

From 1930 to 1968 Hollywood movies were regulated by the Hays Office, which policed the Motion Picture Production Code. Under it:
• nakedness and suggestive dances were banned
• ridiculing religion was forbidden
• depicting illegal drug use and the gratuitous use of liquor was banned
• methods of committing crimes were not to be shown explicitly
• sex perversion, homosexuality, and venereal disease were not to be mentioned
• the use of offensive words and phrases was prohibited
• brutal killings could not be shown in detail
• the sanctity of the home and marriage were to be upheld
• portraying inter-racial marriage and sex was banned
• scenes of passion and lustful kissing were excised
• the United States flag was to be treated with respect
• vulgarity was to be avoided.

bothered with this, dispensing with the G-string and giving her audiences what they had come for. She was proud of her body. 'She'd drop her clothes at the drop of a hat,' recalled Hollywood photographer George Hurrell.

Later in life, ghostwriter Stephen Longstreet recalled turning up at her Ravenswood apartment on the first day of work on her autobiography *Goodness Had Nothing To Do With It* to be greeted by a life-size nude statue of Mae in the foyer and Mae herself in a negligee. 'Feel these,' she said thrusting out her breasts, 'they're hard as rocks.'

As a youngster, Mae and 19-year-old dancer Frank Wallace went on the road with a ragtime dance act, which *Variety* magazine said was 'pretty close to the line'. Frank wanted to marry Mae, but she was content just to sleep with him – it was 'just a physical thing', she said.

Mae was going out with any attractive man who asked her and soon fell pregnant. So on the morning of 11 April 1911 she married Frank in Milwaukee. At 17 she was underage, so she lied about her birth date. But marriage did not suit Mae and she dumped Frank. 'I was born to be a solo act,' she said, 'on and off stage.'

Mae was not big on love either, except in the physical sense. 'I saw what it did to other people when they loved another person the way I loved myself, and I didn't want that problem,' she said. With Frank out of the way, Mae headed for Broadway, stealing the show at the Folies Bergère in red harem trousers and a bare midriff. She soon came to the attention of Florenz Ziegfeld and his casting couch.

DAILY ENEMA

Off stage Mae began giving herself a daily enema because theatre bathrooms were 'so filthy I couldn't face them'. She started every day this way. Throughout her life she had a dread of using public lavatories. People would avoid taking a lift in a car with her because she would not stop to let them use the restrooms in service stations.

Although practically every straight man she met in the theatre made a play for her, she usually kept her lovers outside the stage door – 'bankers, brokers, or merchant chiefs, or maybe just a push-face truck driver with oversize muscles', she said. She also made time for the booking manager for the Loew vaudeville circuit, and for heavyweight boxing champions Jack Dempsey and Jack Johnson. Her penchant for black boxers invited censure at the time. So her next show – called, brazenly, *The Ginger Box Revue* – hinted at sex across the colour line, which was totally taboo in America at the time.

> 'I AM A SHOWMAN AND I KNOW THAT THE PUBLIC WANTS SEX IN THEIR ENTERTAINMENT, AND I GIVE IT TO THEM.'
>
> Mae West

After hours she would hang out at African-American clubs, learning the latest dances. She introduced the shimmy into her act. Wearing a short skirt, she discarded her corset so her breasts could move freely; shaking her top until the sequins flew off, she brought the house down. The dance was declared 'vile' by the Chicago Morals Commission. Even the management complained. But the applause was so thunderous Mae was not to be stopped. Next she wore a black velvet dress that was split to the waistline at the back and cut at either side to display her bare hips.

Cary Grant

1904–1986

Cary Grant became a star after playing opposite Mae West in two of her biggest movies, *She Done Him Wrong* and *I'm No Angel*. When she first saw him walking across the lot in white uniform, she said: 'If he can talk, I'll take him.'

Grant's repressed upper-class Britishness was the perfect foil for her uninhibited low-class American vulgarity. 'I learnt everything from her,' Grant said. 'Well, no, not everything.'

Indeed not. Despite his four marriages, Grant was a life-long bisexual. In his heyday, he lived with Randolph Scott, who usually played a hunky cow-poke. Seeing Grant and Scott wearing matching aprons and doing the washing up in publicity shots for *Hot Saturday*, Carole Lombard said: 'I wonder which one of those guys pays the bills.'

But then nothing about Cary Grant was what it seemed. He was not the Ivy League New Englander he appeared on screen, but a working-class boy from Bristol – possibly even Jewish. His name, of course, was not Cary Grant but Archibald Alec Leach. Nor was he a sophisticated, eligible bachelor, as the women who succumbed to his charms discovered. He would beat, abuse and sometimes injure them.

Gradually Mae moulded herself into a sex goddess. When the sports editor of the New York *World* wanted a picture of her in a bathing suit, she refused. Instead she whipped off her coat to reveal a dress with a hole cut out of the top half. America had just entered the First World War and there was a fad for posing as the French goddess of liberty, who by convention had one breast exposed.

She started her writing career with a play called *Sex*, which soon had fans calling her 'America's Oscar Wilde'. 'People want dirt in plays,' she said, 'so I give 'em dirt.' The play was guaranteed to offend. Kisses abounded and Mae flaunted her body, stopping just short of nudity. 'She undresses before the public, and appears to enjoy doing so,' wrote the New York *Mirror*, shocked. In Chicago, the newspaper ads warned: 'If you cannot stand the excitement – see your doctor before visiting Mae West in *Sex*.'

Sex ran for a year on Broadway, before the New York Police Department closed it down, arresting Mae and the cast 'for corrupting the morals of youth'. The trial drew a bigger audience than the play. Mae was fined $500 and sentenced to ten days in jail. Told to strip and put on prison uniform, she said: 'What? I thought this was a respectable place.'

Mae's next play went even further. It was called *The Drag* and tackled the taboo subject of homosexuality. 'I've got 17 real live fairies on stage,' she boasted. Again Mae and the cast were arrested. She followed this with *The Wicked Age*, *Grand Street Follies* – where she plays a character in prison stripes who seduces every man in sight – *Diamond Lil* and *Pleasure Man*. Then she wrote a novel, *The Constant Sinner*, that dealt with mixed-race sex. The stage adaptation was dismissed as 'filth', though critics were quite taken with a scene in which she crossed the dimly lit stage in a thin chiffon gown and changed into a robe. 'I wasn't really nude,' she said, merely adding to the titillation.

During the Great Depression, many cinemas closed and Paramount was near to bankruptcy until Mae West arrived in Hollywood. People would queue around the block to see her films, which contained as much sexual innuendo as she could get past the Hays Office. Even in old age she would conduct business meetings or press interviews wearing a flimsy negligee.

JUAN PERÓN

GIRL POWER

1895–1974

Juan Domingo Perón was president of Argentina, and is now remembered chiefly because of his wife, Eva, whose life was celebrated in the musical *Evita*. But she was only one among many lovers. Perón was particularly interested in young girls and eventually fell from power because of a girl young enough to be his granddaughter.

At the age of 33, Juan Perón married a schoolteacher, Aurelia Tizon, who translated English-language military textbooks for him. She died ten years later, leaving no children. Immediately before the outbreak of the Second World War, Perón was appointed military attaché in Rome where he could observe Mussolini first-hand. He also travelled to Germany, Austria, Hungary, Portugal and Spain to see how fascism worked there.

In 1943, he joined a clique of military plotters who overthrew the civilian government in Argentina. He became minister of labour. The following year he met 24-year-old actress Eva Duarte, who was already bedding other members of the government. A few weeks later, she marched around to his apartment and evicted his teenage mistress.

> '**MY DEAR BABY GIRL ... I MISS YOU EVERY DAY, AS DO MY LITTLE DOGS ... MANY KISSES AND MANY DESIRES. UNTIL I SEE YOU SOON, PAPI.'**
> Juan Perón

With Eva's help in mustering support among the *descamisados* or 'shirtless ones', Perón became vice-president and minister of war. However, there was another coup in early October 1945, and Perón was arrested. Eva organized a protest by the labour unions. Perón was released and, from the balcony of the presidential palace, addressed a crowd of 300,000. A few days later he married Evita, as Eva Duarte was popularly known. Anti-Perónists said that, when he asked her to marry him, she was so shocked she fell out of bed.

The following year Perón became president of Argentina in an election marked by the repression of the liberal opposition by the federal police and strong-arm squads. Once in power, he set about reorganizing the state along fascist lines.

The Argentine writer, and leading opponent of the regime Jorge Luis Borges said: 'Perón's wife was a common prostitute. She had a brothel near Junín. And that must have embittered him, no? I mean, if a girl is a whore in a large city that doesn't mean too much, but in a small town in the pampas, everybody knows everybody else. And being one of the whores is like being the barber or the surgeon. And that must have greatly embittered her. To be known and to be despised by everybody and to be used.'

Evita got her own back. She had political opponents tortured and killed, and took personal responsibility for the castration of rebel leaders, keeping her victims' testicles in a glass jar on her desk.

She seems to have been faithful to her husband throughout their marriage, except on one occasion. During the Second World War she had met Greek shipping magnate Aristotle Onassis, who was channelling food parcels through Argentina to Nazi-occupied Greece. While Evita was in Europe in 1947, they met at a formal lunch, then arranged a private assignation at her villa

Schoolgirls

Jaded old men have long lusted after schoolgirls. In *The Battles of Venus*, published in The Hague in 1760, the author recommends the reader to visit boarding schools to look for young girls where 'yet no ringlets deck the pouting mount, but all is like her lily hand, both bare and smooth, before the periodical lustration hath stained her virgin shift, whilst her bosom boasts only a general swell rather than distinct orbs, and whilst her tender mind is ignorant of what man can do unto her'.

Once the gentleman has picked one out, he is urged to 'pity a tender virgin's sufferings' and 'not break fiercely in, but to spare fierce dilaceration and dire pangs'.

on the Italian Riviera. As soon as he arrived, they made love. Afterwards he was hungry so she made him an omelette. In return, he donated $10,000 to her favourite charity. Onassis said it was the most expensive omelette he had ever had.

'RECREATION CENTRES'

Perón was just 56 when Evita died in 1952, and Argentina was plunged into national mourning. He began to take an inordinate interest in the Union of Secondary School Students, especially its young female members who were sent to 'recreation centres' where they entertained high-ranking government officials. The centres had teams of doctors who handled unwanted pregnancies and venereal diseases. Perón had his own private recreational centre where he spent the afternoons with teenage girls, watching them swimming and playing basketball. One of them became his full-time mistress.

The daughter of a candy factory worker, her name was Nellie Rivas. She was just 13. Perón set her up in a luxurious love nest with mirrored walls and bear-skin rugs, and showered her with jewels. Though the relationship was primarily sexual, he did care for Nellie, spending time teaching her the rudiments of culture. He even offered to send her to Europe to broaden her horizons, but she did not want to leave him. 'The very thought of leaving the residence brought me attacks of madness,' she wrote later.

Stories about Perón's teenage mistress spread. Soon people were talking about sex orgies behind the high walls of the presidential palace. It was said that Perón was behaving like a Roman emperor, surrounded by willing slave girls ready to do his every bidding. Some of the tales were fanciful, but it was generally believed that Perón was defiling the memory of the saintly Evita.

By 1955, Argentina was an economic ruin and Perón had alienated a large part of his traditional support. There was another coup and Perón was forced to seek refuge on a Paraguayan gunboat that had put into Buenos Aires harbour for repairs. From there he wrote Nellie a hasty goodbye note.

TORRID CORRESPONDENCE

Later the torrid correspondence between Perón and his teenage mistress was published, further besmirching his reputation. He was tried *in absentia* by a military court for his affair with an underage girl and stripped of his rank of general for 'conduct unworthy of an officer and a gentleman'. The judge wrote: 'It is superfluous to stress the horror of the court at the proof of such a crime committed by one who always claimed that the only privileged ones in the land were children.'

Eva Perón

1919–1952

Born Maria Eva Duarte in Los Toldos, Argentina, Evita was the illegitimate daughter of a local landowner. When her father died, her mother earned her living running a boarding house that doubled as a brothel. At 14, Evita agreed to sleep with visiting tango singer José Armani if he would take her to Buenos Aires. Later she claimed that a better-known singer, Agustin Magaldi, was in fact her first lover.

In Buenos Aires she worked as a prostitute and posed for pornographic photographs. At 15 she became the mistress of Emilio Kartulovic, the publisher of the movie magazine *Sintonia*. This gave her a springboard into the world of acting. She toured with the play *The Mortal Kiss*. It was about the evils of sexual promiscuity and was backed by the Argentine Prophylactic League, which hoped it would help cut Argentina's soaring illegitimacy rate.

With the contacts she had made through Kartulovic, Evita landed a part in the boxing movie *Seconds Out of the Ring* and had a brief affair with the star, Pedro Quartucci. She appeared in a few other dire Argentine films and took the occasional modelling assignment. To make ends meet, she went to nightclubs where she picked up wealthy businessmen, who would pay for the privilege of taking her back to a nearby bachelor flat or love hotel.

She landed parts in Argentina's radio soap operas and starred in *The Kingdom of Love*, a series of historical love stories. She played the female leads – Elizabeth I of England, Emma Hamilton, Napoleon's Joséphine, Tsarina Alexandra of Russia and Madame Jiang Jie Shi (Chiang Kai-shek). After the military coup that brought Juan Perón into government, Evita impressed her fellow actors by ostentatiously phoning the president to organize an intimate dinner *à deux*, addressing him by his first name. When the owner of the radio station heard about this, he immediately upped her salary from 150 pesos a month to 5,000. It was a shrewd move as Evita was also having an affair with Colonel Anibal Imbert, the minister of communications in the new administration, who controlled the country's radio network. Colonel Imbert moved his pretty young mistress out of his fashionable apartment on Calle Posadas and moved Evita in.

On 15 January 1944, an earthquake destroyed the Spanish colonial town of San Juan. At a benefit for the victims in Luna Park, Evita spotted Libertad Lamarque – one of Argentina's loveliest actresses – on the arm of a handsome army officer. The officer was Perón. Evita went over to Libertad, whom she knew slightly, and asked to be introduced. And when it was time for Libertad to take her turn at the microphone, Evita slipped into the empty chair beside him. That night, she got him into bed.

Evita was beautiful and energetic. She persuaded Perón to use his position as minister of labour to improve the lot of the *descamisados*. When he was jailed, she organized the demonstration of trades unionists that got him out and, the following year, put him in power. She was his greatest political asset. Her beauty was said to personify Perónist femininity and Perónist posters portrayed her as the Virgin Mary. But still Evita Perón's enemies referred to her as a whore.

One day, while travelling in an official car with an Italian admiral, a jeering crowd mocked and taunted her.

'Do you hear that?' she said. 'They are calling me a whore.'

'I quite understand,' said the admiral. 'I haven't been to sea for fifteen years and they still call me an admiral.'

Nellie was heartbroken. 'He loved me,' she said. 'He could have been my grandfather, but he loved me. He always told me I was very pretty, but I'm not really, am I?' Nellie was sent to a reformatory for eight months. Her parents went into exile in Montevideo. Later she married an Argentine employee of the American embassy. Perón returned from exile and was elected president again in 1973, but he already knew he was dying. He was succeeded by his third wife Isabel.

ADOLF HITLER
VERY NAZI HABITS

1896-1945

When the Second World War broke out, psychoanalyst Dr Walter C. Langer was commissioned to prepare a report on Hitler's psychology by William 'Wild Bill' Donovan, head of the OSS, the Office of Strategic Services, forerunner of the CIA. He collected material from published sources and interviewed all the people he could find who had known Hitler personally, many of whom were then refugees in the United States. His resulting report presents a picture of a man who indulged in the most unpleasant sexual perversions.

Hitler described himself as a mother's boy. For the first 16 years of his life he had watched his father rape and abuse his mother while openly flaunting his own infidelity. When his father died, few tears were shed. Indeed, after the *Anschluss*, which extended Hitler's rule to Austria, the cemetery where his father was buried was turned into a firing range and his grave was obliterated forever.

Four years after his father's death, Hitler's mother died of breast cancer. By then Hitler had moved to Vienna with the intention of enrolling in the Academy of Fine Arts. He visited the Spittelberggasse, a red-light district where semi-naked girls sat behind lace curtains. Many of them were Jewish, and Hitler contracted syphilis there. Later, Hitler would take friends to the Spittelberggasse and rant about the evils of prostitution – and what imbeciles men were to succumb. It is thought that Hitler had a number of homosexual relations during this period, though he also had a fantasy love affair with a woman whom he had never even spoken to.

During the First World War the story circulated that Hitler, though heroic in the trenches, was never promoted beyond the rank of lance-corporal because he had been court-martialled on a charge of indecency that implicated a senior officer. When he came to power, his military records were destroyed by the Gestapo. He showed no interest in women at the time and was hospitalized, possibly with the symptoms of secondary syphilis.

After the war Hitler settled in Munich, where he began a collection of pornographic books and visited life classes to ogle the models. Joining the fledgling Nazi Party, Hitler attracted a number of female followers, despite his dishevelled appearance, body odour and chronic flatulence. His ranting speeches seemed to climax in a verbal orgasm. Many female followers followed suit. At his public meetings, middle-aged women would get so agitated they would require medical attention. On one occasion a women bent down, picked up some gravel Hitler had stepped on and tried to swallow it.

Many of Hitler's early followers, such as Ernst Röhm, the head of the Nazi Party's militia, were homosexuals and assumed Hitler was too. They perished in 1934 in the 'Night of the Long Knives'.

Coprophilia

In *Psychopathia Sexualis*, Richard von Krafft-Ebing records the case of a Russian prince who was 'very decrepit and accustomed to have his mistress turn her back to him and defecate on his breast; this being the only way in which he could excite the remnant of libido'. In another case, Krafft-Ebing mentions a wealthy man who supported a mistress in great style provided she only ate marzipan. He would then come over her faeces. Krafft-Ebing also said that a Brazilian doctor told him of several cases of men who liked women to defecate on their genitals.

> ## 'MY UNCLE IS A MONSTER; YOU WOULD NEVER BELIEVE THE THINGS HE MAKES ME DO.'
> Geli Raubal

Among those who survived were Deputy Führer Rudolf Hess, who was known as 'Fräulein Anna', and Reichsmarschall Hermann Göring, who was a transvestite.

The great love of Hitler's life was his niece, Angela 'Geli' Raubal. Once he had obtained medical confirmation of her virginity, he kept her locked up in an apartment in Munich. The chambermaids who tidied up the apartment talked of the 'strange and unspeakable' sexual practices that were taking place.

Dr Langer interviewed former Nazi Otto Strasser, who had escaped to Canada. He told Langer about Hitler's relationship with Geli: 'Hitler made her undress. He would then lie on the floor. She would have to squat over his face where he could examine her at close quarters and this made him very excited ... When the excitement reached its peak, he demanded that she urinate on him and that gave him sexual pleasure. Geli said the whole performance was extremely disgusting to her and it gave her no gratification.'

Strasser had heard similar tales from Henriette Hoffman, the daughter of Hitler's official photographer, but had dismissed them as hysterical ravings. Pornographic sketches Hitler had made of Geli fell into the hands of his landlady's son. They showed her in every sort of indecent and obscene pose and revealed that Hitler also had coprophiliac cravings. The drawings were recovered by the rabid anti-Semite, Father Stemfle, who also perished in the 'Night of the Long Knives'.

Frustrated by her incarceration, Geli had affairs with Hitler's long-time companion and chauffeur Emil Maurice, a security guard and any other young man who crossed her path. At the age of 23 she was found shot dead. The authorities considered charging Hitler with murder, but the Nazi Party was already strong enough to hush things up. An inquest decided that she had committed suicide, though she was allowed a full Catholic funeral.

FILTHY AND UNCLEAN

Soon after Hitler came to power, 19-year-old German movie star Renate Müller was invited to visit him in the Chancellery. Over dinner, Hitler gloated over the torture methods his men employed on victims to extract a confession. Then they went into the bedroom and undressed. Hitler threw himself on the floor at her feet and begged her to kick him. 'I am filthy and unclean,' he screamed. 'Beat me! Beat me!'

Renate was horrified by the display. She pleaded with him to get up, but he just lay there grovelling and moaning. Eventually, she did kick him and soon found that the harder she kicked him the more excited he got. But that was not the worst of it. Renate told film director Alfred Zeisler that there was something even more unspeakable that she could not bring herself to talk about. Soon after, she fell to her death from the window of her apartment.

Hitler had a thing for movie actresses. He invited Linda Basquette, an American star of the silent movies, to his retreat at Berchtesgaden, where he made a vigorous pass at her. She kicked him in the groin in an attempt to dampen his ardour, but he only became more excited.

In 1929, Hitler had met 17-year-old Eva Braun, who was a laboratory assistant at Heinrich Hoffman's photographic studio where a number of gay men hung out. Hitler was 23 years older than her and kept her on a tight rein. One night she danced with Luis Trenker, who was warned

Benito Mussolini

Adolf Hitler's greatest ally in the Second World War was the Italian dictator Benito Mussolini. Not nearly as kinky as Hitler, he was a straightforward satyr. He told his young mistress Claretta Petacci that the idea of sleeping with only one woman was 'inconceivable' to him, explaining: 'There was a period when I had 14 women, and I'd take three or four every evening, one after the other ... That gives you an idea of my sexuality.'

The 49-year-old Mussolini was married with five children when he met the 23-year-old Claretta, the daughter of a Vatican doctor. In February 1938, he told her: 'Be afraid of my love. It's like a cyclone. It's tremendous; it overwhelms everything. You must tremble.' He added that he wanted to have sex with her on horseback.

In her diaries, she recorded: 'We made love with such force that he bit my shoulder so hard his teeth left a mark. He's mortified; he sits on the bed looking a bit pale and panting: "My love, what have I done to you, look at that mark. One of these days, I'll tear a shoulder off."'

Mussolini's lovers were often well connected. His first steady partner was Angelica Balabanoff, a Russian socialist who had been one of Lenin's lovers. He also bedded Winston Churchill's cousin, the artist Clare Sheridan, who, in their pillow talk, assured Mussolini that Churchill would become leader of the British fascists.

Mussolini was undoubtedly the king of the quickie, launching himself on any woman who came within reach and rarely bothering to take his trousers or boots off. Afterwards, though, he played them a romantic air on the violin. This must have endeared him to Claretta. When they were captured by partisans, fleeing at the end of the war, their captors offered to left Claretta go. She refused and threw herself in front of Mussolini when they shot him. Their bodies were displayed hanging upside down from a lamp-post in Milan's Piazzale Loretto, a well-known haunt of prostitutes.

that he would be shot for trying to steal the Führer's mistress. Eva became hysterical and said, with unintentional irony: 'You don't know what a tyrant he can be.'

Soon after Geli died, Hitler and Eva became lovers. However, her vagina was too small for intercourse and she had to undergo painful corrective surgery. After the procedure was completed, her gynaecologist died in a car accident. Their relationship was not very satisfactory from her point of view and she tried to kill herself several times. In her diary, she records: 'He needs me only for certain purposes ... this is idiotic.'

Hitler liked to watch her sunbathe or swim nude. He was always suggesting that it was too hot for her to wear clothes and would then undress her with trembling hands. He would photograph her nude, but only from the neck down, in case the pictures fell into 'the wrong hands'. However, most of his pictures zoomed in on her buttocks.

Eva was intensely loyal. When the Red Army closed in on Berlin, she left the safety of Berchtesgaden, against Hitler's orders, and joined him in the bunker, where they married, then committed suicide. Interestingly, the Russian autopsy report on Hitler stated: 'In the scrotum, which is singed but preserved, only the right testicle is found. The left testicle could not be found in the inguinal canal.' He really did have only one ball.

That was not quite the end of the story. It is said that Hitler had a child by Tilly Fleischer, the the Nordic javelin thrower who won a gold medal at the 1936 Olympics. She married Dr Fritz Hoser, one of Hitler's aides, and passed off Hitler's daughter Gisela as their own. When Gisela grew up, she married a Jew, the son of a French rabbi who had died in Hitler's death camps, and she eventually converted to Judaism herself.

ALFRED HITCHCOCK

THE VIEWFINDER

1899-1980

Married for 53 years, British movie director Alfred Hitchcock claimed only to have had sex once, producing his daughter Patricia. A recent biographer wrote that Hitchcock was impotent due to his obesity. Even in front of his wife, he told numerous people that he only 'did it with a fountain pen'. However, he did not mind watching.

Hitchcock started in the movie industry in London in 1920, then went to Germany to learn his craft. He was in Munich when he met Anita Donna Dooley, who worked under the name Nita Naldi. An ex-Ziegfeld Follies girl, she had been taken to Hollywood by John Barrymore, co-starring with him in *Dr Jekyll and Mr Hyde*. She had also starred in the movie *Blood and Sand* opposite Rudolph Valentino.

She arrived in Germany with an older gentleman she called 'Daddy', and promptly whisked Hitchcock and his assistant Alma Reville, later his wife, off to a famous brothel that was on her list of tourist attractions. Once there Hitchcock and Alma decided not to join in. On another occasion Hitchcock rejected the advances of two young German girls. Unperturbed, they got into bed together. However, Hitchcock stayed to watch the lesbian encounter in close up. 'It was a very *gemütlich* [easy-going] family soirée,' he said.

Unlike many of his contemporaries, Hitchcock was not fazed by homosexuality. 'He was always at ease with homosexual or bisexual people,' said musical star Elsie Randolph, who appeared in two of his films. 'Hitch often told actors – for what mix of reasons I won't guess – that they really had to be part masculine and part feminine in order to get inside any character.' Indeed, after his marriage to Alma in Brompton Oratory on 2 December 1926, he said: 'I could have been a poof if it were not for Alma.'

According to Hitchcock, the marriage remained unconsummated for over a year. Then came his one experiment with sexual intercourse, leading to the birth of his only daughter Pat on 7 July 1928. Hitchcock said his marriage was celibate and those who knew them said that Alfred and Alma were like brother and sister. He always told actors to address him by his nickname – 'Hitch without the cock'.

However, actress Ann Todd said that Hitchcock had a 'schoolboy obsession with sex'. Playwright Arthur Laurents, who wrote the screenplay for Hitchcock's movie *Rope*, said: 'Hitch lived in the land of kink. Initially, I thought he was a repressed homosexual. The actual word homosexuality was never said aloud in conferences on *Rope* or on the set, but he alluded to the subject so often – slyly and naughtily, never nastily – that he seemed fixated if not obsessed.'

> **'I SOMETIMES WONDER WHETHER I AM NOT – AS ALL MY FRIENDS INSIST – A SADIST.'**
> Alfred Hitchcock

Hitchcock was amused by the fact that, in *Rope*, the actor Farley Granger was playing a homosexual in a film written by another homosexual – and in real life, they were lovers. It tickled him even more that he was in on the secret, and that Laurents knew he knew. 'Sex was always on his mind,' said Laurents, 'not ordinary sex, not plain homosexuality any more than plain heterosexuality. Perverse sex, kinky sex – that fascinated him. He himself didn't strike me as ever having much sex or even wanting sex.' Rumours circulated about Hitchcock's odd tastes, especially when he claimed to have come up with a new cocktail recipe for Laurents – 'a new martini: gin and menstrual blood'. Long-time collaborator Hume Cronyn, who also worked on *Rope*, said Hitchcock enjoyed telling risqué stories, which were 'not very amusing, actually – the kind of jokes schoolboys tell, sniggering and childish'.

'TORTURE THE WOMEN'

There is no doubt that Hitchcock was attracted to women, particularly beautiful blondes. On set he paid little attention to the male actors, but cosseted his female stars. However, he often repeated the advice of 19th-century playwright Victorien Sardou when it came to plot construction – 'torture the women'. 'The trouble today,' said Hitchcock in the 1930s, 'is that we don't torture women enough.' If this were indeed so, the film historian Philip Kemp commented: 'Hitchcock, at least, did his best to make up for the omission.'

Voyeurism

Voyeurism only became a criminal offence in Britain in 2004. However, it did feature in a famous 'criminal-conversation' case in 1782, when Lady Seymour Worsley ran off with George Blisset. Her husband, Sir Richard Worsley, sued, demanding £20,000 in damages. However, it came out in court that Worsley had boasted to Blisset that his wife was a 'Callipygian Venus', that is, one with round buttocks. What's more he allowed Blisset to climb on his shoulders so that he could look through a high window while she was having a bath. Blisset was so impressed that he ran off with Lady Worsley. This evidence destroyed Worsley's case and the jury awarded him just one shilling.

This attitude carried over into the filming. In *The 39 Steps*, Madeleine Carroll spent long periods being dragged around the set, handcuffed to her co-star Robert Donat, and suffered painful bruising. To increase her discomfort, Hitchcock even pretended to lose the key to the handcuffs at one point, when it was, in fact, in his pocket. 'What interests me,' he said, 'is the drama of being handcuffed ... [It] brings out all kinds of thoughts in the audience's minds – for example, how do they go to the toilet was one natural, obvious question. And linking together relates more to sex than anything else.'

Hitchcock took a perverse delight in devising torments for Madeleine Carroll to undergo. She was dragged across country, under a waterfall, over streams and through fences until her hair and clothes were ruined. Her friend Randolph Churchill, visiting the set, complained about her mistreatment. Hitchcock, who called Madeleine the 'Birmingham tart', took no notice and continued. 'We deliberately wrote the script to include her undignified handcuff scene on the bed,' he said, 'and being led out from under the waterfall looking like a drowned rat. But Madeleine was a trouper and turned the tables on us by appreciating the treatment and asking for more.' Hitchcock also had other tricks up his sleeve. When he wanted to capture a shocked expression on her face, he simply unbuttoned his fly.

Handcuffs appeared regularly in Hitchcock's films. During the filming of his first thriller, *The Lodger*, he got the actor playing the inspector to snap the handcuffs on an actress's wrists without warning, so he could film the shock on her face. Years later he said: 'Psychologically, of course, the idea of the handcuffs has deeper implications. Being tied to something – it's somewhere in the area of fetishism, isn't it? There's also a sexual connotation. When I visited the Vice Museum in Paris, I noticed there was considerable evidence of sexual aberrations through restraint.'

Grace Kelly

1929–1982

Hitchcock called Grace Kelly 'the snow princess', but in fact she was hot. In Hollywood it was well known that Grace Kelly had slept her way to the top. Columnist Hedda Hopper called her a 'nymphomaniac'. She lost her virginity at the age of 17, before enrolling in the American Academy of Drama in New York. As well as dating other students at the Academy, she went to bed with Hollywood leading man Alexandre D'Arcy. She used to dance naked to Hawaiian music for him. Although she was from a wealthy family, she made extra money as a lingerie model for the fun of it. Her jewellery came from the Shah of Iran and Aly Khan, who spent time with her when they were in New York.

Grace's big break came in 1951, when she starred in *High Noon* opposite Gary Cooper, whom she immediately bedded. Next came Clark Gable and *Mogambo*. 'I hear you two made Africa hotter than it is,' said Hedda Hopper. There were other actors and amours on the side. During the shooting of *Dial M for Murder*, Grace and Ray Milland became ardent lovers, to the point that his twenty-year marriage was put in jeopardy. 'Hitchcock the voyeur could not have been more delighted,' wrote one biographer.

There were flings with Bing Crosby and William Holden, and with fashion designer Oleg Cassini. James Stewart, her co-star in *Rear Window*, became jealous when he heard of her engagement to Prince Rainier of Monaco, who was taken in by her chaste on-screen persona. She married her prince, but that did not stop her having toy boys later in life.

Even the British Film Institute, when paying a glowing tribute to Hitchcock, noted his 'murderous fascination with blondes'. Film historian Philip Kemp said: 'Like Hitchcock himself, the serial killer in *The Lodger* seems to have it in for blondes ... [and] Hitchcock's mischievous, semi-sadistic treatment of blondes hit its stride in Hollywood, perhaps provoked by the flawless glamour of its screen goddesses.'

None of what Madeleine Carroll went through compares with the physical torment endured by Tippi Hedren during the filming of *The Birds*, or the sexual harassment she underwent during the production of *Marnie*. And it was not just the actresses on set that suffered. When he wanted an assistant to read and summarize stories for him, Hitchcock took on attractive 28-year-old blonde Joan Harrison – but only after he had read her a particularly crude scene from James Joyce's *Ulysses*, which was still banned at the time.

Voyeurism was a staple of Hitchcock's films from *The Pleasure Garden* in 1925 to *Rear Window* in 1954. In 1962, he said: 'I prefer a woman who does not display all of her sex at once. I like women who are also ladies, who hold enough of themselves in reserve to keep a man intrigued. On the screen, for example, if an actress wants to convey a sexy quality, she ought to maintain a slightly mysterious air.'

SHOE FETISHISM

One of the Hollywood blondes whom Hitchcock regularly liked to drag through the emotional mill was Grace Kelly. He was more than a little in love with her and she was happy to gratify his voyeuristic yearnings. She lived a mile down Laurel Canyon from him. He had a powerful telescope and she would purposely leave the curtains open when she got undressed, slowly, at night. On the first day of shooting *Rear Window*, Hitchcock spent half an hour filming close-ups of her shoes. There was no mention of this in the shooting script and the shots were never used in the movie. When questioned about it, Hitchcock said: 'Haven't you ever heard of shoe fetishism?'

TALLULAH BANKHEAD

HEELS OVER HEAD

1902-1968

A southern belle from Huntsville, Alabama, Tallulah Bankhead was an unashamed exhibitionist who loved to take her clothes off at parties and do cartwheels. In an uptight age, she was completely outspoken. A lady reporter in the 1930s asked: 'Miss Bankhead, what is your definition of love?' 'Do you mean fucking?' Tallulah replied. She claimed to have had 5,000 sexual partners. At a society wedding, while the bride and groom were walking down the aisle, Tallulah remarked loudly: 'I've had both of them, dahling, and neither of them is any good.'

Tallulah was a lively and energetic child. There was one particular childhood story she loved to tell in later life. She was having a picnic in the woods with some other children one day when a rattlesnake bit her on the behind. 'Quick as a flash daddy snatched off my panties and sucked the blood from the wound,' she said. He had a cut on his gums and became quite ill. Ever after, in her passport under the heading 'Distinguishing Marks' she would put 'snakebite'.

As a child, Tallulah loved to show off those same panties by doing cartwheels. Once she even did cartwheels in front of the governor of Alabama. In later life she would still do cartwheels at parties, though minus the panties.

At the age of 15, she entered a competition in *Pictureplay* magazine and won. The prize was a movie contract with a company in New York at a salary of $50 a week. She hung out there with the silent movie star Louise Brooks. One night they picked up a black guy in a bar for an evening's troilism.

On a train to Atlantic City, she met John Barrymore and instantly fell for him. When she visited him in his dressing room, he offered her a part in his movie version of *Dr Jekyll and Mr Hyde*, as he locked the door with one hand and led her to the couch with the other. But Tallulah was still young and naive. She declined Barrymore's advances and lost the chance to be in the movie. Soon after, though, she was seen kissing a girl at a party. 'I want to try everything once,' she said. That included marijuana and cocaine – though she had promised her father she would not touch alcohol if he let her go on the stage.

At a party in New York, Tallulah met British aristocrat Lord Napier ('Naps') Alington. She claimed to be a virgin – technically – while admitting to having been introduced to the delights

Lap Dancing

America has a long history of striptease going back to 1896, and a vaudeville trapeze artist's stripping act was captured in an Edison film of 1901. By the 1920s, it was permissible to have topless women on stage, provided they did not move. Then in 1925, in a show at New York's National Winter Garden, Mademoiselle Fifi moved. Following a change in the US law in 1937, striptease artists such as Gypsy Rose Lee and Sally Rand became household names.

In 1964, topless go-go dancing began in the Condor nightclub in North Beach, San Francisco. Five years later, the show went 'bottomless'. San Francisco also gave birth to lap dancing. At the O'Farrell Theater in 1980, the Michael Brothers had girls dancing among the audience for tips, as well as strippers on stage. Although closely regulated, lap dancing has spread throughout the English-speaking world.

of Sapphic love. Alington immediately volunteered to amend her sexual status. She followed him to England when she was offered a stage part there, and Sir Francis Laking – 'a witty young man of cloudy gender' – took her on holiday to Venice. Although Tallulah never bedded John Barrymore, she had better luck with his sister Ethel. While Tallulah was in London, Ethel Barrymore turned up to a party at her flat in Farm Street, intending to stay only a few minutes. She stayed the night, and more nights were to follow.

As Tallulah's fame on the English stage grew, she seems to have gone through half of Burke's Peerage. But she did not confine her favours to the aristocracy. A taxi driver who drove her home one Friday night was invited in for the weekend. When the poor man left, exhausted, on Monday morning, she shouted down to him from her bedroom window: 'Dahling, you're as good as the King of England.'

She was fêted by Augustus John, Winston Churchill, Lloyd George and the then prime minister, Ramsay MacDonald. MacDonald invited her to lunch at 10 Downing Street. Afterwards, he brought his strait-laced sister to visit Tallulah in her dressing room. Tallulah immediately introduced her to a doctor and said, 'You must remember his name, dahling, he's absolutely wonderful at abortions.'

'NOT THAT BRAVE'

She once invited Lawrence of Arabia to visit her, telling him that she loved brave men. Asked what she would do if he turned up, she said 'He's not that brave.'

Tallulah made a habit of sleeping with her leading men, then sending them home to their wives. Leslie Howard, who played opposite her in *The Cardboard Lover*, was one of them. She had an affair with Wimbledon tennis champion Bill Tilden and went to Paris with him when he was playing in the Davis Cup.

Back in England, Tallulah continued her wicked ways. While she was dining with Gerald du Maurier in the Savoy Grill one day, a young woman stormed up to their table and slapped Tallulah across the face for sleeping with her husband. The restaurant fell silent. Everyone expected all hell to break loose. Instead, she turned to du Maurier, a renowned master of the understatement, and said coolly: 'As I was saying, dahling ...'

In 1931, she signed a contract with Paramount Pictures and returned to the USA. On the train to Hollywood she met Joan Crawford and her new husband Douglas Fairbanks Jr. 'Dahling, you're divine,' she said to Crawford. 'I've had an affair with your husband. You'll be next.'

In Hollywood, she began to drink. 'My father warned me about men and booze,' she said, 'but he never mentioned women and cocaine.' Actress Tamara Geva recalled: 'She would get plastered drunk and later on, for no reason whatsoever, she started to take her clothes off.' At MGM, Louis B. Mayer called her in to berate her for 'hibernating' with other women. 'You mean fucking,' said Tallulah. Then she reeled off a list of names of MGM actresses she had been sleeping with. For good measure she added a list of the studio's top actors to whom she had extended similar privileges.

> 'I ONLY BECAME A LEZ BECAUSE I NEEDED THE PUBLICITY – I HAD TO GET A JOB. IN THE TWENTIES AND THIRTIES, A LESBIAN WAS TOPS IN DESIRABILITY.'
> Tallulah Bankhead

Louise Brooks

1906–1985

Silent movie star Louise Brooks came from a peculiar family. Her mother was a frigid man hater, while her father was a ladies' man who was still having sex with the family's black maid well into his 93rd year. He also had his hearing aid specially adapted so that he could eavesdrop on the people making love next door.

At the age of nine, Louise was molested by a 45-year-old house painter. At 14 she had a fling with an artist who wanted her to pose nude for him. At 15 she joined a dance troupe, but was dismissed after it was rumoured that she had slept with the entire backstage crew.

On Broadway, she appeared in George White's Scandals, which was like Ziegfeld's Follies, except that the girls wore fewer clothes. 'There were large quantities of gorgeous costumes on the girls of the chorus,' wrote one critic, 'most of them from the neck up and the shoes down.'

Out on the town with wealthy men, Louise wore revealing gowns. 'Sitting at a restaurant or night-club table,' she recalled, 'I was a nearly naked sight to behold.' She moved on to the Ziegfeld Follies, supplementing her income by posing for nude photographs. She took up with millionaire John Lock. When Lock dropped around one night, he found Louise naked in the passionate embrace of screenwriter Townsend Martin. Not only did they not stop, but Louise invited Lock to join in. Visiting Walter Wanger, the head of production at Famous Players–Lasky, she was asked what made her think she had what it took to make it in the movies. She took off her clothes, lay on the couch and showed him. In her first film, *The American Venus*, she wore very little clothing and became an erotic icon. Entertaining at home, she rarely wore anything more than a bathrobe. When she had an affair with Charlie Chaplin, they often spent the weekend naked in an erotic foursome with Louise's best friend and well-known lesbian Peggy Fears and film financier A.C. Blumenthal. She often wore men's clothing and once spent the night with Greta Garbo.

After Louise had slept her way through Hollywood and the advent of talkies, she headed for Germany where she threw herself into the decadence of Weimar Berlin. She made the silent classic *Pandora's Box*, but it bombed at the box office after a third of the film was cut to get it past the censors. Nevertheless, she rewarded the director Georg Pabst with 'the best sexual performance of my career'. Back in the US, she was seen out with Paul Bern, who committed suicide after marrying Jean Harlow. He took her to the opera and when she slipped off her ermine coat, one witness noted, she was 'practically topless'.

The film parts dried up, but the sex continued. She teamed up with nude model Danny Aikman, who claimed to be the most outrageous man in Wichita. At one of his wild parties, Louise is said to have taken on the entire football team from North High School – though Aikman probably rendered some assistance, since he liked boys too. She started a sadomasochistic relationship with a marine from Fort Dix. She also cultivated a lesbian relationship with a woman called Butch, whom her marine had designs on too.

In 1935, when the young Burgess Meredith became Broadway's newest star, Tallulah invited him to a party. When she opened the door, she kissed him passionately. In his mind, there was no question that they would be making love by the end of the night. Later his eyes popped out at the sight of Tallulah walking naked around the party. None of her friends took any notice.

But even after all this, Tallulah's heart still belonged to Alington. At 35 she went back to England to give him one last chance to marry her. Cecil Beaton recorded the scene in his diaries: 'Tallulah danced frenziedly, throwing herself about in a mad apache dance with Napier Alington. After he left, she wept and bemoaned the fact that he had never married her, then she threw off all her clothes, performing what she called her "Chinese classical dances".'

Tallulah was in the Café de Paris when Alington turned up with his latest conquest. He tried to ignore her, so Tallulah walked up to him and said in front of his lady friend: 'What's the matter? Don't you recognize me with my clothes on?'

SALVADOR DALÍ
THE GREAT MASTURBATOR

1904–1989

Surrealist painter Salvador Dalí's sex life was – well – surreal. His paintings are full of sexual imagery, but he was better at painting than doing. Publicly, he relished all sorts of perversions, but largely to shock. He was always searching for ever-more extreme ways to excite his visual senses, but though he was with his wife Gala for over 50 years, he remained – echoing the title of one of his most famous paintings – *The Great Masturbator*.

Salvador Dalí was fixated with filth. As a child he liked to hide his stools around the house and deliberately wet his bed until his father promised to buy him a bicycle. The sophisticated, well-dressed Dalí even claimed to have enjoyed his military service because he was made to clean out the latrines.

One day in the lavatories he discovered a solitary pleasure he called 'it'. 'One could do "it" all by yourself,' he discovered. '"It" could also be done mutually, even by several at a time, to see who could do "it" quickest.' Whenever he felt sexually aroused, he would go to the lavatories and masturbate. It gave him intense pleasure, but afterwards left him depressed and disgusted with himself. And he repeatedly vowed to give it up. He never did.

Dalí was a lifelong masturbator and rarely if ever came to orgasm any other way. This was partly due to his fear of venereal disease, partly due to his inadequacy. 'Naked, comparing myself to school friends, I found that my penis was small, pitiful and soft,' he said.

Dalí also had other problems. 'You have to have a very strong erection to penetrate,' he said. 'My problem is that I have always been a premature ejaculator. So much so, that sometimes it is enough for me just to look in order to have an orgasm.'

At 15, he fell for a girl named Estela, but she claimed that he was an insatiable sadist who had tortured her with his cold heart. When she found herself a new lover, Dalí followed them about and spied on them.

In Madrid, Dalí became close friends with the gay poet and playwright Federico García Lorca, though he fiercely denied any homosexual leanings himself. That would have been far too normal. Lorca tried to seduce him on many occasions and according to Dalí, he almost succeeded once. They were naked in bed together but, halfway through, Dalí found sodomy much too painful and begged Lorca to stop.

> '**I CONVINCED MYSELF THAT I WOULD NEVER BE ABLE TO MAKE A WOMAN CREAK LIKE A WATERMELON.**'
> Salvador Dalí

On another occasion, Dalí played a cruel practical joke on Lorca. Dalí told him to come to his room late at night. But when Lorca slipped into Dalí's bed he discovered, to his horror, that the body he was caressing was that of a naked woman. Dalí had hired a cheap prostitute and was hiding somewhere in the darkened room, laughing.

THE FEMALE ANUS

Dalí's major source of erotic interest, he said, was the female anus. But his major source of sexual satisfaction remained his own hands. This he freely admitted. After all, one of his best-known paintings is called *The Great Masturbator*, completed in 1929. By that time he had moved to Paris where he met Gala, the wife of the surrealist poet Paul Éluard. When Gala spotted the scatological elements in Dalí's paintings, he asked whether she was a coprophage. The idea of eating excrement was, she said, distasteful. 'I swear I am not coprophagic,' Dalí told Gala. 'I loathe that kind of aberration as much as you can possibly loathe it. But I consider scatology a terrorizing element, just as I do blood or my phobia for grasshoppers.'

Dalí was soon infatuated with Gala. But what good was he, a 24-year-old virgin, to a nymphomaniac? Nevertheless Gala wanted Dalí, but realized that if she made the first move he would flee to his studio and resume painting excrement. So she began wearing white and playing the virgin. Finally, he could hold back no longer. On a windy day on the rocky seashore, he asked her: 'What do you want me to do to you?'

She wept. Overcome with desire, he grabbed her hair, pulled her head back and kissed her. 'Now tell me what you want me to do to you,' said Dalí. 'Tell me slowly, looking me in the eye, in the crudest and the most ferociously erotic words that will make both of us feel the greatest shame.'

'I want you to kill me,' she said.

'Yes,' he cried, pulling up her white skirt. There, tearing his knees to shreds on the rocks, he made love to her.

'My limbs no longer belonged to me,' he wrote in *The Unspeakable Confessions of Salvador Dalí*, 'an unbelievable strength possessed me. I felt myself a man, freed from my terrors and my impotence. By her, I was henceforth gifted with telluric vertical forces such as allow a man to penetrate a woman.' It was probably the first and last time he enjoyed sexual intercourse.

Dalí made two films with Luis Buñuel – *Un Chien Andalou*, which provoked a riot when first shown in Paris, and *L'Age d'Or*. Both featured Dalí's obsessions – hatred of the vagina, buttocks, coprophilia, necrophilia, castration and fear of homosexuality. The outrage they provoked made Dalí and Buñuel famous, and Gala promptly left Éluard and moved in with Dalí. She was convinced that, with her support, he would become very rich.

'THE STAIN, THE STAIN'

Despite his international fame and, in later years, his estrangement from Gala, Dalí never took another lover. A woman friend once took him to a brothel in Barcelona. He liked to watch the girls parading before him but if one tried to touch him he would push her away, muttering 'The stain, the stain.'

Occasionally he would involve a naked woman in one of his surrealist stunts. He modelled the breasts of Ultra Violet, a member of Andy Warhol's factory, with hands on them. And he used

---

The Painting

The Great Masturbator shows a distorted human face in profile looking downwards. A nude Gala rises from the back of the head with her mouth near a thinly clad male crotch. The male figure, seen only from the waist down, has bleeding fresh cuts on his knees. Below the large head, on the mouth, is a locust, an insect of which Dali had an irrational fear. The painting is thought to be a surreal masturbation fantasy indicating Dalí's conflicted attitudes towards sexual intercourse. In his youth, his father had left out a book with explicit photos of the diseased genitalia of people suffering from untreated venereal diseases. These both fascinated and horrified the boy, who carried these images through into adulthood.

Gala Dalí

1894–1982

Born Elena Dmitrievna Diakonova, Russian émigré Gala was a virgin when she married Éluard but soon made up for lost time. After her first taste of sex, she became a nymphomaniac. Both took numerous lovers and she would model nude for anyone who asked her. For a time they lived in a *ménage à trois* with a German painter. Gala's only regret was that she had an 'anatomical problem' that prevented her being sodomized and penetrated vaginally by two men at the same time.

After her marriage to Dalí, she took hordes of young lovers, as well as entertaining Éluard once more. After meeting him again after a long separation, she opened her blouse and said: 'Here, I have a present for you.'

'She was a true nymphomaniac,' said a friend, 'the classic case of a woman who was never satisfied and has to keep on trying with every man she met.' The jealousy that Gala's affairs aroused in Dalí gave him a masochistic delight. He thought it spurred his creativity and he described himself gleefully as 'the King of Cuckolds'. He would line up beautiful men before her. She would take her pick and fondle them openly in front of Dalí.

Gala and Dalí would hold 'sexual experimentation' sessions where they would sit around discussing their sex lives. Gala barred women from these meetings and would regale the assembled throng with graphic details of her amatory exploits, which were always with men.

Everyone, except Gala, was repelled by Dalí's scatological fantasies. She encouraged him, believing that it helped him to come to terms with his sexual inadequacies. She also believed it helped his creativity.

to like to get naked women to crawl through a long red tube he had constructed as if they were being born out of a penis.

He liked having his acolytes pose nude for him, often on a transparent cushion so that he could see their sexual organs in exquisite detail. Or he would get them to stage 'erotic masses'. He pretended to be painting them but, instead, was masturbating behind a blank canvas.

In the chapter of his autobiography entitled 'How to Pray to God without Believing in Him', Dalí relates how he directed the buggery of a young Spanish girl by her lover for the benefit of himself and another spectator. 'I have never been able to tell this story without each time having the wonderful feeling that I had violated the secret of perfect beauty,' he said.

Dalí liked to hover around the couples he got to copulate for him, and then, when it was clear that they were oblivious to anything but their own pleasure, he would make them stop. Then he would throw the humiliated couple out, while he fell to his knees laughing hysterically.

In charge of these entertainments was Captain John Moore, an Irishman who had been a wartime expert on psychological warfare and former head of the Vatican's propaganda department. If Dalí wanted a boy to be sodomized with a plastic dildo, or if he wanted a girl to put lighted straw in her vagina so that he could watch her expression as it singed her pubic hair, Moore arranged it. He would hire palaces and fill them with dwarves, transvestites, trapeze artists, and people of every possible sexual persuasion. All Dalí wanted to do was watch and masturbate.

Dalí also used his surrealism to protect himself from predatory women. He would invite them back to his apartment, get them to strip off and put a freshly fried egg on their shoulder. That was that.

HOWARD HUGHES

FILTHY SEX

1905–1976

A multi-millionaire and movie mogul, Howard Hughes could have practically any woman he wanted. Once established in Hollywood, he went about selecting and seducing all the beautiful women he could find. It has been said that no one in history has spent so much money on their sex life. However, his obsessive fear of germs took over his life, eventually preventing him from having sex with another person for fear of contamination and infection.

Born in Houston, Texas, Howard Hughes was the son of a millionaire manufacturer of oil-drilling equipment. An only child, he was spoilt by both parents. His mother, especially, was over-protective. She had a profound fear of illness and germs and Hughes was rarely allowed to take part in any group activities at school and had only one close friend.

His mother died when he was 16, his father two years later. Hughes persuaded a court to declare that he was legally an adult. He bought the rest of the family out of the Hughes Tool Company and by the age of 19 was a millionaire. Then he headed to Hollywood, where he produced and directed films.

Hughes had a second string to his bow, a passion for aircraft. He founded the Hughes Aircraft Company and bought control of Trans-World Airlines. Serving as a test pilot on the planes he designed and built, he broke transcontinental and world circumnavigation records. During the course of his flying career he crashed three times. Some time in the 1940s he suffered a rather more personal injury. While separating his chow Chang from another dog, he was bitten on the penis. The wound needed six stitches. He was out of action, temporarily, but the bite did not seem to have any lasting effect. However, he never owned a pet again.

FIRST CONQUEST

Hughes married Houston socialite Ella Rice, but he had little time for his wife once they had arrived in California. After three years they divorced and Hughes began his 30-year pursuit of Hollywood movie stars. His first conquest was actress Billie Dove. A former Ziegfeld Follies' girl, she had her first hit in Douglas Fairbanks' *The Black Pirate* in 1926. She became known as 'the American beauty' after the title of one of her films. Even though he was newly married to Joan Crawford, Fairbanks began to take an inordinate interest in his co-star Billie Dove's bust during the filming of *One Night at Susie's* in 1930. But he got annoyed when Joan got her own back by inviting Howard Hughes to a party. Fairbanks had overheard Hughes asking someone to try to get him a date with Joan. When he was reminded that Joan was married to Fairbanks and therefore 'not one of the girls', he said he was prepared to offer her 'a very big present'. Hughes was used to getting what he wanted, whatever it cost. In this case,

> ## Obsessive-Compulsive Disorder
>
> Howard Hughes suffered from an extreme case of OCD or obsessive-compulsive disorder. This is thought to have both psychological and genetic causes. It is the fourth most common mental disorder, affecting 2 to 3 per cent of the US population. These days it is treated by anti-depressant drugs such as fluoxetine or Prozac.

though, he had to make do with Bette Davis instead. Hughes cast her in his movies *The Age for Love* in 1931 and *Cock of the Air* in 1932. But he did not want their affair publicized. When Dell Publications printed a special-issue magazine with Hughes and Billie on the cover, he bought up the entire print run. Then he dropped her.

Hughes used to follow Katharine Hepburn across the country in his private plane, until she dropped him, saying she was bored. Then he had an affair with Ginger Rogers, but she also dropped him after finding him in bed with another actress. His name was also associated with Hedy Lamarr, Ava Gardner, Carole Lombard, Jean Harlow, Lana Turner, Ida Lupino, Ursula Andress and many more.

According to Hollywood fixer Johnny Meyer, although Hughes kept some of the world's most beautiful women under guard all over Los Angeles, he rarely visited them. He had sex with them only once or twice and, probably, never had an orgasm with them. On the quiet, Meyer would fix up rent boys for him. Once, he even set up a date for Hughes with Errol Flynn. Hughes was also thought to have been a lover of Randolph Scott.

Hughes made a huge star out of Jane Russell with his movie *The Outlaw* in 1943. Meanwhile he had agents out looking for fresh material. They would fan out over the country searching for would-be movie stars with perfect faces and perfect bodies – Hughes was particularly interested in breasts. When a suitable candidate was found, she would be shipped off to Los Angeles for a screen test. Hughes had at least five houses in different areas of the city, each occupied by an ambitious starlet or showgirl who was on the payroll of his film company. Hughes would then drop by when he was in the area.

TRAWL FOR TALENT

Hughes would also trawl through magazines for talent, and watch out for new girls on television and on the streets. His detectives would then track them down. On one occasion he sent studio scout Bill Fadiman out to assess Zizi Jeanmaire, the star of the Ballet de Paris, after Hughes had seen a picture of her. When she measured up in Hughes' terms, the entire ballet company was lodged in the RKO Writers' Building while Hughes tried to seduce her. To keep them occupied, he employed a writer to produce a screenplay for them. But after two years, when he still had not got his way, eventually he dropped the project.

Gina Lollobrigida was flown over from Italy to find herself under 24-hour guard in the Town House Hotel. She was permitted to see no one. At the time, she was happily married to a dentist and rejected Hughes' advances. Eventually she escaped and fled back to Italy.

'THE BRASSIERE SHOULD HOLD THE BREASTS UPWARD BUT SHOULD BE SO THIN THAT IT TAKES THE PERFECT SHAPE OF HER BREASTS.'

Howard Hughes

At one time in the 1950s, a Hughes' aide claimed that there were 108 active files on candidates for Hughes' bedroom. Then, in 1960, he watched the Miss Universe contest on TV and signed up seven of the finalists. Waiting around for him in their hotel, they decided that all seven of them could not be destined for stardom and went home.

Hughes favoured teenagers with large breasts. He took a suitable girl to Palm Springs, but her mother tagged

Battle of the Breasts

Jane Russell came to prominence in Howard Hughes' 1943 film *The Outlaw* because of her breasts. Hughes had designed a special cantilevered bra to show off her magnificent bosom to best effect. The idea was that it should look on screen as if she was not wearing a bra. In fact, Russell later claimed that indeed she had not been wearing a bra in *The Outlaw*. She said Hughes' bra was uncomfortable so she did not wear it.

Hughes held the picture back for three years, claiming a ban had been imposed by movie censor Will Hays and the Legion of Decency. The resulting publicity guaranteed that it would be a hit.

In 1954, Jane made another bra-busting epic for RKO. Called *Underwater*, it was merely an excuse to squeeze Miss Russell's considerable bosom into a skin-tight swimsuit. To launch the film, Hughes flew the Hollywood glitterati to Silver Springs, Florida, where he planned to hold the premiere in an underwater theatre built at the bottom of a lake with the first-night audience decked out in aqualungs, flippers and goggles. Afterwards, hand-picked showbiz scribes would get to interview Jane Russell, Debbie Reynolds and an array of other eager starlets from the Hughes stable while they were still dripping wet. However, the party was gate-crashed. A 21-year-old brown-eyed blonde from Pennsylvania had cadged a ticket from columnist Earl Leaf. On the plane out to Florida she sat beside the editor of *Variety*, Joseph Schoenfeld, who was so impressed with her possibilities that he had already made a mental note to give her a puff in one of his columns. After the screening, as the press assembled to await Jane Russell and the other celebrities, the blonde appeared wearing nothing but a pair of high-heeled shoes and a tiny red bikini that was straining at the seams. 'It was the most voluptuous sight I have ever seen,' said one reporter.

The photographers had a feeding frenzy. The stars and Hughes' other Hollywood hopefuls were lost in the scrum. Then, in a fitting climax to the proceedings, the blonde dived into the pool, bursting her bra on the way. Five minutes later, when Jane Russell appeared, the press photographers had run out of film. 'Who's that blonde tomato?' asked Russell.

Annoyed that his star had been upstaged, Hughes' publicity man begged Jane to don a daring bikini. She refused. 'Hell, no,' she said. 'I wear a one-piece. This isn't a cheese-cake competition.' But it was – and she had already lost. The pictures of the near-naked Jayne Mansfield bobbing around in the pool, ineffectually clasping her giant breasts, made the newspapers across the nation.

'Get that girl,' yelled Hughes. 'For a thousand a week, if necessary.' Her agent, however, turned down Hughes' offer as he was well known to have 40 or 50 pretty young actresses under contract stashed in houses around Los Angeles. He slept with them, but rarely got them parts. Instead Jayne started at Warner Brothers for $250 a week.

along. She burst in to find Hughes in bed with her underage daughter. To avoid statutory-rape charges, Hughes settled out of court for $250,000.

In 1957, Hughes was married for a second time to 31-year-old film star Jean Peters, whom he had been dating off and on for 11 years. Hughes liked hair on women and would not allow her to wax, so she appeared in glamour shots looking somewhat hirsute. Jean gave up her career to live in seclusion with him, but during the 1960s he stopped having sex with her for fear of germs. They divorced in 1970 after she had not seen him for three years.

By then Hughes was a hermit, living in seclusion in hotels and penthouses, surrounded by boxes of Kleenex and fighting a losing battle against germs. He had had his first nervous breakdown in 1944 and had become progressively unbalanced. When he died aged 70 in a plane on its way from Acapulco, Mexico, to a hospital in Houston, he weighed less than 68 kilograms (150 pounds) and had long unkempt hair. He was worth $2.3 billion.

ERROL FLYNN

IN LIKE FLYNN

1909–1959

Hollywood actor and heart-throb Errol Flynn was famed for the size of his organ, though witnesses disagreed as to its dimensions. However, he was happy to show it off. Throughout his life he had a penchant for young girls with the merest wisp of pubic hair. And while women flocked to his dressing-room door, in 1942 he was charged with the statutory rape of two minors. The case caused a sensation and enhanced his reputation. He claimed to have spent between 12,000 and 14,000 nights making love, and died exhausted by his efforts at the age of 50.

Errol Flynn was interested in both sexes from an early age. His first love was the family maid in his native Tasmania. When he went to school in Australia, he enjoyed performing a striptease for the other boys, so much so that he always ended up with an erection. He also relished the boys' 'circle jerks'. They would all stand around in a circle masturbating, and the one who came first got the prize – a box of condoms imported from Paris. By this time, Flynn's mother had run off to France, where she took a string of lovers, working her way up to the Aga Khan. Flynn's father, a man of more modest ambition, satisfied himself with the wife of a local tradesman.

The younger Flynn acquired a fiancée, though there was nothing very sexual about their relationship. 'She used to do a bit of grubbing,' he said, 'but I didn't know how to open my fly with a lady present.' Later he was expelled from school for having sex with the daughter of the school laundress. They were caught *in flagrante* in the coal cellar, naked and black, covered with coal dust. He then launched himself into a life of sexual adventure.

To escape the threats of cuckolded husbands, Flynn decided to fornicate his way around the world to England. His travelling companion was a Dutch-American called Dr Gerrit Koets who told Flynn: 'Women are sexier and dirtier than men, bless 'em, and far more perverted – never forget that. They're all sisters under the skin and the foreskin too.' Flynn took on board much of Koets' amorous philosophy.

After shipboard adventures with exotic women and visits to the brothels of Saigon and Calcutta, his real education began in France. 'For example, at Marseilles I saw a braying donkey mounting a French girl,' he said, 'something I can never forget.' He was happy to pay to see such things.

> **'I YIELDED WITH A SMILE TO THE NOW COMPLETE LEGEND OF MYSELF AS A MODERN DON JUAN.'**
> Errol Flynn

PROUD ERECTION

Arriving in England penniless in 1933, Flynn got a job as a leading man in the repertory theatre in Northampton. After the evening performance, young girls aged between 13 and 16 would wait at the stage door for him and follow him back to his digs. Outside, he would line them up and pick the one he would take up to his room. One night, a particularly eager bunch would not disperse and threatened to follow his first choice up the stairs one at a time. So to satisfy his audience, when he had gone upstairs with the girl he had picked, he opened the curtains, stripped naked and showed the gasping girls below his proud erection.

Flynn also had a rich admirer who invited him to her country home for the weekend. 'I was stunned to find myself, late one evening, caught on this bear rug,' he said. 'She had this half-nelson on me. She was so visibly repulsive that I truly felt I was being raped.' He managed to break free, fled to his bedroom, locked the door and slept chastely alone that night.

After appearing in a low-budget British movie, *Murder at Monte Carlo*, he was on his way to Hollywood. Stopping in New York, he visited a club in Harlem, where he stuck his hand up a dress to find more than he bargained for. 'I was paralyzed, holding in my hands ...' he said. 'I didn't know what to do.' He made his excuses and left.

In Los Angeles, he moved in with the movie actress Lili Damita and they married in 1935, but that did not stop him chasing every other woman in town. His one failure was with the virginal Olivia de Havilland. 'I don't think she has a hole between her legs,' said Flynn. In a fit of pique, he put a dead snake in her panties. She found it when she went to put them on and wept.

Exhibitionism

Male exhibitionism or flashing is a relatively mild perversion. Historically it has played a part in fertility rites. In India, 'sky-clad' fakirs would walk the streets naked, ringing bells to summon female devotees from their homes. The women would then pay reverence to the priest's genital organ by embracing it.

The Encyclopedia of Unusual Sexual Practices records an extreme case of exhibitionism. After the end of the Second World War, when ships travelling along the narrow Suez Canal passed a desolate area, as many as 20 naked native men would line up along the shore area. They would thump a drum with their erect penises in a rhythm to a song said to sound like 'Hubba hubba – thump thump – hubba hubba – thump thump.'

Flynn liked to collect souvenirs from his lovers – jewellery, even wedding rings, and items of underwear. He kept these around the house, never even bothering to hide them from Lili. He took more risqué pleasures with underage girls, usually between 13 and 16. His relationships were furtive and intense. He also went for boys between 17 and 19, usually indulging his bisexual tendencies south of the border in Mexico. However, once at a party Flynn took a male prostitute into his bedroom and fellated him. The boy returned the favour, confessing later that he was genuinely turned on by the encounter. Flynn also had a long affair with Tyrone Power.

In Mexico, Flynn also indulged his voyeuristic tendencies. He went to places where men could watch women making love through peepholes in the wall. He also went to a nightclub that featured live sex acts on stage. For a price you could see men and women having sex with animals. Flynn liked to watch other men making love, often in groups, while he made love to a woman. He also installed a two-way mirror in his home so he could watch other couples making love.

Flynn was not averse to an audience himself. At a fancy dress party at William Randolph Hearst's castle at San Simeon, Flynn made off with the young socialite Eloise Ann Onstott, and made love to her in front of 14 security guards. He also got a tremendous kick out of exhibiting himself – with a full erection – to his 'straight' male friends.

'SAN QUENTIN QUAIL'

Flynn had his friend Johnny Meyer find gay actors for him, putting him on the payroll as a full-time pimp. He attended gay orgies, though he preferred bisexual ones where he could pick a man or woman on a whim. There were also trips to the Hollywood High School to check out the young girls – 'jailbait' or 'San Quentin quail', as Flynn would call them.

The Trial of Errol Flynn

In November 1942, Errol Flynn went on trial in Los Angeles for the statutory rape of 17-year-old Betty Hansen and 15-year-old Peggy LaRue Satterlee. Flynn's attorney, Jerry Giesler, was a wily trial lawyer. He picked a jury of nine women and three men, reasoning that women loved Flynn. Betty Hansen told the court that she thought Flynn was undressing her to put her to bed because she was unwell.

'Did he remove all your clothing?' asked the assistant DA.

'All, except my shoes and stockings.'

'And then what happened?'

'He undressed himself.'

'Did he remove all his clothing?'

'Everything except his shoes.'

'What happened next?'

'We, well...'

'What happened next, Miss Hansen?'

'We had an act of intercourse.'

'You state that you had an act of intercourse with Mr Flynn right there in that upstairs bedroom?'

'Yes.'

'And this act was forced on you. I mean to say, it was against your will.'

'It was against my will.'

But Giesler managed to get Betty to admit she was provocatively dressed and that she thought Flynn might help her get a job in the movies. He then asked if she had been held at Juvenile Hall, charged with performing oral sex on her boyfriend – oral sex was a felony in California.

'Did you not admit, Miss Hansen, under oath before the grand jury that you have performed two acts of sexual perversion with a man?' he asked.

Sobbing, Betty Hansen admitted she had. Then it was time for Peggy Satterlee to take the stand. She said that Flynn had come to her cabin and got into bed with her. He had pulled her underskirt up and her panties down and had sex with her, twice. She claimed that on both occasions she resisted. Afterwards, he had brought her a glass of milk and had called her 'JB' – jailbait – in other words he knew that she was underage.

She mentioned that she had seen the moon through the porthole of the cabin. Giesler called in a noted astronomer, who demonstrated that Peggy could not possibly have seen the moon through the porthole of the cabin. It was on the wrong side of the boat.

Giesler then established that Peggy worked in nightclubs as a showgirl and frequently said she was 21 to get work. He also got Peggy to admit that she had had extra-marital relations with another man and an illegal operation – that is, an abortion.

With five jiggers of vodka inside him, Flynn took the stand and simply denied everything. In his summing up, Giesler said that his handsome, rich, famous, movie star client was as pure as the driven snow. His two accusers were lying to avoid prosecution for other felony charges.

The jury was out overnight. The women believed Flynn was innocent. Rape in a narrow bunk four feet off the ground on board the *Sirocco* was impossible, they figured. Two of the men thought he was guilty. Eventually, they gave in and Flynn was acquitted.

Afterwards, women pursued him even more. and his popularity soared. Ironically, his next two films were *Gentleman Jim* – which some joked should be called simply *Jim*, because he had not taken his shoes off before having sex with Betty – and *They Died with their Boots On*. It was then that US servicemen coined the expression 'in like Flynn'.

The rows between Flynn and Lili got worse. One night, columnist Hedda Hopper, who lived next door, complained about their shouting. Flynn came storming out of his house masturbating and ejaculated all over her front door. When he spotted her peeping out of the window, he shouted: 'Will you invite me to come again?' On his yacht *Sirocco*, his mates, known collectively as the Shit Club, would gather under the insignia FFF – Flynn's Flying Fuckers. They held a contest to see who could have sex with the greatest number of young girls. After having sex with 15-year-old Peggy Satterlee, Flynn had to pay off the DA and was warned to check girls' birth certificates in future. It was advice he did not take and he was caught with 17-year-old Betty Hansen.

FRANCIS BACON

THE GILDED GUTTER LIFE

1909-1992

When Francis Bacon began showing signs of effeminacy as a boy, his father, an Irish landowner, had him horsewhipped regularly by his grooms. This was a source of erotic pleasure for Bacon, who responded by having sex with his tormentors. When his father then caught Bacon trying on his mother's underwear, he kicked him out. But indulging a passion for wearing female lingerie was the least of Bacon's artistic habits, and he spent a long life guzzling up a surfeit of debauchery and deviant excess.

Bacon referred to himself as 'completely homosexual' and never contemplated any other option. He recounted only one youthful flirtation with heterosexuality, featuring a prostitute who used to eat chips while her clients went about their business. There was also a rumour that he had once attempted sex with his friend and model Isabel Rawsthorne. It was unsatisfactory.

In 1927, Bacon's father made one last misguided attempt to save him from himself. An uncle, who was a byword for masculinity in the family, was taking a trip to Berlin and was inveigled into taking young Francis with him. During the declining years of the Weimar Republic, Berlin was the European capital of decadence. Every type of sexual temptation was openly on offer. There were 170 homosexual brothels licensed by the police. Young men in full make-up sashayed down the Kurfürstendamm, many of them schoolboys earning a little extra pocket money. And there were clubs where you could watch nude wrestling or government ministers chatting up sailors. Berlin was, as the poet W.H. Auden put it, 'the bugger's daydream'. Bacon was like a kiddie in a sweetshop. His uncle went off in pursuit of women and Bacon went to it. 'Berlin showed me how to follow my instincts,' he said.

After a brief stay in Paris, Bacon returned to London and began living with Jessie Lightfoot, his childhood nanny. And he began to paint. He supported the two of them and his painting by a little casual prostitution. He would advertise himself in *The Times* as a 'gentleman's companion'. The replies poured in. 'My old nanny used to go through them all and pick out the best ones,' he recalled. 'I must say she was always right.'

Bacon flaunted his homosexuality, even though it was against the law. He used to dye his hair with boot polish and wear make-up. One old queen said of Bacon: 'When I knew her, she was more famous for the paint she put on her face than the paint she put on canvas.' Bacon also indulged his passion for sado-masochism. He was famed for his ability to withstand pain. When visiting the doctor's, he would refuse an

Love Is the Devil

In 1998 a film was made about Bacon called *Love Is the Devil*. It told the story of his affair with George Dyer. Bacon, played by Derek Jacobi, surprises a young working-class burglar breaking into his flat and invites him into his bed. The intruder is Dyer, played by Daniel Craig, who later played James Bond. Although Dyer dominates their sex life, as Bacon was a lifelong masochist, Dyer is no match for Bacon socially. Excessive drinking, pill-popping and Bacon's casual infidelities send Dyer into a terminal depression, and he eventually commits suicide. The film was based on the book *The Gilded Gutter Life* by Bacon's drinking buddy Dan Farson, and it won three awards at the Edinburgh International Film Festival.

anaesthetic. Only once did his courage fail him. Fearing that a particularly violent lover was going to kill him, Bacon fled into the street wearing only a pair of fishnet stockings.

In 1935, he gave up painting and threw himself with renewed vigour into a life of brutal sex, excessive drinking and reckless gambling. When he got into financial difficulties, wealthy businessman Eric Hall helped him out, became his lover and encouraged him to paint again. They stayed together for 15 years, even though Hall was married with two children.

NON-STOP ORGY

The war years and the London blackout were a non-stop orgy for Bacon. The prospect of imminent death sharpened everyone's sexual hunger. London's urinals heaved with bodies. 'It was often quite impossible for anyone who genuinely wanted to relieve himself to get in,' he reported. 'In the darkness exposed cocks were gripped by unknown hands, and hard erections thrust into others. Deep inside, trousers were forcibly – or rather tender-forcibly – loosened and the impatient erections plunged into unknown bodies, or invisible lips.'

Curiously, Bacon did not like having sex with other homosexuals. He preferred seducing straight men, who for money or on a sudden whim might succumb. The dislocation of the war provided plenty of opportunities.

Despite his louche lifestyle, Bacon was aware of the death and destruction going on all around him. After volunteering for the ARP (Air Raid Precautions), he was often involved in pulling mangled bodies out of bombed houses, which provided the degenerate images that infused his paintings.

When Bacon no longer needed Hall's money, he replaced him with Peter Lacy, who satisfied his masochistic needs. They met in the newly opened Colony Room, a drinking club in Soho, and, for the first time, Bacon fell in love. 'Of course it was a disaster from the start,' he said. 'Being in love in that extreme way – being totally, physically obsessed by someone – is like having a dreadful disease. I wouldn't wish it on my worst enemy.'

Lacy was very beautiful. The problem was that he liked little boys. Bacon was over 40 by then and did not fit the bill. Nevertheless, Lacy asked Bacon to move into his cottage in Berkshire. 'You could live in the corner of my cottage on straw,' Lacy said. 'You could sleep and shit there.'

'He wanted to have me chained to the wall,' said Bacon. 'He liked to have people watching us as we had sex. And then he liked to have someone bugger me, then bugger me himself right after.' Bacon's relationship with the kinky and neurotic Lacy opened a new well of creativity. In jealous rows Lacy would beat Bacon up, which he loved, but he also slashed Bacon's canvases.

> **'I HAVE BEEN BUGGERED SO OFTEN, IF I BEND DOWN AND OPEN MY MOUTH, YOU CAN SEE DAYLIGHT.'**
> Francis Bacon

In 1967, homosexuality was legalized in Britain. Bacon did not like this. 'Being queer was really so much more interesting when it was illegal,' he said.

CHAINS AND RAZOR BLADES

Bacon loved what he called his 'gilded gutter life' in low dives, preferring it to the increasingly dizzying social circles he was now moving in. One night at a party given

Bacon in Tangier

When Francis Bacon's long-time lover Peter Lacy went to Tangier to indulge his passion for paedophilia, Bacon pursued him there and mingled with the likes of Tennessee Williams, Truman Capote, Nöel Coward, Paul Bowles, Ian Fleming, Allen Ginsberg and William Burroughs. His main hang-out was a bar called Dean's. Ian Fleming, the creator of the fiercely heterosexual James Bond, described it as 'a cross between Wiltons and the porter's lodge at White's'. 'There's nothing but pansies,' Fleming wrote to his wife Ann, 'and I have been fresh meat for them.'

Bacon tried to continue his work in Tangier, sometimes dashing out pornographic paintings for celebrity sitters. But, as in London, Lacy destroyed many of his canvases. However, Bacon did not return to London empty-handed. The poet Allen Ginsberg had given him some pornographic photographs of himself and his latest lover in various hotel bedrooms. Bacon used them as the basis for a series of nudes.

Lacy was drinking increasingly heavily and fell in love with an Arab boy. He phoned Bacon to tell him it was all over between them. Then, much later, he sent Bacon a telegram, begging him to return. When Bacon arrived at Lacy's villa in Tangier, Lacy was not there. There was only Lacy's Arab boy up a tree, picking figs. Lacy came home to find Bacon and the boy in bed together and smashed everything in the place. Eventually he drank himself to death.

for Cecil Beaton and choreographer Frederick Ashton, Bacon was eager to get off to meet his date, a Teddy boy, at Piccadilly Circus. The party's hostess, Ann Fleming, persuaded Bacon to go and pick up the Ted and bring him back. Beaton was terrified. Knowing Bacon, he feared that the Ted would be carrying bicycle chains and razor blades.

In 1964, Bacon began another serious relationship with George Dyer, a small-time crook whom he used as a model and who was 30 years younger than him. He embarked on a series of portraits of Soho bohos, which he felt uniquely qualified to paint. 'Homosexuals are obsessed with the physique,' he said. 'They simply never stop looking at the body. That's why if I want to know what someone really looks like, I've always asked a queer.'

Through Dyer and the actor Stanley Baker, Bacon met the homosexual gangster Ronnie Kray, who fascinated him. He would frequently come around to Bacon's studio, but his men started stealing paintings and Bacon had to pay large sums of money to get them back.

Bacon continued his life of heavy drinking and sexual excess through his sixties and seventies', but Dyer could not keep up the pace. Eight years after meeting Bacon, at the age of 38, he killed himself. Bacon then found a new companion, pub manager John Edwards. But he still went out on drinking sprees which often ended in serious injuries inflicted by sadistic lovers he had picked up along the way.

In 1989, when Bacon was 80, he received several fan letters from a young Spaniard. He was handsome and well educated, very different from the rough trade that Bacon usually preferred. They became passionate lovers, despite an age difference of nearly fifty years. Bacon's new lover flattered his vanity and gave him a new lease of life. He nursed Bacon after he had a kidney removed. Ill again in 1992, Bacon flew to Madrid, against his doctor's advice, to see his young lover. There he was admitted to hospital where he was nursed by nuns. Given the demolition job he did on the Catholic Church in his *Popes* paintings, this was his worst nightmare. Five days after arriving in Spain, Bacon died.

YUKIO MISHIMA
SUICIDE - THE ULTIMATE IN MASTURBATION
1925-1970

For Japanese novelist Yukio Mishima, death was a sexual act. In 1970, he led a raid on the offices of the Self-Defence Force in Tokyo, where he then disembowelled himself and was beheaded. Friends said that, for Mishima, *hara-kiri* was the ultimate in masturbation. A would-be samurai and lover of transvestite geishas, the author had always been a strange fellow, beset by weird fantasies and fetishes.

Born Hiraoka Kimitake, Mishima came to fame at the age of 24 in 1949 with the autobiographical novel *Confessions of a Mask*. In it, he revealed that he was a man incapable of feeling passion or even feeling alive unless he was embroiled in a sadomasochistic fantasy, dripping with blood and death. He said that he had written the book to channel his own homicidal instincts and the pen-name he chose – Yukio Mishima – could be written so that the characters also read 'mysterious devil bewitched with death'.

In *Confessions of a Mask*, the first-person protagonist has his first ejaculation at the age of 12 over a reproduction of the death of Saint Sebastian. The tense agony of the dying saint's arrow-pierced body drives him to ecstasy. The protagonist then dons the mask of homosexuality to hide his own dark feelings. Towards the end of the novel he goes to a brothel to demonstrate to himself, with some satisfaction, that he is not aroused by women.

Mishima was not troubled by women, even as an adolescent. 'Having attained puberty, other boys seemed to do nothing but think immodestly about women,' he said. 'I, on the other hand, received no more sensual impression from "woman" than from "pencil".' Indeed, he was horrified to discover that another picture that stimulated him as a boy – Joan of Arc being burnt at the stake – actually showed a girl. From then on, he hated the sight of women in men's clothing and, when he forced himself to get married, reprimanded his wife for wearing trousers.

DEATH AND CANNIBALISM

At school, Mishima fell in love with a male classmate. As a result he developed three life-long fetishes – for male armpit hair, sweat and white gloves. He also became a frantic masturbator, fuelling his fantasies with images of death and cannibalism.

With the royalties from *Confessions of a Mask*, Mishima could give up work and spend his time cruising gay bars. He fell in love with Akihiro Maruyama, a chanteuse in drag who was called the Edith Piaf of Japan. 'He was as pale as death, so pale that he had a purplish tint,' said Mishima. 'And his body seemed to float in his clothes. Yet he was a narcissist and had a true eye for beauty. In those days, before he began the body building, when he looked at himself with those eyes that could really perceive beauty – and he looked at himself constantly – he was filled with disgust at what he saw.' They were often seen dancing together. Mishima immortalized Maruyama in his novel *Forbidden Colours* and his play *The Black Lizard*.

In 1951, Mishima went to the carnival in Rio, where he could be openly gay. He also enjoyed courting women, but avoided the 'final act'. This was sometimes difficult. One afternoon he had

> 'THE MURDERER KNOWS THAT ONLY BY BEING MURDERED CAN HE BE COMPLETELY REALIZED.'
> Yukio Mishima

to call a friend and beg him to come round to rescue him from the wife of a Japanese businessman who seemed determined to seduce him.

From Brazil he went to New York, where he tried to find his ideal white male partner. Then he headed for Paris, where he met the composer Toshiro Mayuzumi, who took him to a 'bar for pederasts'. Mishima was not best pleased that Mayuzumi hogged all the boys because he could speak French. After a flying visit to London, Mishima made the mandatory gay trip to Greece.

Mutilation

Hara-kiri – ritual disembowelment – is an extreme form of self-mutilation. While seldom performing it themselves, women can be aroused by viewing it. During the Sparticist uprising in Berlin in 1919, the German sexologist Magnus Hirschfeld, author of *The Sexual History of the World War*, wrote that he 'accompanied a woman to the mortuary where, among the hundreds of bodies, some of which were shockingly mutilated or had their throats slit, we discovered her son ... In the identification hall an endless stream of people, mainly women, were filing past the unidentified bodies and an attendant who knew me called my attention to some girls who had for several days continually rejoined the queue, evidently because they could not tear themselves away from the sight of the male bodies which lay, entirely stripped, before them.' He compared their expressions to those seen on the faces of women watching a bullfight.

Hirschfeld also reported that he had attended an execution a few years earlier. 'Next to me,' he wrote, 'stood the State Attorney's wife, who followed the horrible scene – the condemned man screamed and fought the executioners who were dragging him to the scaffold – with a heaving chest and ecstatic groans that sounded almost lustful. As the axe fell, the woman behaved as though she were passing through the moment of orgasm.'

'Greece cured my self-loathing,' he said.

Back in Japan, Mishima tried to woo the daughter of a wealthy industrialist, but brought his mother along with him on dates. He consoled himself with sorties on the gay scene, favouring both the slender, young intellectual type as well as swarthy, hirsute gangsters.

At his 30th birthday party, he told the guests that he was going to kill himself as he could no longer be a beautiful corpse. Instead he took up body-building, going to the gym three times a week. He also took up boxing, but was hopeless and regularly beaten senseless. This was all the more masochistic as he was plagued with stomach cramps and had to inject himself in the belly.

Thinking he had developed a near-perfect body – except for his skinny legs – he posed for magazines and newspapers naked from the waist up. These pictures were swooned over by his fans, whom he called 'literary virgins'. He enjoyed telling the story of how he was almost suffocated by the breasts of an American woman who insisted on dancing with him at an embassy party. Mishima was a mere 155 centimetres (5 ft 2 in) tall. But his real erotic interest was a painful, gory death.

His family put pressure on Mishima to marry, convinced that it would cure him of being gay. He tried to hide his sexuality from his wife, burning his diaries on the eve of his wedding. But he refused to pay up when he was blackmailed and told her everything. A dutiful wife in the geisha tradition, she accepted the situation. However, she objected to the body-building parties he held, where the boys from the gym came around, stripped off and oiled each other's bodies. She was also annoyed when Mishima posed nude for the photographic study *Punishment by Roses*. By then, they had two children.

The Death of Yukio Mishima

Mishima planned his death meticulously. In September 1970, he posed for a series of photographs called *Death of a Man*. These show Mishima as Saint Sebastian, tied to a tree and bristling with arrows, Mishima drowning in mud, Mishima crushed under the wheels of a cement truck. Then there is a picture of Mishima squatting naked on the floor with a short sword buried in his belly, while behind him is seen a long sword ready to decapitate him. These were to be included in a photographic retrospective he planned which would also show a number of earlier nude studies.

Mishima said goodbye to his comrades at the Misty Sauna Baths, telling them that he had now thrown away the pen and had decided to die by the sword. On 25 November 1970, Mishima and his men made for the headquarters of the Self-Defence Force, the only army the country was allowed under the terms of surrender that ended the Second World War. His idea was to shame members of the force with a display of the true samurai spirit.

The party arrived at the headquarters at 10.50 a.m. and took the commandant hostage. A number of officers tried to storm the commandant's office but Mishima and Morita drove them back with a display of swordsmanship. Mishima then gave a short speech to members of the Self-Defence Force drawn up outside. Afterwards he squatted down in front of the window and unbuttoned his uniform jacket.

With Morita behind him, Mishima took a short sword and plunged it into his left side, then drew it across to his right. He had intended to write the character for 'sword' in his own blood but the pain was too debilitating. He slumped forward and Morita brought down a long sword on his neck. Unfortunately Morita was not a skilled executioner, and Himomasa 'Furu' Koga, who was looking on, shouted: 'Again!'

But Morita was paralyzed, so Koga grabbed the sword and despatched Mishima. Then he swung around and beheaded Morita with a single blow.

In his work, Mishima began to mix together erotic desire, patriotism and a quest for death into some kind of mystical cocktail. He began to wear uniforms and founded the Tate no Kai – Shield Society – a small private army of young men with whom he went to training camp. Military and imperial fantasies blended with masochistic visions of a bloody death. He wrote a play called *My Friend Hitler* and posed by a swastika for the poster. Another play featured *seppuku* – ritual suicide by disembowelling. At the dress rehearsal, Mishima stopped the action and asked for more blood. He also wrote the play *Madame de Sade* in 1965.

WARRIOR CODE

Mishima would take out hand-picked recruits from the Shield Society to get to know them better. One he was particularly attracted to was Masakatsu Morita. They spent a lot of time together and a friend said that, in Mishima's company, Morita was 'like a confident fiancée'. There is a tradition of homosexuality in the Japanese warrior code. One of Mishima's favourite books, which he kept always on his desk, was *Hagakure* – 'Hidden among the Leaves' – by the 17th-century samurai Jocho Yamamoto. In it, Yamamoto says: 'Homosexual love goes very well with the way of the warrior.'

By the spring of 1970, Mishima and Morita had decided to die together in what they said would be a 'lovers' suicide'. Previously, Mishima had talked about *kirijini*, the samurai tradition of going down fighting, sword in hand. Now he began to talk only of *seppuku*.

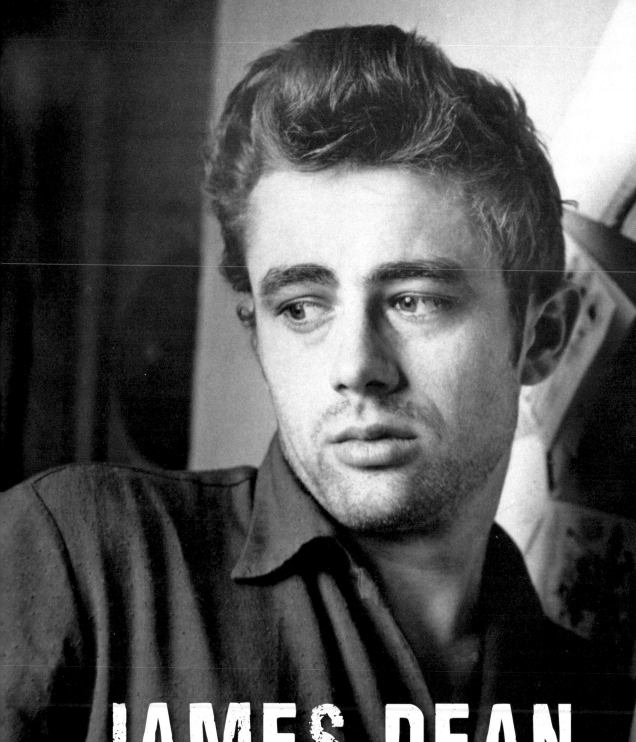

JAMES DEAN

THE HUMAN ASHTRAY

1931-1955

In 1955, actor James Dean appeared as a moody teenager in *East of Eden* and *Rebel Without a Cause* and struck a chord with disaffected youth worldwide. In September that year, he died in a car crash. 'Dean died at just the right time,' said Humphrey Bogart. 'If he had lived, he would never have been able to live up to his publicity.' The heart-throb had become a legend. But ever since there has been speculation over his sex life – aspects of which were very perverted indeed.

James Dean was nine years old when his mother died and his father sent him to Indiana to be brought up by a kindly uncle and aunt. At high school, he was called a sissy and could never get a girlfriend or a date. A lonely boy, he sought the companionship of the Reverend James A. DeWeerd, the local Wesleyan pastor who was then 30. They read poetry together and listened to Tchaikovsky. A war hero, DeWeerd had a huge shrapnel wound in his stomach. One day, he asked Dean whether he would like to put his hand inside the wound. It was almost big enough to accommodate Dean's whole first. This act of intimacy frightened and excited him.

DeWeerd encouraged him to become an actor. At school, he played the lead in *Our Hearts Were Young and Gay*, about the misadventures of two 19-year-old college girls in Paris. But the thing Dean liked most about acting was the make-up.

He dodged the draft by pretending to be gay, then considered feigning a mental illness. Later when Hedda Hopper asked him how he had avoided service in Korea, he said: 'I kissed the medic.' Following his artistic bent, he sketched bountifully endowed young men and produced a candleholder shaped like a woman's vulva. Gleefully, he inserted a candle and lit it.

One of Dean's closest friends and his first biographer, William Blast, admitted having a homosexual affair with him. 'He dabbled in everything,' a girlfriend said. 'He wanted to experiment with life.'

In New York he lived with producer Rogers Brackett. They shared a bed. 'If it was a father–son relationship, it was also incestuous,' said Brackett. 'I loved him and he loved me.' Thanks to Brackett's contacts, Dean soon had a string of introductions to important men who were eager to take him out and give him jobs. Those who knew him said that he only slept with them 'for trade' – that is, to advance himself in the business. Others said he was basically asexual, getting his kicks from acting, motorbikes and fast cars. When asked whether he was gay, he said: 'Well, I'm certainly not going through life with one hand tied behind my back.'

> 'I'VE HAD MY COCK SUCKED BY FIVE OF THE BIG NAMES IN HOLLYWOOD, AND I THINK IT'S PRETTY FUNNY BECAUSE I WANTED MORE THAN ANYTHING TO GET SOME LITTLE PART.'
> James Dean

MOTHERING

Dean had sex with women too. One friend said that basically he just wanted to be mothered. His favourite seduction technique was to curl up with his head in a woman's lap and let her cuddle him. 'All women want to mother you,' he said. 'Give them the chance and before you know it you're home free.'

Amputees

Having a sexual fetish about amputees is called acrotomophilia. If acrotomophiles cannot actually find someone with a missing limb to have sex with, they sometimes manage to get a partner to wrap a hand or a foot with bandages. In his book *Strange Loves: The Human Aspects of Sexual Deviation*, Dr Eustace Chesser reported the case of a man who got his wife to limp across the bedroom on crutches before making love to her. If she did not do this, he was impotent.

This succeeded with the singer-dancer Elizabeth 'Dizzy' Sheridan. He may have loved Dizzy, but he did not give up Brackett, who got him TV work, usually walk-ons. This gave him a new chat-up line when he hung out late at night in bars in the West Village.

Dean continued to bounce between gay and straight sexual partners. One night he turned up to a party with fellow actor Jonathan Gilmore, in drag, as his date. 'Jimmy was neither homosexual or bisexual,' said Gilmore. 'I think he was multisexual.'

Signed to Warner Brothers for *East of Eden*, Dean moved to California, where he bought a motorbike – to scare the hell out of anyone who rode with him – and a 1953 MG, which he soon traded in for a Porsche Spyder. One of the girls he picked up was 17-year-old Arlene Sachs, who said she was a virgin. He went back to her apartment anyway. 'I guess he didn't realize I was telling the truth until I screamed, and suddenly there was blood all over,' she said. He mumbled an apology and left.

Later, Arlene invited him to an 'orgy'. It was a tame affair. The boys took off their shirts. The girls removed their blouses and they all got under a blanket together. But Dean called their bluff. 'Okay, if you want to stage a so-called orgy, I'll show you orgy,' he said. And he got his penis out and began masturbating. 'That is not what I wanted to happen,' said Arlene.

She teased him about his homosexual tendencies, but did not take them seriously. One day she overheard him on the phone to a male movie star, saying: 'I really want to cock you.' On another occasion, he complained that his 'ass hurt'. When she asked why, he said: 'It was Rogers. I shouldn't have been with Rogers.'

Arlene closed her ears to all this. She did not want to believe that he was having homosexual affairs while he was making love to her. The affair ended when Arlene invited him over to dinner and he arrived with a hat-check girl called Barbara. Arlene went out to the grocery store to get some things. When she returned, it was clear that Dean had made love to Barbara. 'I went into the kitchen and thought I was going to faint and throw up at the same time,' she said.

THE MEAT RACK

In 1954, Dean fell for the Sardinian beauty Pier Angeli, but her mother objected because he was not a Catholic. She married Vic Damone instead. Rejected, Dean dated a string of other girls. But at night he would cruise the gay meat rack of Hollywood Boulevard. In the oral history of the small leather and chains clubs there, it was said that he was 'an instant hit with the fist-fuck set' because he would do things that no one else would do.

One night in a bar on Sunset Strip, Dean was with Jonathan Gilmore when they met a girl who had lost a leg in a motorcycle accident. They took her back to Dean's place where they drank and smoked dope. 'Then Jimmy drew a face on the stump of her leg with lipstick,' said Gilmore. 'He draws the eyes, the nose, the mouth. And he starts kind of relating and talking to

Rock Hudson

1925–1985

At the same time that James Dean was getting into pictures, Rock Hudson was Hollywood's rising star. The fan magazines identified Dean, Hudson and Tab Hunter, who was also homosexual, as Hollywood's most eligible bachelors, all on the lookout for the right woman. Hudson starred in Dean's last picture, *Giant*, along with Elizabeth Taylor.

Hudson had been born Roy Sherer in Winnetka, Illinois, and at the age of eight, after seeing a Jackie Cooper movie, he decided to become a film star. After wartime service in the US navy, he went to Los Angeles and moved in with the immaculately coiffeured Ken Hodge, the 36-year-old producer of Lux Radio Theater, who suggested he change his name to Rock Hudson. He allowed himself to be seduced by talent scout Henry Wilson, who got him a part in *Fighter Squadron*. Universal then put him under contract. Soon he was getting 150 proposals of marriage every week.

Hudson played the suave, handsome boyfriend in his films opposite Doris Day. It was a role he honed off the screen too, though he was in constant danger of being exposed. *Confidential* magazine offered one ex-lover $10,000 for his story. Wilson got it spiked. When appearing at premieres with starlets did not quash the rumours surrounding his sexuality, Wilson arranged for Hudson to marry Wilson's secretary, Phyllis Gates. He went into the closet and did not come out for 14 years. Meanwhile he had affairs with other boys behind her back.

When the Hudsons split, Rock moved into a new home, the Castle, where he had all-boy parties around the pool. He also spent time in the bath-houses of San Francisco. The inevitable happened. He contracted AIDS, dying of the disease in 1985.

the face. Next he wants me to fuck her and he's going to sit in a chair and watch while I fuck her. So I fucked her while he watched. Then he had me take her to where she was living. And when I came back he was gone.'

During the filming of *Rebel Without a Cause*, Dean was involved with co-star Natalie Woods after a hairy trip up Mulholland Drive. 'We did the impossible,' he said. 'We made love in the Spyder.' There were rumours that both of them were sleeping with director Nicholas Ray. They were both close to Dennis Hopper. One night the young night clerk at the El Paisano Lodge recalled seeing Dean and Hopper rushing through the hotel brandishing a woman's panties, bra, slip, blouse and skirt. Outside in a car, he found a waitress from El Paso, naked. 'They talked me out of my clothes, then ran off,' she whimpered. The night clerk got a blanket, which the nude girl wrapped around herself, and then she disappeared into the night. Dean also had an affair with Ursula Andress, before Howard Hughes took her off his hands.

At six o'clock on the afternoon of 30 September 1955, Dean ran his Porsche full speed into the side of a black-and-white sedan that was crossing Route 466 near Cholame, California. His neck was broken. The coroner noted that Dean's torso was covered in scars. Towards the end of his life he had entered the twilight world of S&M. In an East Hollywood leather bar called The Club where he was known as the 'Human Ashtray', Dean would bare his chest and beg people to stub their cigarettes out on him.

While the world mourned the loss of a great movie star, few in the business missed him, partly because he gave crabs to half the cast and crew of *Rebel Without a Cause*.

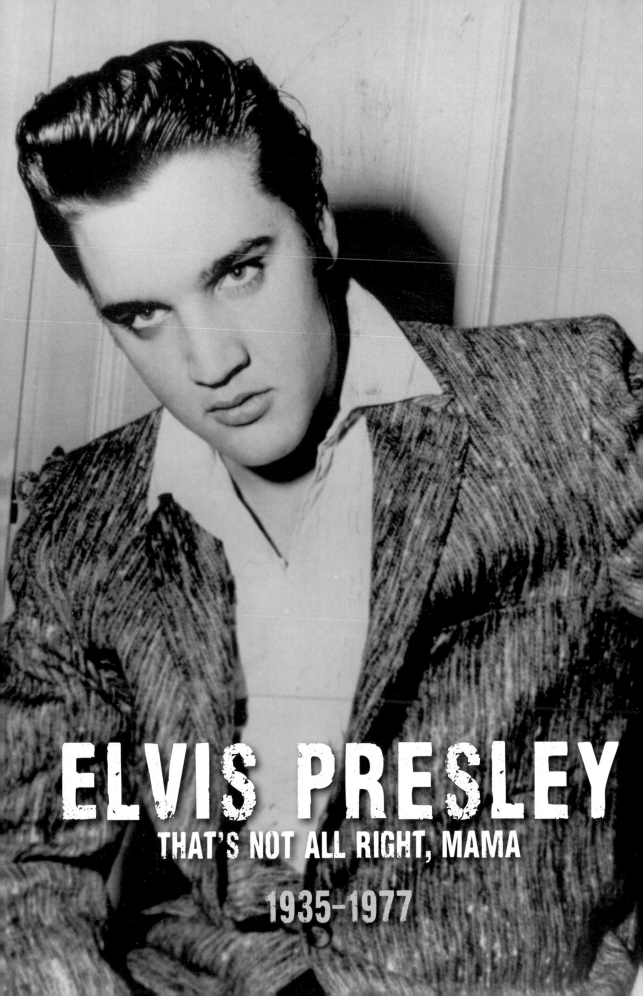

ELVIS PRESLEY

THAT'S NOT ALL RIGHT, MAMA

1935–1977

As a young rocker, Elvis Presley was considered to be a moral threat to America. Hedda Hopper called him a 'menace to young girls'. He was denounced from countless pulpits and, when he appeared on *The Ed Sullivan Show* in 1956, the cameras only showed him from the waist up. Initially shy, he soon found he could have any woman he wanted. But as he grew older, fatter and addicted to drugs, he needed more specialized turn-ons to arouse him.

Born to a poor family in Tupelo, Presley was an identical twin, but his brother, given the name Jesse Garon, was stillborn. Brought up an only child, he became extremely close to his mother Gladys, particularly after his father went to jail. During his eight-month incarceration, the family lost its home and Gladys and her son moved in with relatives. They were good God-fearing folk and Presley's first musical influences were the hymns sung in the Assembly of God church he attended with his mother.

At school, he was bullied by his classmates as a 'mama's boy'. His mother lived for him and told him that, despite the family's poverty, they were as good as anyone. At the age of ten he appeared on stage for the first time at the Mississippi–Alabama Fair and Dairy Show, singing 'Old Shep'. At the age of 11 his parents bought him a guitar, because they could not afford the rifle he wanted. Soon afterwards the family moved to Memphis, where he became influenced by the music of African-Americans, including Ike Turner who, in 1951, had made the first rock-and-roll record, 'Rocket 88'.

After high school, Presley got a job as a truck driver and, for $4, made a record as a birthday present for his mother. This brought him to the attention of producer Sam Philips at Sun Records, who famously said: 'If I could find a white man with the Negro sound and the Negro feel, I could make a billion dollars.'

'ELVIS THE PELVIS'

Philips was right. Presley's recording of Arthur Crudup's 'That's All Right (Mama)' was a local hit. But it was his stage performances that women found electrifying. The animal sexuality of his gyrating hips sent women into a frenzy. He became known as 'Elvis the Pelvis' and 'Sir Swivel Hips'. Many were outraged. In 1955, the Florida police forced him to perform without moving.

By 1956, Presley was a millionaire. His first appearance on *The Ed Sullivan Show* was seen by 54 million people. His TV ratings were higher than President Eisenhower's. He was America's most eligible bachelor, but when it came to marriage, he was not keen. 'Why buy a cow when you can get milk through the fence?' he said. The following

Candaulism

Candaulism involves three people, two of whom have sex while the third looks on. In the early 20th century in France, men would take their wives to brothels to watch shows where prostitutes had sex, some wearing strap-on penises and playing the part of the man. The men would then arrange for another customer to have sex with their wives while they looked on. If a man had not brought his wife, he would pay another man to have the prostitute of his choice while he watched.

year he moved his family into Graceland, a 23-room mansion in Memphis. Just after Presley had begun his Hollywood career in 1957, he was drafted into the army. Before he was posted overseas, his mother died. Stationed in Germany, he met 14-year-old Priscilla Beaulieu, the daughter of a US army officer. When Presley returned to the USA, her father allowed Priscilla to go with him. Before she arrived in Memphis, Presley showed her photograph to his stepmother and said: 'I've been to bed with a thousand women in my life. This is the one, right here.'

> ## 'I DON'T FEEL SEXY WHEN I'M SINGIN'. IF THAT WAS TRUE I'D BE IN SOME KIND OF INSTITUTION AS SOME KIND OF SEX MANIAC.'
> Elvis Presley

According to Presley's secretary, he started sleeping with Priscilla, who was then 15, as soon as they arrived at Graceland. Years later, Priscilla made discreet references to having sex before they married when she was 21. The marriage in 1967 put an end to an affair that Virginia Sullivan – a cashier in a movie theatre – claimed she had been having with him since 1953. At 14 years, that would make it easily his longest sexual relationship.

Presley did not take Priscilla with him when he filmed in Hollywood. His name was linked with an endless list of actresses, including Ann-Margaret and Tuesday Weld. In Graceland, Priscilla had to put up with the constant presence of the Memphis Mafia, 15 of his redneck buddies who were employed as bodyguards, valets, chauffeurs and panders. They were ordered to stay away from any woman Presley wanted. On the other hand, their girlfriends were fair game for him.

Exactly nine months after he married Priscilla, their daughter Lisa Marie was born. The strains in the relationship began to show. Presley had a life-long aversion to married women, especially those who had children. He once dropped a girlfriend flat when he discovered that she was a mother.

GIRL-TYPE GIRLS

After five years of marriage, Priscilla left him for her karate teacher, Mike Stone. Presley settled $2 million on her, then sought comfort in food, drugs and women. Throughout his life, Presley liked young girls, preferably girls that were inexperienced, so they could not make comparisons. He liked 'girl-type girls' – slim, petite and feminine women. He did not like big breasts, preferring shapely legs and buttocks. But his biggest turn-off was big feet. And despite surrounding himself with almost exclusively male company, he hated homosexuals.

After Priscilla left, he took up with Linda Thompson, Miss Tennessee 1972. She was still a virgin when she met him and was utterly devoted. They stayed together for several years. But when he started dating other women and inviting Linda along too, the relationship started to peter out.

In the last year of his life he had an affair with 19-year-old Ginger Alden, Miss Memphis Traffic Safety 1976. Like his other mistresses, he gave her an $85,000 ring and a Cadillac. Although women all over the world still wanted to sleep with him, he became uninterested, saying: 'Bed is for sleeping in.' The women who made it as far as his bedroom found themselves disappointed when the drug-raddled Presley lost interest. Even when Presley no longer wanted sex himself, he did like watching. He had two-way mirrors installed so that he

Michael Jackson

1958–2009

Elvis Presley's daughter Lisa Marie moved from a father who was the 'King of Rock' to a husband who was the 'King of Pop' when she married Michael Jackson in 1994. This was the year after the first allegations of child sex abuse had been levelled against Jackson.

In the summer of 1993, 13-year-old Jordan Chandler claimed that Jackson had touched his penis. Jackson denied this and refused to settle with the Chandlers. However, his deteriorating health left him in no state to face a long trial. In the face of further allegations of kissing, masturbation and oral sex, Jackson submitted to a strip search. Doctors concluded that his genitals did not match the detailed description given by Jordan Chandler. Friends said he never recovered from the humiliation.

The press remained unconvinced and continued to paint him in an unfavourable light. On 1 January 1994, in an attempt to draw a line under the coverage, he paid off the Chandlers with a $22-million settlement. Five months later he married Lisa Marie. They divorced after less than two years, but remained friends.

In 1996, Jackson married a dermatological nurse, Deborah Rowe, who gave him two children. He had a third child from another mother. In 2003, in a series of TV interviews with Martin Bashir, Jackson was seen holding hands and discussing sleeping arrangements with 13-year-old Gavin Arvizo, who later accused him of sexual abuse. Jackson was charged with seven counts of child molestation and two counts of administering intoxicating substances to Arvizo.

On 13 June 2005, Jackson was acquitted on all counts. But the strain had taken its toll. He reportedly became dependent on Demerol. The settlement with the Chandlers and legal fees in the Arvizo case had eaten into his fortune. He was finally forced to close his Neverland ranch.

To recoup his finances, Jackson announced that he would play a comeback concert at London's O2 arena. The demand for tickets was so great that it had to be extended to 50 dates. This, he said, would be his 'final curtain call'. However, just three weeks before the concerts were to begin, he died in Los Angeles of cardiac arrest.

could watch other couples making love, or women undressing or going to the bathroom. He would also videotape them so he could review the action later. In his later years he became a dedicated voyeur. When he got a girl into his bedroom, he would give her a sleeping pill. Then he would slip into a nearby room where he would watch two especially pretty prostitutes he had picked having sex. Once he was sufficiently aroused, he would 'make a dead run to his bedroom and make it with his girl'.

TWO OR THREE A DAY

There is no record of exactly how many women Presley went to bed with but when he told his stepmother in 1960 that he had slept with a thousand women, no one thought he was exaggerating. Between the ages of 20 and 30, when he was young and fit, he often went through two or three women a day.

At the age of 42, Presley was found dead in his bathroom. The cause of death was a heart attack – not an overdose – though ten different drugs were found in his bloodstream. Mass hysteria followed his death. Women flocked to Graceland, saying they did not want to live in a world without Elvis. Others claimed to have made love to his ghost.

DENNIS NILSEN

KILLING FOR COMPANY

B. 1945

Dennis Nilsen was a necrophile killer – one of the rare cases of a man who murders to have sex with a corpse. He would lure his victims home, strangle them, then have sex with their dead bodies. That way his lover could not leave him. During the day he would keep the body hidden in his small flat, then bring it out at night for sex. After a while, though, it would begin to decay and he would have to dispose of it. This proved to be his downfall.

Dennis Nilsen was obsessed with death from an early age. He was born in Fraserburgh, a small town on the bleak northeast coast of Scotland, where his father, a Norwegian soldier who had escaped to Scotland after the German invasion of his homeland in 1940, had married local girl Betty Whyte in 1942. The marriage ended in divorce a few years later. Nilsen grew up with his mother, elder brother and younger sister, but the strongest influence on him were his mother and his stern, pious grandparents.

The young Nilsen was sullen and intensely withdrawn. The only person who could penetrate his private world was his grandfather, Andrew Whyte. A fisherman, he was Nilsen's hero. He would regale the little boy with tales of the sea and their ancestors lost beneath its churning waves. When Whyte died of a heart attack at sea in 1951, he was brought home and laid out on the dining-room table. Nilsen was invited to see his grandfather's body. At the age of six, he got his first glimpse of a corpse. From that moment, the images of death and love fused in his mind.

Nilsen left school at 15 and joined the army. After basic training he was sent to the Catering Corps. There he was taught how to sharpen knives – and how to dissect a carcass. During his life in the army, Nilsen only had one close friend. He would persuade him to pose for photographs, sprawled on the ground as if he had just been killed in battle.

One night in Aden, Nilsen got drunk and fell asleep in the back of a cab. He awoke to find himself naked, locked in the boot. When the cab driver returned, Nilsen played dead. Then as the Arab manhandled him out of the boot, Nilsen grabbed a jack handle and beat him around the head. Nilsen never knew whether he had killed the man or not, but the incident had a profound effect on him. Afterwards he had nightmares of being raped, tortured and mutilated.

SEEING DEATH FIRST-HAND

After leaving the army, Nilsen joined the police force. Part of his training included a visit to a mortuary so that new recruits could become accustomed to seeing death first-hand. The partially dissected corpses he saw in the morgue fascinated Nilsen. Death became an obsession. At home, he would pretend to be a corpse, whitening his skin with talcum powder and smearing blue paint on his lips. Looking at himself in a mirror, he would then masturbate.

Eleven months after joining the police force, Nilsen caught two men committing an act of gross indecency in a car park, but he could not bring himself to arrest them and resigned. He settled in north London, where he took a job in an employment agency. He did well at work, but began to crave a lasting

> **'I'LL TELL YOU EVERYTHING. I WANT TO GET IT OFF MY CHEST, NOT HERE BUT AT THE POLICE STATION.'**
> Dennis Nilsen

relationship. He had been aware of his attraction to other men in the army and the police force, but had repressed it. Now he felt free to act on his urges. In 1975, he met a young man called David Gallichen outside a pub. They moved into a flat together at 195 Melrose Avenue. But after two years Gallichen left, plunging Nilsen back into a life of loneliness.

On New Year's Eve 1978, Nilsen met a teenage Irish boy in a pub and took him home, but they were too drunk to have sex. In the morning, Nilsen was afraid the boy would want to leave when he woke up. To make him stay, Nilsen put a tie around his neck and strangled him. Then he gave the dead boy a bath and lay for a while on the bed, just holding him. The following day he masturbated over the naked corpse. After a week, he hid the corpse under the floorboards.

Necrophilia

The Greek historian Herodotus noted that the bodies of beautiful women in Egypt were not given to the embalmers immediately after death. Instead they would be kept for three or four days, because it was feared that the embalmers would have sex with the corpse.

At one time a fiancé in India was expected to have sex with the corpse of his intended bride if she died before they were married.

During the French campaigns in Morocco between 1919 and 1926, and during the Russo-Turkish wars, soldiers would sodomize the dying so that they could enjoy the anal spasm that occurs at death.

Nearly a year later, Nilsen met Kenneth Ockenden, a Canadian tourist, in a pub in Soho and took him home. Realizing that Ockenden would soon be returning to Canada, Nilsen strangled him. He stripped and washed the body, then put it to bed so that he could sleep next to it. The following day, he took photographs of Ockenden's corpse. He would sit the body in an armchair so he could pretend they were watching TV together. Then, when it was time for bed, he would undress the body and have sex with it.

While Ockenden's disappearance had made the news, no one came knocking on Nilsen's door. He now thought he could get away with his crimes and began going out looking for fresh victims. He lured 16-year-old runaway Martin Duffey home, partially strangled him and drowned him in a sinkful of water. Then he stripped and bathed the corpse, took it to bed and masturbated over it. Nilsen did not even fancy 27-year-old Billy Sutherland, but Sutherland followed him home one night. Nilsen vaguely remembered strangling him. There was certainly a dead body in the flat in the morning.

Nilsen did not even know the names of some of his victims. He was not interested in them – only in their bodies, their dead bodies. The murder routine was always much the same. That part was mechanical. But once they were dead, they really turned him on. Touching the corpse would give him an erection. One victim had fought him off and went to the police, but they took no action, considering the incident a domestic disagreement.

EVIL-SMELLING GREY SLUDGE

When the hiding places in the Melrose Avenue flat were full, Nilsen began cutting up the corpses. He left the internal organs out in the garden for the rats and birds to dispose of. The rest he burnt on a bonfire, putting a car tyre on top to disguise the smell. He then moved to a small attic flat at 23 Cranley Gardens, Muswell Hill, in a deliberate attempt to stop the murders. But they did not

Jeffrey Dahmer

1960–1994

Milwaukee mass murderer Jeffrey Dahmer went one step further than Dennis Nilsen in his murderous perversion. To dispose of the bodies of his victims, he turned to cannibalism.

As a child Dahmer would ride around the neighbourhood looking for dead animals that he could dissect. At the age of 18, he picked up 19-year-old hitchhiker Steven Hicks, and brought him back to his empty house. When Hicks wanted to leave, Dahmer hit him with a dumb-bell, then strangled him. He dragged Hicks' body into the crawl space under the house and dissected it. Later he stripped the flesh and pulverized the bones with a sledgehammer, scattering the remains around the garden.

In 1982, Dahmer moved in with his grandmother in the West Allis district of Milwaukee. Soon afterwards he was sentenced to a year's probation for masturbating publicly in front of two 12-year-old boys. Six days after the end of his probation, he picked up 24-year-old Stephen Tuomi in a gay club. They went to the Ambassador Hotel to have sex. When Dahmer awoke, he found Tuomi dead and realized he must have strangled him. He took the body home in a suitcase, cut it up, put the bits in plastic sacks and left them out for the garbage collector.

Dahmer then began taking young homosexuals back to his grandmother's basement for sex, before strangling and dismembering their bodies. But his grandmother began complaining about the terrible smell that persisted even after the garbage was collected. Dahmer moved into a small apartment in a run-down, predominantly black area. On his first night there, he lured Keison Sinthasomphone, a 13-year-old Laotian boy, back to the flat and drugged him. The boy somehow managed to escape. Dahmer was arrested and charged with sexual assault and enticing a minor for immoral purposes. While out on bail, he picked up 26-year-old bisexual Anthony Sears. Fearing that the police were watching his apartment, he took Sears back to his grandmother's basement for sex. Then Dahmer drugged him and dismembered his body, keeping the skull as a macabre souvenir.

He began offering young African-American males money to pose for nude photographs. Back at his apartment, he would drug them, strangle them and perform oral sex with the corpse, which he would then dismember. He began photographing the dissections, keeping body parts in the fridge.

Dahmer's next victim was by chance Keison Sinthasomphone's older brother, 14-year-old Konerak. Dahmer drugged the boy, stripped him and raped him but then, instead of strangling him, Dahmer went out to buy some beer. On his way back to the apartment, Dahmer saw Konerak out on the street. He was naked, bleeding and talking to two black girls. One of them had called the police and two patrol cars arrived. Dahmer convinced the police that Konerak was 19 and they had had a lovers' tiff. Back at the apartment, Dahmer strangled Konerak and dismembered him.

More victims followed and Dahmer began sodomizing the corpses. After he had killed at least 17 men, Tracy Edwards, a young black man who had just arrived from Mississippi, managed to escape, even though he was drugged and handcuffed. He directed the police to Dahmer's apartment, where an officer opened the fridge door to find a human head.

Dahmer was convicted of 15 murders and sentenced to 15 life terms, totalling 957 years in prison. On 28 November 1994, he was beaten to death by another inmate.

stop. Now he had no floorboards to hide the bodies under and no garden where he could dispose of the pieces. Instead, he began dissecting the bodies, boiling the flesh from the bones, then dicing the remains and flushing them down the lavatory.

Unfortunately, the drains in Muswell Hill were not built to handle bodies. When a workman came to clear a blockage, he found an evil-smelling grey sludge that he suspected was human flesh. The police were called. That evening they interviewed Nilsen, who quickly confessed to killing 15 or 16 men. More body parts were found in his flat. When his lawyer asked him why he had done it, Nilsen replied: 'I'm hoping you will tell me that.'

GLOSSARY

Acomoclitic: preference for hairless genitals

Acousticophilia: arousal from sound

Acrophilia: arousal from heights or high altitudes

Acrotomophilia: arousal over a partner with a missing limb

Adolescentilism: cross-dressing or playing the role of an adolescent

Agonophilia: arousal by a partner who pretends to struggle

Agoraphilia: arousal by open spaces or having sex outdoors

Agrexophilia: arousal from others knowing you are having sex

Albulophilia: arousal from water

Algophilia: sexual gratification through pain

Alloerasty: the use of the nudity of another person to arouse a partner

Allopellia: reaching orgasm from watching other people having sex

Allorgasmia: arousal from fantasizing about someone other than one's partner

Allotriorasty: arousal from partners of other nations or races

Alphamegamia: arousal from partner of different age group

Altocalciphilia: high-heel fetish

Alvinolagnia: stomach fetish

Amatripsis: masturbation by rubbing labia together

Amaurophilia: preference for a blind or blindfolded sex partner

Amelotasis: attraction to absence of limb

Amokoscisia: arousal or sexual frenzy with desire to slash or mutilate women

Amomaxia: sex in a parked car

Amychesis: act of scratching partner during sexual passion

Anaclitism: arousal over activities or objects associated with infancy

Anaelitism: arousal from items used as infant

Analinctus: licking of the anus

Analingus: rimming or penetration of the anus with tongue

Androgyny: having both male and female characteristics

Androidism: arousal from robots with human features

Andromania: nymphomania

Androminetophilia: arousal from female partner who dresses like male

Androsodomy: anal sex with a male partner

Angelism: the inability to make love to an idealized partner

Anililagnia: arousal from older female sex partner

Anisonogamist: attraction to either older or younger partner

Anomeatia: anal sex with a female partner

Anophelorastia: arousal from defiling or ravaging a partner

Anophilemia: kissing of the anus

Anoraptus: rapist who only attacks elderly women

Antholagnia: arousal from smelling flowers

Anthropophagolagnia: rape with cannibalism

Anthropophagy: cannibalism

Aphrodisiacs: drugs stimulating a sexual response

Apotemnophilia: person who has sexual fantasies about losing a limb

Arachnephilia: arousal from spiders

Arborophilia: arousal over trees

Asceticism: religious self-denial often including celibacy

Asphyxiaphilia: arousal from lack of oxygen

Asthenolagnia: arousal from weakness or being humiliated

Autagonistophilia: exhibitionism, arousal from exposing naked body or genitals to strangers while on stage or while being photographed

Autassassinophilia: arousal from orchestrating one's own death by the hands of another

Autoerotic asphyxia: arousal from oxygen deprivation and sometimes risk of dying

Automysophilia: arousal from being dirty or defiled

Autonepiophilia: infantilism; arousal from dressing or being treated like an infant

Autopederasty: person inserting their own penis into their anus

Autophagy: self-cannibalism or eating own flesh

Autosadism: infliction of pain or injury on oneself

Avisodomy: breaking neck of a bird while penetrating it for sex

Axillism: stimulation from the penis penetrating an armpit

Barosmia: arousal from smell

Basoexia: arousal from kissing

Bell dancing: self-flagellation with bells or other ornaments hanging from the skin

Belonephilia: arousal from use of needles

Bestiality: sex with animals

Bestialsadism: cruelty or mutilation of animals

Biastophilia: preference for violent rape of victims

Bigynism: sex between one male and two females

Bihari surgery: cutting ligament above the penis to make it appear longer

Bisexuality: sexual attraction to both sexes

Bivilism: sex between one female and two males

Blastolagnia: person aroused by young females

Blood sports: sex games which involve blood; borderline self-mutilation; automasochism

Bondage: physical or mental restriction of a partner

Bordellos: houses of prostitution

Bouginonia: female masturbation from the use of objects such as dildos that stretch open the vagina

Brachioprolic eroticism: a deep form of fisting where the arm enters the anus

Buggery: anal sex

Butt plug: anal inserts used for masturbation

Candaulist: spouse who gets arousal from watching their partner having sex with someone else

Capnolagnia: arousal from watching others smoke

Castration: removal of the scrotum, testicles or penis

Cat fighting: women fighting without rules and often tearing off each other's clothing

Catamite: a boy kept for homosexual practices

Cataphilist: male submitting to female

Catatasis: stretching of the penis

Catheter: plastic tube inserted into urethra

Catheterophilia: arousal from use of catheters

Chastity belts: leather or metal belts used to prevent genital penetration

Chastity: sexual purity

Chemise cagoule: long heavy night shirt with hole for penis

Chezolagnia: masturbation while defecating

Choreophilia: dancing to orgasmic release

Chrematistophiliac: person aroused by having to pay for sex or having sex partner steal from them

Chronophilia: arousal from passage of time; arousal from older partner

Chubby chasers: people who are aroused by obesity in partner

Circumcision: the removal of foreskin on genitals

Clamps: metal, plastic or wood fasteners used on nipples or genitals

Claustrophilia: arousal from being confined in small space

Clitoridectomy: surgical removal of the clitoris

Clitorilingus: licking of the clitoris

Clitoromania: nymphomania

Cock rings: rings placed around the base of the male genitals to maintain erections

Coitobalnism: sex in a bathtub

Coitophohia: fear of sexual intercourse

Coitus: sexual penetration with orgasm

Coitus à cheval: couple having sex on the back of an animal or one acting out role of horse

Concubinage: use of female slaves as sex partners; living with sex partner without being married

Coprography: writing obscene words or phrases, usually in public toilets

Coprolagnia: arousal from faeces

Coprolalia: arousal from using obscene language

Coprophilia: arousal over faeces and defecation

Cynophilia: sex with dogs

Defilement: arousal from partner or self becoming dirty or wet

Dogging: sexual activity in a car while others watch from outside

Doraphilia: arousal from animal fur or leather

Douche: to rinse out the anus or vagina

Drag queens: gay men who dress in female clothing

Emetophilia: arousal from vomit, *see* Roman showers

Endytophilia: arousal only from partners who are clothed

Enema: insertion and expulsion of fluids into/from the anus

Entomophilia: arousal from insects or using them in sex play

Ephebophilia: attraction to adolescent sex partner

Eproctophilia: arousal from flatulence

Erotica: sexual literature and photos

Erotographomania: arousal from writing love poems or letters

Erotomania: unreasonable love of a person not interested in the lover

Erotophobia: fear of sexual love

Eunuchs: castrated men

Exhibitionism: compulsion to display one's genitals in public

Felching: sucking semen out of vagina or anus; or inserting animals into anus or vagina

Fellatio: oral sex on a male

Fetish: an object that replaces people as primary object of love

Fetishism: arousal by objects or activities not directly involved in sex

Fisting: inserting a fist or hand into the vagina or anus

Flagellation: whipping for religious reasons or for sexual gratification

Fratrilagnia: arousal from having sex with one's brother

Frottage: rubbing your body against partner or object for arousal

Gang bangs: sex with a series of partners, not necessarily consensually

Gerontophilia: attraction to a partner whose age is that of different generation

Golden showers: urinating onto a partner's body

Gomphipothia: arousal by the sight of teeth

Graphelagnia: arousal from photographs of nudity or sex

Gregomulcia: arousal from being fondled in a crowd

Group sex: sex with more than one partner or in close proximity of others

Gymnocryptosis: females talking about sex life of husbands

Gynecaeum: area where Greeks kept wives at home and separated from other men

Hebephilia: men aroused by teenage boys

Incest: sex with a close family member

Incubus: a spirit who was thought to lie on top of women and have sex while they slept

Infantilism: cross-dressing as a young child for sex play

Infibulation: closing vagina with suture

Lactaphilia: arousal from lactating breasts

Lesbianism: sexual love between two women, see Sapphism

Lupanar: brothel

Masochism: sexual arousal through pain

Massage: rubbing of the body to increase circulation

Masturbation: orgasm not involving penetration of partner; self pleasuring

Ménage à trois: a husband and wife having sex with a third party

Misogynist: a man who hates women

Misogyny: hatred of women by either sex

Mixoscopia: orgasm dependent on watching others having sex

Narcissism: self-love

Narratophilia: person who is aroused by discussing sex with others

Nasophilia: nose fetish

Necrophilia: having sex with corpses

Necrosadism: mutilation of corpses

Nymph: young woman or nature goddesses

Nymphomania: uncontrollable desire of women for sex

Omniphiliac: lover of all varieties of sexual activity

Onanism: masturbation or withdrawing penis from vagina before ejaculation

Oral sex: contact between the mouth and genitalia; the use of the mouth in sex play

Orgasms: climax of sexual excitement

Paedophilia: sex with minors

Pander: a procurer

Paraphilia: arousal by unusual or socially unacceptable object or act

Perineum: the area between the genitals and the anus

Perversion: sexual acts that differ from the norm

Phone sex: arousal by conversation between partners on a phone

Polygyny: having multiple wives

Pornography: explicit depictions of sex

Procurer: a person who solicits or provides prostitutes for clients

Prostitution: sex performed for financial gain

Pygmalionism: a statue fetishism where person rubs their body against statue

Red light district: area with bordellos and perhaps street prostitutes

Roman showers: vomiting on a partner, usually after drinking wine or urine

Sadism: sexual arousal through inflicting pain

Sapphism: sexual love between two women, see Lesbianism

Satyriasis: excessive craving for sex in the male

Snuff film: pornographic movie that portrays an actual murder

Sodomy: anal intercourse

Spintriae: homosexual prostitutes in ancient Rome

Swinging: group sex or swapping sexual partners

Teledildonics: arousal from computer sex games

Transsexual: person who is in the process of physically changing sexes

Transvestite: person who is aroused by cross-dressing

Tribade: a lesbian, particularly when one woman lies on top of another and simulates heterosexual sex

Tribadism: lesbianism

Troilism: arousal by being third party in sex scene

Uranism: homosexuality

Urophilia: sexual pleasure gained from urine and urination

Vampirism: consuming blood of partner for arousal

Virgin: person not having experienced penetrative sex with another person

Voyeurism: sexual pleasure gained from observing nudity or sexual activity

Whipping: striking or flagellating a partner for sensory enhancement

Zoophilia: arousal from animals

INDEX

INDEX

Quercus Publishing Plc
21 Bloomsbury Square, London, WC1A 2NS

First published in 2010

A catalogue record of this book is available from the British Library

ISBN: 978-1-84866-061-8

Printed and bound in China

10 9 8 7 6 5 4 3 2 1

Acknowledgements

The publishers would like to thank the following for permission to reproduce illustrations and photographs:

8 Alamy/The Art Archive; 12 Picturedesk.com/ONB Bildarchiv; 16 Photo Scala Florence/Heritage Images/Stapleton Historical Collection, 2010; 20 Topfoto/HIP/Stapleton Historical Collection; 24 The Bridgeman Art Library/Whitford Fine Art, London, UK/Private Collection; 28 Lebrecht Music & Arts/Leemage; 32 Corbis/Bettmann; 36 Corbis/The Gallery Collection; 40 Alamy/The Art Gallery Collection; 44 The Bridgeman Art Library/Scottish National Portrait Gallery, Edinburgh, Scotland; 48 akg-images; 52 The Bridgeman Art Library/Hermitage, St Petersburg, Russia; 56 Corbis/The Gallery Collection; 60 Getty Images/George Eastman House/Etienne Carjat; 64 Getty Images/Hulton Archive/APIC; 68 Corbis/Bettmann; 72 Getty Images/Hulton Archive/Rischgitz; 76 akg-images; 80 Getty Images/Hulton Archive/W & D Downey; 84 Getty Images/Hulton Archive/Stringer; 88 Lebrecht Music & Arts Photo Library/RA; 92 Corbis/Bettmann; 96 Corbis/Bettmann; 100 The Bridgeman Art Library/Ken Welsh/Private Collection; 104 Corbis/Bettmann; 108 Topfoto/Roger-Viollet; 112 Getty Images/Hulton Archive/APIC; 116 Getty Images/Hulton Archive/Walery; 120 Lebrecht Music & Arts Photo Library/Rodway; 124 Rex Features/Roger-Viollet/Lipnitski; 128 Corbis/Bettmann; 132 Getty Images/Time Life Pictures/Alfred Eisenstaedt; 136 Rex Features/Everett Collection; 140 Corbis/Hulton-Deutsch Collection; 144 Corbis/Bettmann; 148 Getty Images/Picture Post/Thurston Hopkins; 152 Corbis/John Springer Collection; 156 Corbis/Bettmann; 160 Getty Images/Pictorial Parade; 164 Getty Images/General Photographic Agency/Elmer Fryer; 168 Photo12.com/Carlos Freire; 172 Corbis/Bettmann; 176 Corbis/Bettmann; 180 Getty Images/Michael Ochs Archives/Stringer; 184 Mirrorpix.